GOD'S BLUEPRINTS

GOD'S BLUEPRINTS

A Sociological Study of
Three Utopian Sects

John McKelvie Whitworth

Department of Sociology and Anthropology,
Simon Fraser University, British Columbia

Foreword by
Professor David Martin

0355910

Routledge & Kegan Paul
London and Boston

59031

First published in 1975
by Routledge & Kegan Paul Ltd
Broadway House, 68–74 Carter Lane,
London EC4V 5EL and
9 Park Street,
Boston, Mass. 02108, USA
Set in Monotype Bembo
and printed in Great Britain by
The Camelot Press Ltd, Southampton
© John McKelvie Whitworth 1975
ISBN 0 7100 8002 6

For my father, Alan Whitworth,
and in memory of my mother,
Helen Whitworth

Contents

Contents

Foreword

In the last quarter of the twentieth century there are few more important topics of study than the forms and styles and fate of utopianism. It is very easy to suppose that a scholarly study of three utopian sects provides mere footnotes to 'real' history and to 'normal' society. In fact, the footnotes to history often provide its most instructive material. One has only to recollect that for Tacitus and Suetonius Christianity itself had the status of an obscure footnote to see the force of this point. And the sects here described are part of the persistent undertow of Christian aspiration and expectation.

There are many ways of viewing utopian sects. There is, first of all, the point of view adopted by the sect itself. For the members of the holy community its boundaries form a colony of heaven, and the world outside is an overgrown untidy garden within which sin and corruption rage. Against that world they attempt to create the Lord's garden through what Dr Whitworth calls 'viable isolation'. To achieve 'viable isolation' you must first build a wall to protect the planting of the Lord. For some sectarians this is enough: they avert their eyes from the world outside, and cultivate their own enclave of salvation. They have discovered how a garden should be run and they will now proceed to run the garden that way to all eternity. This form of perfectionist aspiration is, as Dr Whitworth shows, inherently stagnant and usually produces a 'peasant' character: heavy, repetitious and circumscribed, though not necessarily uncreative or resistant with regard to specific economic and agricultural techniques.

Not all sects look inward towards the tiny enclave of perfection: some look over the wall, signal to the world outside and even make carefully controlled forays into the uncultivated mess brought about by sin. These belong to the kind of sect described with such scholarly care by Dr Whitworth. He gives us a historical account of three such sects and a sociological analysis of their origins. He also describes the sequence of their development, their techniques of social control, their options and limitations, and their ways of monitoring the traffic across their boundaries with the outside world.

Within a general category of 'utopian sect' certain problems are solved in different ways, each involving specific opportunity costs and achieving a characteristic partial mesh with the solution of other problems. For example, two central difficulties are rooted in sexuality and property: which of these is to be held in common, or are both? Is sexuality to be denied, heavily restricted, or opened up to wider permutations than those available in 'ordinary society'? All the central problems of community size, local economic viability, social stability and innovation, the ownership of goods and the expression of sexuality can be examined instructively within the context of utopian sects.

I have already trespassed on the second way of viewing sects: that of the social analyst. For the analyst of social arrangements there is more to the study of utopian sects than the balance of options within what are called 'system problems'. There is also the interest belonging to the 'uncontrolled experiment'. For the sectarian himself, of course, his experiment is incomparable and unique; for the sociologist the sectarians' sense of uniqueness is an item in a set of marginal variations between one example of a sub-category of sect and another example. The sociologist carefully moves through the superabundant data of religiosity and isolates a sub-class within which he observes the variant forms and their empirical correlates. The 'uncontrolled experiment' of a given sect becomes an item in the vast laboratory of human history. The sociologist observes that solution to system problem X in a particular sub-category of sect S is susceptible to $a, b, c \ldots n$ solutions, of which a and e are peculiarly congruent and empirically likely in conjunction with external circumstances of such and such kind. He then asks why this is so, i.e. he enquires why the socio-logic of *this* solution to a problem is congruent with *that* solution to another problem. And by working over all the extant examples he begins to approximate the likely sets of congruences, the possible incompatibilities, and the conditions under which the heavy congruences are likely to recur and those under which the incompatibilities are relatively likely. This approach is based on categorization, cross-categorization and comparison over time and over social and geographical space. To be quite short about it: Dr Whitworth employs the 'comparative' method, the logic of which (as distinct from certain practical limitations) is identical with statistical logic. That is why Dr Whitworth begins with the problem of categorization.

The sociological study of sects teases the analyst with problems which transcend either issues of optimal size, economic viability, sexual regulation, boundary maintenance, or of what is involved in the logic of comparison. One is confronted by further questions about which most of us are too ill-informed to attempt a confident answer. The sect clearly sees itself in several roles: as exemplary and as anticipatory, as both set aside and potentially universal It is small, but God will use the small things of the world to confound the mighty. These varieties of self-conception are in sober fact varying empirical possibilities in human history. The sociologist wants to know whether these experiments are in their present form or in some transmuted form a marginal development permanently incapable of being universalized or whether they are nuclei which indicate the form of the future. He is teased by the issue as to whether they are inherently and for ever parasitic on the fact that other men are not as they are, or whether all mankind will one day come together on some basis pre-figured by the utopian sect. This set of queries fits into an enormous intellectual task: the role and place of utopian sects within the general schemata of social development. Given the vagueness of criteria, the lack of adequate knowledge, the disjunctions and partial disconnections of human history, and the reappearance of problems at higher levels which seemingly belonged to lower levels, there is room for varied answers, including maybe the answer which rejects the very notion of social development. Quite a lot begins to turn on one's *own* theological or philosophical position and the way this meshes in with and selects from the empirical data.

Thus the 'theology' or social philosophy and philosophical anthropology of the observer itself plays a role in reflecting on the long-term implications of the theology, social philosophy and philosophical anthropology of the sectarians. It is not a determining role and it is one partially controlled by the data. When someone who does not believe in any of the varieties and transmutations of the notion of the Kingdom of God on earth is confronted by sectarian phenomena he views them quite differently from someone who believes that sectarianism is the preliminary essay in a perfection which must eventually be revealed to us. So far as I am concerned sectarian utopias represent the impossible possibility without which very little is possible. Their failures are endemic and inherent and are part of the ineradicable paradoxes of human organization. These paradoxes may be manœuvred past with greater or less skill, and their worst consequences can in certain circumstances be ameliorated, but they are as implacable as Scylla or Charybdis. And those who deny this implacability, sociologists included, are themselves creatures of delusion identical with, analogous to and partly derived from the kind of utopian thought they are studying. Unfortunately, every generation has partly to relearn and re-cognize these paradoxes in its bitter experience, and by the time the lesson is relearnt the suffering of human beings has been that much the greater. Yet, of course, it is utopian to lament the fact that each generation has to relearn the limitations governing its own existence, though one may well protest at those modern systems of education which positively encourage an ignorance of limitations. A book like Dr Whitworth's should be read because it is both a primer of limitations for those with the wit to understand, as well as a commentary on those signals of transcendence which point beyond themselves and make faith the substance of things hoped for. Sociology does not encourage us to give up hope, but it does show us – or rather it is capable of showing us – what the genuine limits of hope are.

There are, if I may simplify, two schools of thought about Utopianism. One is that we move instalment by instalment along the way that leads to

New Jerusalem. The road is one and the destination clear even though the way is rough and wayfaring men 'err therein'. The other is that we are constantly running against points or limits at which the aims that took us up to that point begin to turn their sharp edges progressively against us. As we push harder and harder the complex, many-sided blades of reality bite us more and more cruelly. This is why systems of liberation encountering a limit and a boundary begin to resemble and eventually approximate systems of oppression. Their own potentialities are not expanded but eroded by their extension according to some paradigm of persistent advance. There *is* advance, or rather there has been and can be advance, but this is only possible on the basis of experience of limitation and of the paradoxes attendant on alternative options, which are in part at least, mutually exclusive. Of this, Utopians whether Christian or Marxist or whatever, understand too little, but history and society are the arena within which, inevitably, they are forced to learn. If they won't co-operate they will be dragged. They might save themselves a certain amount of trouble by reading about previous Utopians, without using the characteristic Utopian trick of supposing that those they see as precursors are imperfect imitations of a reality yet more perfect to be embodied and exemplified in themselves.

There is one final question which leads me back to the point made at the beginning about Christianity. Whoever reads the literature of Utopianism, whether based on a swift, divine transition to New Jerusalem or on the more gradualist, semi-reformist notions so expertly discussed in those pages by Dr Whitworth, asks himself a question about Christianity. Is the Galilean movement of the first century merely the most remarkable and celebrated instance of these impossible possibilities? In one sense it clearly is. Christianity constantly creates enclaves of perfection: those inside the church described in various works on religious orders and those outside the church described here. But the seeds of perfection clearly blow over the enclosed garden wall and fructify in the most unpredictable manner in the social world outside. And there is also in Christianity the element of limitation and of a sombre celebration of the sharp blades which sink deeper and deeper in all human beings who advance towards the perfect society. Christianity is itself double edged: New Jerusalem yes, *and* the impalement of man. No one organization can fully contain within itself both this hope and this ineluctable sorrow, except at the symbolic level. Utopianism is one arm of the Christian thrust, separating itself off, and fruitfully impaled on the limitations of the world.

David Martin
Professor of Sociology,
London School of Economics

Acknowledgments

My major debts of academic gratitude are owed to two persons. Professor Ilya Neustadt of the University of Leicester and Dr Bryan Wilson of All Souls College, Oxford. Professor Neustadt first whetted my interest in sociology and subsequently guided (and sometimes goaded) me in my career as an undergraduate at Leicester, and greatly encouraged my burgeoning interest in the sociology of religion. This book was initially inspired by Dr Wilson's empirical research and conceptual formulations in the sociology of sectarianism, and would never have been completed without his extraordinarily helpful and sympathetic guidance, advice and encouragement.

I am also grateful to the staff of the British Museum, Bodleian and Nuffield College Libraries, and for the support provided by Nuffield College and the President's Research Grant Committee of Simon Fraser University, British Columbia, which enabled me to complete the research on which this book is based.

Many persons directly or indirectly assisted me in this work, and among them I should specifically like to thank Barbara Abad, Elizabeth Baker, Alan and Susan Budd, Michael Davies, Donald Field, Tony and Nina Lambert, Valerie Levens, Jill Staples, Penelope Tims and Robert Wyllie. Denis Bevington kindly read the manuscript and made many very helpful suggestions. Finally, I should like to thank Professor David Martin of the London School of Economics for writing the Foreword to this book.

Chapter 1

Introduction

The utopian sect is an extremely rare, complex and hitherto scarcely differentiated and largely unexplored form of sect. In this work three religious groups which are regarded as individuals of the utopian type of sect are analysed. These groups are: the Shakers, who emerged in England in the middle of the eighteenth century, migrated to America, and are now apparently dwindling to extinction; the Oneida Community, which appeared as a distinct religious grouping in New England in the eighteen forties, and abandoned its religiously inspired communal life more than thirty years later; and the Bruderhof, a sect which was founded in Germany shortly after the First World War, and which now maintains three communistic communities in the eastern United States.

In the sense of Sir Thomas More's coinage, Utopia was a non-existent place, an imaginary island blessed with perfect social arrangements, and, consequently, with a happy and harmonious population. In more cynical usage the adjective 'utopian' has come to be applied to any vision of the future, proposal for reform or general plan of action which is judged to be unrealistic because it rests on an over-optimistic or ingenuous view of the malleability of human institutions and of man's capacity for goodness and improvement.

Here, the adjective 'utopian' designates a particular type of sectarian response to the world, and implies an aspect of the original meaning of Utopia, but the later pejorative connotations of the term are eschewed. The three sects are described as utopian because their members believed that God had revealed to them the essential nature of His Kingdom, and that it was their task to establish this Kingdom throughout the earth.

The hallmark of utopian sectarianism is not simply a conviction of the corruption of earthly society and a vision of an infinitely better world, but the existence of a distinct conception of how the new world is to be brought into being. The utopian sectarian does not believe that the Kingdom of God will be established on earth merely as a result of divine fiat, but that such establishment is conditional upon human action performed under divine tutelage and surveillance. The sectarians' action is in part oriented towards spiritual improvement – they must demonstrate their capacity to receive ever-renewed outpourings of God's grace – but the utopian conception also implies that the sectarians must establish a nucleus of the Kingdom of God on earth.

The pristine vision which inspires religious utopians is not one of an improved but minuscule community existing permanently on the margins of depraved society, but rather a conviction that, once the prototype of the new order of society has been established, the mass of mankind will quickly come to realize its superiority and divine provenance and will abandon the institutions and vices of the world. The vision is gradualistic, but it is none the less radical. The earth will eventually be transformed into the Kingdom of God, and will be inhabited by that portion of mankind which is capable of the spiritual rebirth necessary for participation in the new and final order of society.

The utopian sect exists in a peculiarly equivocal relationship to the external society – the world. Such a sect regards the world as a place in which corrupt social institutions almost inevitably foster the corruption of individuals and their estrangement from God. Viewing the world with abhorrence, the members of a utopian sect seek to isolate themselves from its influence in order to construct a new, perfect society according to God's blueprint. However, the sectarians also regard themselves as divinely commissioned to demonstrate the perfection and joy of their lives to persons in the world.

The sects analysed below were inspired by such a vision of a totally regenerated world, although of course the principles on which God's King-dom was to be based, as well as the clarity, detail and immediacy of the vision varied greatly between the three groups. All three sought to establish communities as demonstrations of the principles which they believed God had revealed to them as his chosen élite – the first settlers of the new earth. While communitarian world-building was the primary concern of each group once its utopian vision was articulated, it must be emphasized that colony-building was not the sole aspect of the utopian mission. The sectarians did not attempt to isolate themselves completely from the surrounding society, but rather they established their communities in intimate connection with evangelism, and sought to induce men to adopt their social principles and communal life-styles.

A religiously inspired commitment to the maintenance of communal isolation and to evangelism creates a high degree of ambiguity and ambi-valence in the response to the world of a utopian sect. In the analytical chapters which follow it will be argued that a clear appreciation of this ideologically generated ambivalence is among the factors which are crucial to an understanding of the characteristic forms of organization of utopian sects, and the complex patterns of their development.

This work is rooted in the sociology of religion; more specifically, its principal focus and intellectual genealogy is the sociological study of sectarian-ism. Not all of the work in this field is directly relevant to the present study, but the origins and development of the sociological concept of the sect and of the specific type of utopian sect must briefly be indicated.

The sociological study of sectarianism

In recent years sustained attempts have been made to develop a conceptual framework sophisticated enough to facilitate comparative analysis of varieties of sects in the Christian tradition (although as yet few attempts have been made to extend such analysis to sectarian groupings in other religious traditions). Practically all such developments in the study of sectarianism derive from, or represent partial reactions to, a dichotomous ideal-typical distinction established by Troeltsch (1912).

Troeltsch distinguished between the church and the sect both as styles of Christian thought and as related forms of religious organization. He stated that the social doctrines of the Early Church had an inbuilt dualistic tendency which caused them to split apart under the pressures of the secular world. The church embodied the conservative aspects of the teachings of the Early Church; the sect the radical aspects of the same teachings.

Troeltsch characterized the church as universalistic in its self-conception and aims. It claimed to be imbued with God's grace, and to have the task of bringing all men within the realm of this grace, which was administered by the priesthood through the sacraments. The church sought to dominate society and to compel every individual to accept its ministrations, but in so doing it necessarily accommodated itself to the prevailing social order, and became closely associated with, and dependent upon, the state and the ruling classes of society.

In contrast, Troeltsch maintained that the essence of the sect was individualism and voluntarism. The individual entered the sect as a result of conviction and free choice, and his spiritual progress was dependent not upon the impartation of grace through sacraments, but on his own efforts in the context of a directly personal fellowship. The sect actively sought to avoid compromise with the external society, to which it was indifferent or hostile. It was, in its own self-conception, a select group – one placed in opposition to the world.

Troeltsch asserted that the legalism, radicalism and world rejection of the sect had an especial affinity with the most oppressed and most idealistic sections of the lower classes. This statement was elaborated by Niebuhr (1929), whose discussion of the general types of denomination and sect represented little more than a popularization, and translation to an American context, of Troeltsch's original distinction. Niebuhr summarily presented a general interpretation of sect dynamics – the denominationalization thesis – which, although challenged by subsequent observations and investigations, is still frequently asserted as if it were applicable in all cases and contexts.

Niebuhr stated that sectarian forms of organization typically arose among the socially and religiously disinherited poor. He argued that, with the emergence of the second generation of sectarians, and small but cumulative improvements in their socio-economic position, the pristine vigour of the group's rejection of the external society declines, and it gradually takes on the world-accepting aspects of a denomination. Niebuhr recognized that some members of the sect (usually the poorest) might resist this process of accommodation and establish schismatic groups. The picture emerging from his work is one of pullulating sectarianism, and of the almost inevitable movement of the majority of any sect towards a denominational position.

Niebuhr's sweeping thesis was accepted with only very minor reservations in the works of Becker (1932), Clark (1937) and Pope (1942), but an important qualification was subsequently put forward by Yinger (1946) who coined the term 'established sect' to denote groups resistant to the pressures leading to denominationalization. An established sect has developed a *modus vivendi* whereby over several generations it has managed to maintain a considerable measure of aloofness from the world. Such a group still sees itself, and is seen by others, as a group apart. The membership of an established sect is usually small relative to that of a denomination, and the established sect to a large extent dominates the lives of its members, and provides them with their primary context of identification and loyalty.

In the nineteen fifties the Niebuhr thesis was the subject of a number of critical, exploratory and programmatic articles, the most significant of which were those by Berger (1954), Johnson (1957) and Wilson (1958). Niebuhr was said to have over-simplified Troeltsch's much qualified statements, and to have unduly focused attention on the endogenous factors making for sect transformation, while overlooking the influence of exogenous factors on sect development. Wilson in particular drew attention to the reciprocal and dynamic relationship existing, on the one hand, between the wider social milieu in which a sect emerged and developed and, on the other hand, its belief system, organizational structure and the pattern of the group's relationships with the wider society.

The three authors deplored the absence of any coherent theoretical framework for the study of sects. They insisted that adequate preliminary definitions and more explicit, logical and comprehensive typological formulations were necessary if the existing mass of empirical data was to be made subject to systematic analysis. Berger presented a tentative typology of sectarian groups, but subsequently it was Wilson who, in two important articles (1959, 1963) and one major analytical work (1961), developed and demonstrated the sociological utility of an elaborate typology of sectarian groups.

In summary, Wilson described the sect in ideal-typical terms as being a voluntaristic, ideologically oriented religious institution which tends towards totalitarianism, and is committed to maintaining a relatively high degree of separation from other religious bodies and from the world in general.

From this broad characterization Wilson developed a typology of seven

4

sub-types of sect which, he argued, was at least potentially applicable to the analysis both of Christian and of non-Christian sectarian groups.

Wilson based his classification on the various types of mission and closely associated responses to the world exhibited by sectarian groups. He stated that he had selected this taxonomic basis in the hope that it would facilitate not only the comparative study of the structure of sects, but also of their mutations – the changes in their response to the world from one sectarian position to another.

Wilson indicated that a sect's response to the world is influenced, but not wholly determined, by doctrine (the response to the world can change without formal doctrinal changes). He argued that this criterion gave due recognition to the ideological character of sects without diverting attention from the developmental significance of changes in the life circumstances of the sectarians, or more generally, from the multivarious facets of the relationship which exists between the world and the sect.

Wilson described seven sub-types of sect – the adventist, gnostic, thaumaturgical, conversionist, introversionist, reformist and utopian types. The latter three merit more detailed discussion as the utopian sect is the explicit concern of this work, and as it will be argued that mutation to an introversionist or reformist position has been the characteristic fate of those utopian sects whose members have despaired of effecting the total transformation of worldly society.

The members of introversionist sects regard themselves as having a mission to cultivate and deepen their spirituality, and seek as far as possible to avoid contamination by the world. Typically such groups are little concerned with the orthodox eschatology, but the Holy Spirit is believed to be manifested to the individual believer in and through the 'gathered fellowship' of believers. In consequence high value is set on communalism, and the desire to escape the world may lead an introversionist group to intensify their isolation by embracing full communitarianism usually in association with a move to the margins of civilized society. Recruitment in such sects is almost entirely internal, they are indifferent to social reform, to other religious groups and to persons in the world, all of whom are regarded with some measure of pity as being 'tainted with perdition' and hence to be avoided.

Wilson introduced his discussion of reformist sects by admitting that they were in some respects a special category, but argued that they represented a case which, from the standpoint of a dynamic view of sectarian groups, merited recognition. Reformist sects are groups whose earlier responses to the world have undergone transformation, but which still retain markedly sectarian characteristics, including a strong sense of their own identity. They seek to do good works in the world, or more abstractly, simply to exert an influence for good on the world, while to some extent remaining apart from the surrounding society.

The reformist sect appropriates to itself the role of a social conscience; the sectarians regard themselves as 'the leaven in the lump' – an especially inspired and enlightened group who, by their efforts and example, can draw men upwards to their own level. Wilson intimated that such a response appears to develop when the circumstances which earlier led a group to a vehement rejection of the world have largely disappeared, while a strong organizational structure and sense of past and present identity persist.

Finally, Wilson provided a characterization of the type of sect which is the concern of the present work. He stated tentatively of the utopian sect (translated from the French of Wilson, 1963, p. 55):

> Its response to the external society consists partly in withdrawing
> from it, and partly in wishing to remake it in accordance with
> a better model. It is more radical than the reformist sect, potentially
> less violent than the revolutionary sect, and more concerned with
> social reconstruction than the conversionist sect.

It is important to emphasize the distinction between the response to the world of the introversionist and the utopian sect. The introversionist sect is largely indifferent to the world and to people in it, its members shun the world in order to cultivate their spirituality. The utopian cares passionately about the plight of persons suffering in a corrupt world and offers them a panacea, a world reconstructed according to the model revealed by God to his elect.

Wilson distinguished carefully between communitarianism adopted as an expedient to escape the world (as by many introversionist sects) and communitarianism as the deliberate end product of religious vision. He stressed that, while communitarianism might initially be embraced for expedient reasons, it might also subsequently be invested with ideological significance. However, he said virtually nothing of the circumstances of origin of utopian sects, or of their characteristic structure and patterns of mutation.

The task undertaken in this study is inspired by Wilson's conceptual work, and is that of conducting an investigation of the utopian sub-species of sect. This investigation involves the examination of empirical material which is sociologically largely unexplored. Before turning to consider the three sects it is necessary to consider some of the difficulties attendant upon the study of religious sects in general and of the utopian sect in particular.

The empirical study of sectarianism

Until very recently there has been a dearth of intensive empirical studies of sects undertaken from a sociological perspective. The scarcity of such studies is the more remarkable when it is realized that established sociologists have alluded to the rich veins of sociological ore which they believe to be lying untapped in apparently insignificant religious protest groups (as an early example of the genre see Faris, 1955, originally published 1928). However, very few of the authors of these hortatory pieces have followed their own advice and undertaken the detailed analysis of a religious sect.

One of the conclusions which can be drawn from this rather disappointing state of affairs is that religious sects exert immediate attractions as objects of sociological study, but on closer inspection they prove to have drawbacks which are sufficiently severe to dispel superficial enthusiasm and investigatory zeal. The attractions of the study of sects are fairly obvious; the difficulties are perhaps less immediately apparent and require slightly more detailed consideration.

The primary attraction of sects for the sociologist stems from the fact that they are self-consciously boundary-maintaining groups which strive to establish a high, sometimes totalitarian, degree of control over their members. An individual sect is thus, potentially, a kind of sociological laboratory. It is a small group which provides the essential meaning and the focal point of its members' lives, and in which, consequently, a wide range of social processes can be observed in a state of 'artificial' purity and isolation.

Implicit in the statement that all sects to a greater or lesser extent reject the world, is the fact that, inevitably, they also in a sense reflect the world which they reject. Adherence to a sectarian group implies that the individual is repelled by or dissatisfied with at least some aspects of the wider society. Consequently, sects may attract the sociologist not simply because of their 'microcosmic' aspects, but also because the study of any particular sect is likely to provide an acute depiction of the aspirations and frustrations of the members of the socio-economic group or groups from which its adherents are primarily drawn. The study of sects may thus illuminate (possibly un-suspected) tensions and conflicts existing in the wider society.

Sectarians are not necessarily in the usual sense of Niebuhr's designation a 'heroic' minority (although they often display a capacity for heroism in conjunction with a taste for martyrdom), but those sects whose rejection of the world is extreme are heroic in the more general sense of 'attempting great things'. The attempt to construct alternative societies or worlds is fraught with difficulties, especially when such attempts are made in genuine independence of the wider society and with the intention that the new social forms should not be merely temporary refuges, but should permanently replace the old social arrangements.

As objects of sociological study utopian sects exert in the highest degree the attractions general to all sects. They are typically small, largely but not entirely separated from the world, and are truly radical attempts to replace the institutions of the world by institutions which the sectarians believe to be of divine provenance, but which inevitably bear the stamp of the society which gave them birth.

The problems attendant upon the sociological study of sects arise from just those very totalitarian and world-rejecting aspects of sectarian organizations which render them attractive to sociologists. Two broad areas of difficulty can be distinguished; on the one hand is the problem of gaining access to information regarding sectarian groups, on the other that of evaluating and interpreting such information as can be gained.

Information regarding sects may be obtained from six main sources: from interviews with members of the sect and open participation in its activities; by participating disguisedly in the group's activities; from apostates; from the group's publications; from secondary published material relating directly to the sect; and finally from published material which discusses the sect tangentially – as marginal to, or illustrative of, the main subject of the work.

In the case of extant sects it may in some cases be possible for the sociologist *qua* sociologist to gain access to the sect and to be freely received and admitted by the sectarians, but the idea of being subjected to sociological investigation is anathema to most sects.

The sectarian is oriented to a world beyond the secular – to truths and principles which he believes are superior to worldly knowledge. For him the world is a place to be shunned and the sociologist appears as the incarnation of the secular – someone who would number God's elect and who would seek to categorize and explain in mundane terms what, for the sectarian, is explicable only by persons possessing a high degree of spiritual awareness, or insofar as God in his wisdom has revealed his intentions to men.

To the utopian sectarian the sociologist is likely to appear as a somewhat pathetic, benighted and impudent figure who, himself the corrupt product of a corrupt form of society, attempts to assess the worth of God's Kingdom on earth in terms of the moral standards and institutions of the degenerate world.

For these reasons, the sociologist who wishes to undertake an intensive investigation of an existing sect is usually forced to resort to subterfuge to derive first-hand information, and may engage in 'disguised participation' in the activities of the sect – usually by presenting himself as a potential convert. This technique of investigation poses moral problems for the individual sociologist which must be solved according to his conscience, and (assuming that the moral problems have been resolved, shelved or simply not recognized) also presents practical difficulties.

It is in fact extremely hard for the sociologist to maintain the guise of an intending convert for more than a few hours at a time. The sociologist may know more of the past history, doctrine and social characteristics of the sect than any genuine aspirant to membership, who will usually have 'felt drawn' to the sect as a result of a concatenation of personal social circumstances. Moreover, the enthusiasm of the typical convert is extraordinarily hard to counterfeit.

In terms of his attitude to the sect, the sociologist is likely to be watchful rather than involved, interrogatory rather than receptive, and, even in those groups which encourage questioning by visitors, the style of questions asked by the sociologist, even when he is exerting himself to the fullest to disguise his identity, may well betray him as a representative of the secular forces which besiege the sect.

Apostates and persons expelled from sects are potentially a rich source of information for the sociologist, but in practice many apostates may have only a superficial knowledge of the group, and their accounts of its teachings, social practices and of the iniquities they believe themselves to have suffered are often grossly distorted and hysterical in tone. Some persons expelled from a sect may cherish ambitions to return, or to be allowed a measure of contact with the group, and in any case may well remain hostile to the world and refuse to collaborate with sociologists.

In the case of non-contemporary sects the sociologist is forced to rely primarily on literary sources for his information. If it exists, the literature published by sects is frequently of an ephemeral nature and may be extremely hard to trace. On the other hand, if the sectarians were of a literary turn, and especially if literary evangelism was among their main activities, the investigator may well be daunted by the volume of their works.

Sheer bulk aside, the sociologists may have to struggle through literally hundreds of pages of closely written and obscure exegesis before finding a single illuminating fact, or a statement betraying some significant modification of social practice. What is important to the sociologist is frequently of little interest to the sectarians (or may be so well known as to be taken for granted) who are characteristically extremely vague in regard to dates and statistics. Further, some groups (including the utopian sects analysed here) may deliberately keep aspects of their beliefs and social attitudes secret from the world, and sometimes even from the less senior members of the group.

Among the varieties of the secondary literature are accounts by apostates, by representatives of other religious bodies, historical accounts by persons living in the world and a wide range of journalistic literature. Finally there exist numerous works in which some aspects of the teachings and practices of various sects are adduced as illustrative material. For example, religiously-inspired communitarian groups are frequently cited as at once crude forerunners of, and sources of inspiration for, socialist communitarian groups or secular communal experiments in general.

On occasion apostates provide rounded and balanced accounts of the groups from which they have seceded or been expelled but, especially in the latter case, the majority of such works are extremely biased, violently phrased sensationalistic diatribes against the group which has cast the author into the darkness of the world. Accounts of sects produced under the auspices of other religious bodies usually pay only scant attention to the sect's beliefs, which are dismissed as crude heresies or as based on manifest errors. Such accounts tend to be either condescending, or violently condemnatory.

Historical and journalistic accounts of sects vary greatly in their quality and comprehensiveness, but usually are markedly lacking in objectivity, being written either from an extremely sympathetic or antagonistic position. Sympathetic discussions of sects frequently rest on good intentions and only scanty information, and are often marred by whimsy, credulity, romanticism and a total inability to appreciate the subtleties of the sectarian mind. Frequently the complexities of the inter-relationship between doctrine and social practices are overlooked, and the authors of these works often display the same disdain for chronological accuracy as do their subjects.

Antagonistic accounts of sects exhibit many of the above-mentioned substantive defects, and are further marred by their authors' cynical refusal to attribute any but the basest of motives to the sectarians – and especially to their leaders. In the final type of literary source, those works which cite sectarian groups as illustrative or exemplary material, the very marginality of such references generally precludes anything more than gross characterizations of the groups considered.

Such are some of the factors which may have damped sociologists ardour to investigate sectarian groups, and it is now necessary to point to some of the specific difficulties associated with the analysis of the three sects which are the subject of this study: the Shakers, Oneida Community and the Bruderhof.

The literary output of the Shakers from the late eighteenth century to the early decades of the present century was extremely large, and these primary sources are supplemented by a voluminous body of secondary works which range from the scurrilous outpourings of deranged apostates, to sentimental reminiscences of childhood visits to the declining Shaker colonies.

Fortunately, this secondary literature includes a number of serious and reasonably comprehensive studies which, although deficient in some ways (none for example provides a comprehensive account of the development, systematization and social implications of the sect's religious beliefs), none the less provide an initial appreciation of the range and complexity of Shaker history and culture: an appreciation which is deepened by consideration of the sectarians' own theological works, statements of social principle and later apologetics and memorabilia.

The literary output of the Oneida Community was also voluminous, and a considerable body of secondary literature was generated by the group's intermittent zeal for publicity and, more especially, by its religiously inspired reconstruction of social arrangements governing sexual relations and the upbringing of children. In addition, the literature of the sect underwent considerable editing and rewriting in the forty years of the group's existence.

Special problems of interpretation are also posed by the secrecy which surrounded aspects of the group's communal life, and by the enigmatic character of its founder – who was at once forceful and vacillating, morally courageous and physically cowardly, but who was able to command the devotion and, literally, the bodies of several hundred followers for more than three decades.

The literature of the Bruderhof is much less extensive than that of the other two groups, but is still considerable. In this case, library research was supplemented by a short period of disguised participation in one of the group's communities in the eastern United States. This participation yielded little new information, but provided an important 'feel' for the atmosphere and style of the communal life of the sectarians. Further information was derived from interviews and correspondence with informants now living in Britain, Canada and the United States.

Analytical procedure

In the chapters which follow, discussion of each sect proceeds according to a broadly similar pattern, and is divided into several major analytical sections. First, the circumstances of emergence of the group and the nature of its original religious teachings are discussed. Second, its more fully developed belief system and theologically derived self-conception is examined. In the third and longest section, the formal organization of the group is considered. Subsequently, the social composition of the group is discussed, and in the fifth section the nature of the sect's relationships with the external society is considered. In the concluding chapter comparisons are drawn between the three sects, and this dicussion is presented in broad correspondence to the analytical scheme outlined above.

The three sects are individually considered as approximations to the utopian type in that in the early stages of their development, a leader, or succession of leaders, endowed them with a utopian mandate or mission, a mandate which it is argued has been an important determinant of each group's subsequent development.

Critics of attempts to construct typologies have pointed to the danger that types may be proliferated without regard to their usefulness in ordering and analysing empirical data. Put another way, it is argued that the heuristic functions of types tend to be neglected, and that the types themselves are often reified – they are invested with reality, and so are rendered into Procrustean beds on which empirical data is stretched and distorted. Such criticisms are in many cases perfectly valid and, while it is possible to speak of sub-types of sect, it must always be remembered that the degree of approximation of each individual sect to a particular sub-type is itself a matter for empirical investigation.

The particular mode of analytic procedure outlined above has been adopted in the interests of clarity and comprehensiveness, but in view of the complexity of the belief systems and organizational forms of the three sects some summary repetition is inevitable. The length of the analytic chapters is another function of the task undertaken – that of sociologically dissecting three religious groups whose members, for a considerable period of time, attempted to construct and promulgate complete and genuinely alternative worlds. (To assist the reader chronologies of each sect are provided in the appendices.)

Chapter 2

Origins and expansion of the Shakers, 1747–1835

Ann Lee, the woman whose religious teachings were to become the funda-mental doctrines of the Shaker sect, was born in Manchester, England, in 1736, the second of the eight children of John Lee, a blacksmith and jobbing tailor. Little is known of her youth, but she appears to have had no formal schooling, and to have worked from an early age in a textile mill and, later, as a cook in a public infirmary.

In 1758, she joined a group of religious dissidents led by the Quaker apostates Jane and James Wardley of Bolton, whose ecstatic manner of worship had led them to be called 'Shaking Quakers' or, more colloquially, 'Shakers'. The doctrines of this group were the chief source of the ideas which the illiterate Ann Lee later developed in the light of her experience and her conviction of personal divine inspiration.

In 1747, accompanied by some thirty followers, Jane and James Wardley broke away from the Society of Friends. The earliest substantial Shaker theological work (Youngs, 1808) indicates that their secession was influenced by contact with the doctrines of the group known in France as the 'Cami-sards', and in England as the 'French Prophets'. This sect had developed in France after 1685, in which year Louis XIV revoked the Edict of Nantes, which had guaranteed liberty of conscience to Protestants. After this revoca-tion the Protestant minority was subjected to extreme persecution which was intended to force them to embrace Catholicism.

Their resistance was, at first, only passive, but in 1700 the peasants of the Cevennes region retaliated violently against their persecutors and, in 1702–5, waged a full-scale guerrilla war against the Catholic forces. The Protestants were encouraged by the appearance of numbers of male and female prophets who claimed to be directly inspired by God, and who prophesied in ecstatic trances, foretelling the imminent destruction of 'Babylon and Satan' – the Roman Catholic Church and the Papacy. In 1705, an amnesty was granted to the Camisards and, in the following year, several of the prophets arrived in England.

In London, which for some years was the sole centre of their operations, the Camisards' anti-Catholicism developed into general anti-clericalism and, in 1707, several prophets were pilloried after they had attacked the

Established Church. Their denunciatory millennial prophecies, accompanied by trances, seizures and glossalalia, won the French Prophets much notoriety and many followers, chiefly of artisan background. Numbers of indigenous prophets arose in direct imitation of the Camisards, and the movement quickly passed into English hands.

In 1708, the disappointment attending the non-fulfilment of their millennial predictions led to a rapid decline of interest in the sect, and its numbers fell sharply. In the period 1709 to 1713 the remaining leaders of the various schismatic groups made evangelical journeys to Edinburgh, Glasgow and Manchester. They succeeded in attracting small numbers of followers in these cities, but with the exception of these obscure, and probably short-lived, groups, the teachings of the French Prophets appear to have merged into the 'underground tradition' of proletarian millennial thought.

Although it is impossible to trace the exact nature and degree of influence of the French Prophets on the Wardley group, the latter's manner of worship and teachings closely resembled those of the Prophets. The central tenets of the Wardley group appear to have been belief in the imminence of the millennium, and in the continuance of revelation, manifested in prophecies accompanied by physical seizures. The dominant figure in the group, Jane Wardley (the wife of a weaver), was the recipient of the members' periodic confessions, and appears to have combined strongly anti-clerical sentiments with general calls to repentance.

Ann Lee joined the Wardley group in 1758, but for some years did not play an important part in its activities. In 1762, she reluctantly married a blacksmith, Abraham Stanley, and in four years bore him four children, all of whom died at birth or in their infancy. As a result of these repeated tragedies, Ann Lee developed a horror of all sexual relations and of the institution of marriage. In her own words, she shunned her husband's bed 'as if it had been made of embers'.

After the death of her last child Ann Lee became increasingly prominent among the Shakers, and her abhorrence of sexual relations first coloured, and then dominated, their teachings. She was twice imprisoned for Sabbath breaking and, in 1772, during her second spell of imprisonment, she had a vision of the original self-indulgent sexual act, which took place in the Garden of Eden, and was 'the cause wherein all mankind was lost and separated from God' (cited in Andrews, 1963, p. 11).

From this time, Ann Lee considered herself to be directly inspired by God, and to be the female counterpart of Christ. She believed herself divinely commissioned to reveal sexual relations as the source of all sin, and celibacy as the door to regeneration and eventual salvation. Her claims to special inspiration appear to have been accepted by most of the Shakers, and Jane Wardley dropped into obscurity. Ann Lee was regarded by her followers as the herald and inaugurator of the new and final 'dispensation' or era of mankind, and the Shakers believed themselves to be converts to teachings which would eventually be accepted by the world at large.

The style of worship of the sect, and their testimonies against sexual relations, brought the Shakers much local notoriety, and on several occasions they were mobbed and beaten. The group had earlier made several converts, mainly artisans and factory labourers, but Ann Lee's rise to prominence brought no significant increase in its numbers.

Evangelical failure appears to have turned Ann Lee's thoughts abroad, and in 1773 she received repeated revelations urging her to travel to the American Colonies, and prophesied that such a migration would be rewarded by a great expansion of the sect. Consequently, in May of 1774, financed and accompanied by John Hocknell, a relatively wealthy convert, Ann Lee, her husband and seven other followers (at least three of whom were directly related to Ann Lee) sailed for America.

On their arrival in New York the Shakers separated to look for work. Ann Lee found employment as a washerwoman, and her husband as a blacksmith. After some months Hocknell bought a tract of land at Niskeyuna, seven miles from Albany, New York. Early in 1775, Ann Lee, who had remained in New York City, was deserted by her husband, who presumably resented her abhorrence of 'fleshy relations', and for some months she suffered great poverty. Her position improved after John Hocknell returned from England with his family and, by the autumn of 1776, the group had reassembled at their Niskeyuna purchase.

During the period immediately following their settlement at Niskeyuna, the sectarians were preoccupied with the problem of subsistence, and their isolation and poverty rendered evangelism practically impossible. The communism of this period consisted of a simple sharing of goods among people engaged in a common endeavour, and probably stemmed from poverty rather than from ideological conviction, although the Shakers certainly drew parallels between their social arrangements and those of the early Christians. For more than three years the group made no converts, but Ann Lee constantly exhorted her followers to labour, and encouraged them with revelations which promised that soon thousands would flock to the sect and that the Shakers' testimony would 'overcome all nations' (Evans, 1859, p. 150).

The first group of Shaker converts was drawn from among the subjects of a religious revival which took place in 1779 at New Lebanon, a town in the vicinity of Niskeyuna. The excitement and sense of urgency generated by the New Lebanon revival was greatly heightened by the War of Independence, which many persons interpreted as heralding the 'last days', and took to be a skirmish preliminary to Armageddon. Consequently, when the fervour of the revival had passed, the disappointment and despair of the more zealous converts was unusually extreme.

In 1780 Joseph Meacham, one of the most influential of the New Lebanon revivalistic preachers, was informed of the teachings of the Shakers, and travelled to Niskeyuna to interview and appraise them. After much scriptural argument, Meacham and his immediate followers were convinced of the genuineness of Ann Lee's inspiration and adopted the Shaker faith. Inspired by this initial success, the Shakers held public meetings and made many converts among the persons who had been 'agitated' by the New Lebanon revival.

Public testimony brought the Shakers converts but also engendered much persecution. As the leading Shakers were English, and preached non-resistance (presumably a legacy of the Wardleys' original Quakerism), they were accused of being agents of the British government, and of diverting the meagre donations they received from converts to the aid of the British forces. In July of 1780, Ann Lee and several of her English followers were arrested and jailed in Albany and Poughkeepsie on vague charges of 'being nnfriendly to the patriotic cause', but they were released five months later, after agitation by the other Shakers and by several local dignitaries.

The imprisonment of its leaders on unfounded charges brought the sect much publicity and considerable sympathy, and word of the Shakers' doctrines spread rapidly throughout New York and into neighbouring states. Consequently, in May of 1781, Ann Lee and two of her original followers set out on a missionary journey which was to last two years and was to sow the seeds of the Shaker faith throughout New England.

The three 'witnesses' made many converts, but evangelical success again generated much antagonism and persecution. Although the earlier charges of sedition had been dismissed they were frequently repeated, and public feeling against the Shakers was deliberately fomented by apostates and by ministers who felt that their congregations were susceptible to the Shakers' teachings. The missionaries were violently assaulted on several occasions, Ann Lee once being stripped by a mob who at first maintained that she was a male British agent in disguise. Conversions and persecution increased throughout 1782 and the early part of 1783, and in the autumn of the latter year the three witnesses returned to Niskeyuna where, weakened by her exertions and sufferings, Ann Lee died in September 1784.

Despite the large number of converts made, there was no immediate change in the organizational structure of the group. At Ann Lee's death, the Shakers' 'church' consisted of a loose charismatic association of perhaps a thousand individuals, with a central nucleus of the original Shakers at Niskeyuna, and widely scattered recent converts. Persons were admitted to the sect after confessing their sins to Ann Lee or one of the senior members, and renouncing sexual relations. Presumably, after the excitement caused by the novelty of the Shakers' doctrines and worship had abated, there were many apostates. Where individuals were free from immediate want, they continued in their occupations and remained with their families, even when their relatives were not members of the sect.

The success of the evangelical journeys of the three witnesses exacerbated internal and external pressures making for the development of a more formal organizational structure. Ann Lee's successor, James Whittaker, realized the need to unite the scattered converts in some form of congregational system in order to prevent indiscipline and apostasy. He greatly restricted the missionary activities of the sect, warned converts that they would be subjected to remonstrance and abuse by their relatives and friends, and stressed the need for the Shakers to sever all affective ties with persons who were not members of the sect.

Whittaker died after only three years as leader of the sect, and under the later leaders, Joseph Meacham and Lucy Wright, the institutionalization of Ann Lee's charismatic legacy was completed, and communism and communitarianism were established as the fundamental organizational principles of the Shaker Church. From being simply expedient devices, these social principles and forms were gradually invested with intrinsic ideological significance and were sanctified by an elaborate theological system.

Religious teachings and self-image of the sect

For about a decade after the death of Ann Lee the energies of the Shaker elders were primarily devoted to the task of strengthening the convictions of the original converts, but in 1797 the Shaker testimony was 'reopened to the world', and the membership of the sect increased rapidly in the first years of the nineteenth century.

This increase, which was mainly the result of evangelism among the subjects of the Great Kentucky Revival of 1799 to 1806, gave rise to new problems of communication and social control, as the societies established in Kentucky and Ohio were, geographically and environmentally, widely separated from the north-eastern communities. The expansion of the sect in the south-west was accompanied by as vigorous persecution as had been experienced earlier, and in the first two decades of the nineteenth century, the Shaker societies generally were assailed by pleas or legislation intended to challenge or destroy the legality of the sect's membership covenant.

The Shakers' original preoccupation with subsistence and proselytization, and subsequently with the practical implementation and defence of the organizational principles implicit in their belief system, explains the lateness of their development and formal statement of a comprehensive theological system. However, in the first quarter of the nineteenth century the sectarians produced three works (Youngs, 1808; Dunlavy, 1818; Green and Wells, 1823) which together provide a comprehensive statement of the central beliefs of the Shakers and their related historical exegesis and eschatology.

In common with all charismatic leaders, Ann Lee's authority was based on her ability to convince some of her hearers that her message was important, and that it was their duty to act in accordance with her teachings. By their allegiance, her followers legitimized both her claim to inspiration and her explicit teachings, which rested on one fundamental tenet – the idea that sexual relations were the source of all sin – and the subordinate conception of continuing progressive revelation.

The Shakers taught that the duality of the incarnate expression of the deity in the male (Christ) and in the female (Ann Lee) was a reflection of the essential duality of God, who was believed to have two aspects – that of the Holy Father, whose primary attribute was infinite power, and the Holy Mother, whose attribute was infinite wisdom.

This duality of an infinitely righteous and loving God was mirrored not only in Christ and Ann Lee, but generally, in the division of the sexes. Although they rejected any idea of corporeal resurrection, the Shakers believed that distinctions between the sexes persisted in the spiritual world. The sexes were regarded as fundamentally equal, if differently endowed, a concept which, while theological in derivation, was of crucial importance for the authority structure, recruitment and later development of the sect.

Salvation from the sin engendered by sexual relations could be gained only by making a full confession of sins to the elders of the sect, and by embracing 'the cross' of celibacy. The convert thus entered into the 'regenerate life' which, if maintained, led progressively to complete freedom from sin, and ultimately to salvation.

Immense importance was attached to the act of confession. The convert was required to describe his past life and sins in great detail, and confessions were frequently deemed insincere or insufficient and had to be repeated. Confession was believed to expiate sins and to purify the convert, while symbolizing his rejection of the world and its temptations. Further, the act of confession mortified the convert and so encouraged the development of humility and submissiveness, qualities which the Shaker leaders held to be essential for all believers.

The Shakers' religious conceptions were optimistic and perfectionist, but their perfectionism was distinctive in that it was gradualistic, evolutionary, conditional and, doctrinally and socially, strictly disciplined. After the death of Ann Lee, the basic beliefs outlined above were encapsulated in an elaborate theological system which included a detailed discussion of the interplay of the forces of good and evil throughout history, the culmination of which was the emergence of the Shakers as God's final emissaries to the degenerate world.

Discussion of the idea of progressive revelation must necessarily start from an examination of the Shakers' conception of the Fall, and of the nature of original sin. They believed that, prior to the Fall, man was sinless and, like other animals, employed his sexual organs seasonally, and solely for purposes of procreation. This natural pattern was perverted by the temptation and Fall of Eve, as a result of which sin and death entered the world and man succumbed to unbridled lust, which 'corrupted the nature and disposition, and degraded the dignity of man' (Youngs, 1808, p. 48).

The result of the original transgression was that the human species had become 'devilish, beastly and unclean', but despite this virulent condemnation the Shaker theologians rejected any idea that the perpetuation of this corruption was inevitable. Rather, they claimed that man had free will to choose between the paths of salvation and of damnation, but they admitted that such a choice was seldom recognized and rarely exercised, as men were 'born into a fallen state', and so were led to sin by the example of others.

Interesting evidence of the psychology of the Shaker theologians can be found in the instances of the 'practical evils' deriving immediately from sexuality, which they cited to illustrate the corruption and misery of life in the world. These evils included excessive child-bearing (the 'curse of women') and the power of 'unseasonable lust' to master and degrade otherwise controlled and rational men.

Further, despite the fact that the Shakers believed that sexual relations always resulted in disappointed expectations of pleasure, they also argued that indulgence in sexual relations led almost inevitably to ungovernable excesses. For them, sexuality was the root of all evil, moral and social, and they staunchly maintained that scarcely any person had 'run deeply into criminal practices, who has not first quaffed largely of libidinous indulgences' (Green and Wells, 1823, p. 142).

On the basis of their conception of the nature and implications of the Fall, the Shaker theologians presented a total interpretation of man's past and future religious development. They described this development in terms of four historical 'dispensations' or cycles, each governed by a distinctive revelation, and each having its appropriate heaven and hell.

In the first, the Antediluvian cycle, men's religious conceptions were at their most primitive, and God was understood only as a remote Great Spirit. The second, Mosaic dispensation, was regarded as a 'preparatory work' intended to discipline men for the third dispensation, that of Christ, who revealed the deity to be not the remote and arbitrary God of the Jews, but a father to mankind. Christ enjoined the virtues of celibacy and established the 'earthly Heaven' of his cycle, the Primitive Church.

Finally, the fourth dispensation was that of Ann Lee, who revealed God as the mother of mankind, and announced the possibility of earthly salvation for all men. Her dispensation was the 'completing work' embodying all the valid teachings of the former cycles, and would result in the world-wide establishment of the true Shaker Church, which alone could lead the individual to salvation (Youngs, 1808, p. 427):

> The Church of Christ is the kingdom of heaven, a state, habitation,
> or society, necessary to prepare mankind for heaven itself; and is
> placed in such a line of order from the source of true happiness, that
> no soul can enter heaven, but through the kingdom of heaven or
> Church of Christ.

This outline of the progressive revelation of God's plan to offer the chance of redemption to all men, was paralleled by a discussion of the forces of evil in the world. The Shaker theologians adopted one component of the millennial 'drama', the idea of the cumulative development of the forces of Antichrist, but they rejected the normally associated apocalyptic conceptions of Armageddon and a dramatic Advent.

It has been shown that the Shakers believed the earthly heaven of the third dispensation was embodied in the Primitive Church of Jerusalem, whose essential principles were economic communism, celibacy, pacifism and separatism, and whose divine origin was evidenced by the healing powers of its members. The Shaker theologians dated the rise of Antichrist from the abandonment of these principles, and attributed the responsibility for this abandonment to the theologians of the Alexandrian School and to the Emperor Constantine.

They dismissed Constantine as an agent of Antichrist who, despite his good intentions, was corrupted by the priesthood, and who so perverted the teachings of the Primitive Church as to make persecution, slavery and war essential elements of Christian theology. The Catholic Church and the Papacy had furthered these developments and, by insisting on the alliance between Church and State, had reduced religion to a travesty, making it a subordinate tool of the civil government. To the Shakers the Catholic Church was a totally corrupt hierarchy – 'the habitation of devils, and the hold of every foul spirit, and a cage of every unclean and hateful bird' (Youngs, 1808, p. 18).

It is interesting that, in his concern to establish the total iniquity of the Catholic Church, Youngs, the author of the 'Shaker bible', condemned the religious orders and levied charges against them which were as wild and paradoxical as the charges made against the Shakers themselves. Far from praising the celibacy, communism and general asceticism of monks and nuns, Youngs asserted that monasticism was 'productive of millions of lazy, useless beings, who for ages were a common pest to civil society', and who were all guilty of self-pollution and secret debauchery (Youngs, 1808, pp. 265–6).

Although the Reformation had destroyed the hegemony of the Catholic Church, the Shakers felt that it represented merely a division in the forces of Antichrist. Arising from 'wrangling and animosity' it had resulted only in an increase in suffering, bloodshed and superstition. The Catholic and Protestant Churches were alike in their intolerance, their acceptance of war, and in lacking the Pentecostal power of healing which the Shakers believed was only to be found in those bodies which were directly guided by divine inspiration and revelation.

The Protestant Churches not only retained the corrupt principles of the Catholic Church, but also, by allowing their clergy to marry, had removed the taint of worldly impurity from the institution of marriage. By completely legitimizing marriage, they had increased the moral ignorance and degenerate state of mankind (Youngs, 1808, pp. 331–2):

The fact is, the reformation opened the very last and most effectual door for the unrestrained and full gratification of every unclean, and worse than brutal lust both in man and woman, under the name of a holy ordinance, by making the woman a proper object of worship, or setting her up, openly and avowedly above all that is called God. . . . And they have enjoined it upon all, as a solemn duty to marry, in their way, with the licentious prospect of living in the full gratification of their lusts, without any respect to times or seasons, but with full liberty to defile and abuse each other in the most scandalous, incestuous and debauching manner.

In sum, the Shakers felt that the cumulative growth of the forces of evil had led to an almost complete perversion of the original spirit of Christianity.

The Shakers did not claim that they and the Primitive Church had together monopolized divine inspiration, but felt that, even in the period following the establishment of the Catholic Church, 'in the night of apostasy and wilderness state of the truth', some measure of 'the light' was vouchsafed to such groups as the Manichaeans, Bogomils, Waldenses, Cathars and Quakers. The common characteristic of these sects was their initial rejection of the formalism of the established church or churches.

These earlier 'Witnesses of Truth' had suffered persecution in proportion to the strength of their testimony and their degree of spiritual power but, although they had the 'spirit of the prophets', they lacked the 'building power of the apostles', and had gradually lost or perverted their original inspiration. This had even been the fate of the Quakers, who had possessed the highest degree of spiritual light accorded to any group in the time between the apostasy of the Primitive Church and the commencement of the ministry of Ann Lee.

Arguing from the general Christian conception of an infinitely wise, powerful, loving and righteous God, the Shaker theologians rejected the deterministic dogmas of the New England Calvinist Churches. They dismissed the belief that God had totally pre-determined every action of man, and insisted that man had free will within the limits of the decrees of God, which had established the immutable laws of the universe and of man's physical and psychological nature.

The Shakers repudiated the doctrine of pre-determined election and reprobation as being illogical and blasphemous; a loving and righteous God was morally incapable of creating whole classes of men who were involuntarily and inescapably doomed to eternal torment. The Shakers preached the possibility of gaining this worldly salvation guided by divine revelation, and flatly contradicted the Calvinistic conception of justification by faith, by asserting that 'all must finally be judged and rewarded according to their works' (Green and Wells, 1823, p. 115).

The Shakers' reaction against Calvinism did not lead them to reject the conventional belief in hell as being a place of eternal torment, but, in accordance with their conception of continuing revelation adjusted to the spiritual condition of mankind, they believed that salvation and damnation were progressive. Those persons who had lived before Ann Lee's teachings had been revealed, and who had been condemned to the hell of their dispensation, would, in the spiritual world, be acquainted with God's ultimate message, and would have the final choice of accepting or rejecting this message and of being saved or damned accordingly.

The Shaker theologians did not expect the world to be immediately and cataclysmically converted to Shakerism. Their conviction of the deep-rootedness of the corruption of its institutions and inhabitants precluded this. They asserted that the Advent dated from the commencement of Ann Lee's ministry, which would result, not in the destruction of the world by fire and brimstone, but in the destruction of worldly things by the 'consuming fire' of their testimony against lust and pride. Ann Lee had inaugurated the final era of human history, and the task of her followers was to resist being contaminated by the world, and to promulgate her teachings until such time as God's work was completed and all men would have been offered the chance of salvation (Green and Wells, 1823, p. 317):

> This work having already commenced, will continue its progressive
> influence till all souls shall have seen and felt its purifying effects; or,
> through wilful disobedience shall have rejected their day of trial,
> because of the cross [of celibacy], and numbered themselves with the
> impenitent and rebellious, as vessels of wrath fitted for destruction.

The comprehensive belief system presented in the Shakers' earliest doctrinal works was a synthesis of diverse theological elements crystallized around Ann Lee's idiosyncratic teachings. The Shakers' rejection of the dogmas of Calvinism stemmed from their revivalistic perfectionism, and from their associated belief in the existence of free will and of the importance of the 'spiritual gifts' which they believed denoted divine inspiration and approval. However, in contrast to the antinomianism of many of the North American Perfectionist groups, the exercise of these gifts and the conduct of the individual member was strictly disciplined, and this discipline was justified in terms of the sect's religious mission.

Members of all sectarian bodies regard themselves as numbered among God's elect, but the Shakers considered themselves to be, not merely an elect who would receive heavenly rewards for their piety and suffering, but the inhabitants and custodians of God's Kingdom on earth. They were the sole heirs of the spiritual enlightenment which had increased progressively throughout all history. Ann Lee promised her followers not simply elevation to heaven, but elevation within heaven, where they would be 'kings and priests unto God' (Evans, 1859, p. 152).

The task of the Shakers was to establish, maintain and promulgate a form of society in which the individual could live unspotted by the world, and so attain salvation through leading a life of 'virgin purity'. They were committed to evangelism as a necessary preliminary to selective recruitment, and they rejected almost every aspect of the values and institutions of the external society.

The early Shakers considered themselves to be the vessels of ˌdivine inspiration and the agents of God, and their societies to be the nucleus of the Kingdom of Heaven on earth. When God's plan for the world had been fulfilled, and the majority of mankind had embraced Shakerism, the final judgment would occur and God would reign over his spiritual Kingdoms, the earth and heaven.

The Shakers made frequent reference to the organizational and religious principles of the Church of Jerusalem – in particular to its economic communism, and to the celibacy and brotherliness of its members. They cited the Primitive Church not as an inspiring but unattainable ideal, but rather as being the highest spiritual product of the third dispensation, and as such necessarily inferior in spirituality and organization to their own 'Millennial Church'.

In their historical exegesis the Shaker theologians attributed the moral decline of the Primitive Church to individual heresy, backsliding and factionalism. From this analysis they drew practical conclusions applicable to themselves. Being directly inspired by God and having one common aim to 'crucify one root of evil, which is the flesh with all its affections and lusts', it followed that the essential properties of the Shaker Church must be unity and purity, 'for Christ is not, nor can he be divided' (Youngs, 1808, p. 427).

The Shakers were guided by one spirit and so must have one government, and it behoved all members to submit to those individuals whom God had elevated within his Church. The members of the sect were enjoined to strive constantly to develop the twelve true Christian virtues: faith, hope, honesty, continence, innocence, simplicity, meekness, humility, prudence, patience, thoughtfulness and charity, and so become worthy to receive the gifts of God's grace which were evidence of true Christianity.

While striving to develop all of these virtues, each Shaker was to be guided in every moment of his life by reference to seven moral principles, and to the precepts derived from them. He was to perform his duty to God by rendering Him praise, and to his fellows by acts of love and charity. He was to live in peace and separate from the world, swear no oaths, be diligent and, above all, lead a life of virgin purity, according obedience to God and to the manifestations of God's spirit.

The institutionalization of communitarianism

Immediately after Ann Lee's death at Niskeyuna in September of 1784, her closest disciple, James Whittaker, assumed the leadership of the sect. Although Ann Lee had never claimed to be immortal, her death caused many to abandon the faith and increased the vigour of its opponents. Whittaker sought to strengthen the belief of those who remained faithful, urging them to gather at New Lebanon or at the informal centres at the homes of the more wealthy members in Maine, Massachusetts and Connecticut.

In 1785 the 'Shaker testimony' was withdrawn from the world, and proselytization was temporarily abandoned. For three years, Whittaker travelled ceaselessly among the incipient communities, inveighing against sexual temptation and the snares of ambition and political involvement, and luridly invoking the torments which awaited apostates and backsliders. Presumably, his health was broken by his endeavours, for he died in 1787, at the age of thirty-six.

It is difficult to assess the degree to which Whittaker was responsible for the subsequent organizational structure of the sect. His short ministry was an interregnum between Ann Lee's purely charismatic authority, and the extensive routinization effected by Joseph Meacham.

Evans (1859, p. 177) claimed that Whittaker had left directions regarding the establishment of 'Gospel Order', but it seems likely that such directions took the form of injunctions to continue his work rather than of specific instructions. The later Shaker authors sought to sacralize the formal structure of the group – to demonstrate that this structure was directly inspired by the three witnesses. Consequently, they emphasized those aspects of the disparate early teachings which appeared to legitimize the subsequent development of the sect.

Joseph Meacham, who succeeded Whittaker, was certainly the most influential and gifted of the converts made after the New Lebanon revival, and had been hailed by Ann Lee as her 'firstborn son in America'. At the first religious service following Whittaker's death, a youth, speaking 'in inspiration', proclaimed Meacham to be the new leader, and this occurrence, in conjunction with his pentecostal gifts and his standing in the group, was thought to legitimize his claims to the leadership and, consequently, to be the pre-eminent recipient of divine inspiration.

The first 'gift' received by Meacham in his capacity as leader was to appoint Lucy Wright to the female 'Lead', thus giving concrete organizational expression to the sexual dualism of Shaker theology. The New Lebanon Ministry was later expanded by the addition of an elder and eldress, who remained subordinate to Meacham and Wright.

In September 1787, Meachan summoned all those who were free from familial and financial ties to New Lebanon and, in 1788, commenced the 'gathering' of the sect, the formal institutionalization of communitarianism. The New Lebanon society was the first to be gathered, and provided a model for the subsequent societies and, as the permanent home of the Ministry, was the locus of authority of the sect.

Originally, the society at New Lebanon was modelled on the temple at Jerusalem, and consisted of three 'courts', the members of which varied in terms of their spirituality and degree of commitment to the sect. The inner court was composed of persons who were free from worldly ties, and who had given convincing proof of their sincerity by donating their property to the sect. The second court was made up of younger members, who were judged to be less advanced in spirituality, and the outer court consisted mainly of elderly and infirm persons, most of whom were probably dependants of persons in the 'more inward' courts.

As the number of persons gathered at New Lebanon and the other centres increased, Meacham delegated trusted individuals to found subordinate societies until, by the end of 1795, a total of eleven societies had been established in New York State and New England. In the course of this expansion the original loose temple pattern of organization was replaced by a more rigid, contractually based, stratification system, which persisted with only slight modification throughout the life of the sect.

Each society eventually consisted of three 'orders': the senior or church order, the junior order and the novitiate or gathering order. Before outlining the distinctions between these orders, it is necessary to indicate the content of the written covenant which was adopted in 1795, and signed by all existing members and subsequent converts to the group.

The preamble of the written covenant affirmed the belief that the only truly christian form of church was one based on a 'joint interest', that is, on common ownership and use of all goods and property. The signatories declared that they entered the sect, and submitted themselves to the authority of its elders, of their own free will. Similarly, they dedicated their labour and, in the case of the senior members, their property, to the Church, expecting in return only that, as a 'religious right', all persons, regardless of the amount of their contribution, should have a just and equal 'privilege' in the use of all things belonging to the sect.

When an individual professed a desire to embrace the Shaker faith, an assessment of his enthusiasm and of the nature of his external ties was made, and, if the assessment was favourable, he became a member of the society novitiate. The novice continued to live and work in the world, but was privileged to worship with the other novices and with the elders of the novitiate order.

When the elders judged that the individual was suitably prepared, he was expected to settle all his worldly affairs in readiness for enrolment in the junior order of his society. Married persons who entered singly were (usually) only admitted when they separated by mutual agreement and, in the case of a husband entering the society alone, only after he had made settlements upon his wife and children. All entrants had to agree to undertake manual labour, and the Shakers refused responsibility for debts which were not settled or disclosed before entering the sect. Children were only accepted into the care of the sect when this was freely requested by the parents or responsible parent or guardian of the child.

On entering the junior order, the individual covenanted to donate his labour to the sect without payment and, when possessed of property or money, usually dedicated all or part of this to the group, reserving the right to reclaim his property or its equivalent should he leave the sect, but relinquishing all claim to the interest accrued to consecrated monies during the period of his membership.

It was generally expected that, after the convert had proved his faith and capacity for spiritual improvement in the course of several years in the junior order, he would enter the church order of his society. On entering the church order he was required to consign his goods irrevocably to the sect, and promised to make no future claim for recompense for the value of his labour, or for the restitution of consecrated goods.

The Shakers recognized that not every member possessed the abilities or self-control necessary for a continuous ascent through the hierarchy of the sect. However, each member was expected to struggle to attain that degree of moral excellence necessary for him to 'travel' upwards in the group, and much attention was directed to persons who were judged to have stayed over-long in the junior order.

The terms 'order' and 'family' appear to have been at first used synonymously but, concomitant with the expansion of the gathered societies, the meanings of the terms changed. As the societies increased in size the junior orders (and very occasionally the senior orders) were divided into 'family' units, which were usually named after their location within the society, and which contained from fifty to a hundred persons of both sexes.

Thus the maximum membership of the New Lebanon society was approximately six hundred, these members being divided among eight separate families. An individual's membership of a particular order broadly indicated his standing in the total hierarchy of the sect, in terms of his degree of spiritual elevation and commitment to the faith. His society and family membership additionally indicated his spatial location within the group.

Supreme authority in matters spiritual and temporal rested with the central Ministry at New Lebanon. More precisely, such authority was vested in the pre-eminent member, or 'Chief Elder', of the Ministry, who was believed to be in direct spiritual communication with Ann Lee and the other early leaders, and whose decisions and utterances were believed to be gifts from the Holy Spirit.

To question a decision of the Chief Elder was implicitly to question his inspiration, and so to challenge the fundamental tenet of continuing inspiration and the conception that the sect was the vehicle of the divine plan for the redemption of the world. The Shakers believed that God's word and God's church could never be divided, and persons who laid claim to inspiration without ministerial sanction and condonation as 'lesser vessels', were not suffered to remain within the sect.

The Ministry was self-recruiting; when death created a vacancy, the

Chief Elder co-opted another member to the position, and he appointed his own successor without any formal consultation with the mass of the members. However, important appointments were usually submitted to the members for their approbation, which gave formal expression of the unity of the Church and the members' unanimous submission to the Holy Spirit (Youngs, 1808, p. 503):

> Neither Ministers, Elders nor Deacons, nor any others, either in spiritual or temporal trust in the Church, are appointed to their several callings, either by their own individual choice, or by a majority of votes among the people, but by a spontaneous spirit of union which flows through the whole body, by which every created talent, and every special gift of God given to individual members, is mutually preserved in the Church.

In 1792, the Ministry appointed two elders and two eldresses to the leadership of each of the New Lebanon families. As subordinate societies were established, Meacham appointed two members of each sex to the ministries of these societies, the chief elder of the society ministry usually being the individual who had been entrusted with the gathering of the particular society. Where several societies existed in proximity to each other, they were grouped in 'Bishoprics' with one central ministry and subordinate society ministries, and with one chief elder, or 'Bishop', responsible for the several societies.

Elders and eldresses were subsequently appointed for each family within the societies, each elder being responsible for the spiritual development, purity and orderly conduct of the members of his or her sex in the family. The economic authority structure was subordinate to the spiritual hierarchy. In each family two 'deacons' and two 'trustees' of each sex were appointed, the deacons being responsible for the management of the different departments of labour, and the trustees for the allocation of goods within the family and for dealings with other families and with the external society.

The day-to-day affairs of each family were supervised by its elders, but the elders were in all matters subordinate to the society ministry, who periodically examined each family's accounts and appointed deacons and trustees.

Social control

The communitarian structure institutionalized by Meacham had a rigid, hierarchical authority structure which was defined and legitimated in spiritual terms. The Shaker sect was a theocracy, in which the work, general conduct and spiritual progress of every non-ministerial member was under the constant surveillance of a superior to whom, by virtue of his closer proximity to the 'fount of revelation', respect and unquestioning obedience were owed.

An apostate who, after fifteen years in the church order, remained in many ways favourably disposed to the sect, drew this comparison (Elkins, 1853, p. 21).

> The Shaker government, in many points, resembles that of the military.
> All shall look for counsol [sic] and guidance to those immediately
> before them, and shall receive nothing from, nor make application for
> anything, to those but their immediate advisers.

The resemblance of the sect to an army was increased by the deliberate regimentation of every aspect of conduct, and by the unremitting surveillance to which the sectarians were subject. The *Millennial Laws* . . . , which regulated virtually every aspect of Shaker life (reprinted in Andrews, 1963), appear to have been originally framed by Joseph Meacham and were probably largely a codification of Ann Lee's practical and moral strictures. In order to illustrate the degree of control to which the sectarians were subject, some of the regulations concerning their relations with the world and the internal order of the societies will be briefly examined, before considering the wider aspects of social control in the sect.

The Shakers believed the external society to be an antechamber to perdition, and sought to insulate themselves from its contamination. Members were obliged to ask the permission of their elders if they wished to leave the grounds of their society, and such permission was refused if the reasons for leaving were judged to be frivolous. All members returning to the societies were required to present an immediate and full report of their doings to their elders and, if necessary, were to purge and purify themselves by confession before joining in communal worship.

Normally, the ordinary members had little contact with the world, but the trustees, who were responsible for all the financial dealings of each family, occupied a pivotal position between the sect and the outside world, and their every action in the external society was minutely regulated. They were forbidden to enter into any conversations not directly concerning their business, were to shun the company of apostates, and were only to shake hands with non-believers when not to do so would cause offence. The trustees were to wear the distinctive Shaker dress at all times, to kneel in prayer twice daily (by the roadside if need be), and were to eat, drink and lodge together. Presumably to symbolize their unity in the face of evil, they were to maintain such close physical proximity that there 'would not be room for even as much as a dog to run between you and your companion' (cited in Andrews, 1963, p. 258).

The Shakers regarded their ability to maintain sexual purity while living in families composed of both males and females as a standing demonstration of the potency of their faith. However, despite their conviction that they could subdue and extinguish 'the Old Adam', relations between the sexes within the societies were minutely regulated. The brothers and sisters of a family worshipped together and ate in the same hall, but at separate tables, and their living apartments and workrooms were separate. All forms of unnecessary contact between the sexes were forbidden, as was any kind of conduct which was thought conducive to the development of particular affections, as distinct from the spiritual love which all were required to feel for their co-religionists.

Constant supervision and lack of privacy greatly reduced the possibility of clandestine relationships or of deviance of any kind. The retiring rooms of the brothers and sisters were shared by from two to six persons, and the sexes were segregated at work which, especially in the case of the women, was frequently performed in groups. From 1793, contact between the sexes was institutionalized by 'union meetings' which were held four times weekly. In these meetings between four and ten persons of each sex gathered to discuss general topics, each individual being matched with a person of the opposite sex who was judged to be his equal in spiritual development. The author of the *Millennial Laws* stated that 'real flesh hunters' preferred to absent themselves from such orderly and obligatory meetings, and to rendezvous with their 'peculiar favourites' in private (cited in Andrews, 1963, p. 267).

Within each society separation was enforced, not only between the sexes, but between members of different orders and of different families of the same order, and members were forbidden to tell persons from other families of the rules by which the elders governed their own families. Further, the regulations specified the conduct expected of members before, and during, religious services, in the dining hall, in their retiring rooms, as well as their style of speech, the furnishings permitted for their apartments, and even the correct, or orderly, way to lie in bed. 'All should retire to rest in the fear of God, without any playing or boisterous laughing, and lie straight' (Andrews, 1963, p. 270).

The ordinary members were effectively isolated from any but rare contact with persons in the 'world of generation', and the leaders of the group also sought to protect the sectarians from any opinions or knowledge that might provide a basis for challenges to their authority or to the sect's doctrines. Members were permitted to receive visitors only at the trustees' office, where their conversations could be overheard; their letters were opened, and all but the most rudimentary education was frowned upon.

The primary source of information about the external society appears to have been occasional readings from newspapers at mealtimes. According to the accounts of apostates, the items read mainly concerned economic disasters and criminality, and served to strengthen the members' conviction of the degeneracy of the world and of their own good fortune in being saved from it.

In addition to restricting information about the external society, the elders appear to have had no compunction about concealing news of internal disruption from the ordinary members. Thus the Shaker authoresses White and Taylor (1905, pp. 69–70) blithely reported the temporary suppression of all information concerning the secession of two of the English members who refused to believe that the succession of James Whittaker was divinely ordained.

The common member was physically, socially, economically and intellectually isolated from the world. Subject to constant moral exhortation, and frequently warned of the dangers and varieties of temptations to selfishness and disobedience, it is likely that many unhappy members were unable to command the moral courage necessary to leave the sect, and rationalized their discontent in religious terms as being the last lingering vestige of their 'unregenerate personalities'. Mary Dyer, an apostate who ceaselessly campaigned against the Shakers, graphically summed up the situation of dissident individuals: 'though all are in trouble, none knows of any but their own' (1818, p. 18).

The above discussion indicates some of the formal regulations which governed the conduct expected of the sectarians in virtually every foreseeable situation and moment of their lives. However, the mere existence of regulations is seldom, if ever, sufficient to control individual behaviour absolutely and to ensure total conformity to group norms. Behavioural regulations, no matter how explicit, must be supported by positive sanctions to reward conformity, and by negative sanctions to punish non-conformity.

Among the Shakers, the most important positive sanctions were of a supernatural kind. A person who adhered strictly to the norms of the group would be likely to win the approval of his elders, and to 'travel' rapidly upwards in its hierarchy to occupy a prestigious and powerful position in the sect, and, most important, in the world to come. Even the most humble member who strove to 'live up to the light accorded him', could expect other-worldly elevation to a position far above that of the vainglorious princes of the earth. Additionally, all faithful members enjoyed the mundane, but none the less gratifying, approval of their elders and fellows.

Some of the early apostates (several of whom were probably half-crazed by repeated exposure to revivalistic excitement and disappointed millennial expectations) claimed that recalcitrant members were cruelly punished and prevented from leaving the group, but there was probably little truth in these rumours. The apostate Elkins (1853, p. 30) reported that corporal punishment was only used on small boys, and the hymns of the sect stressed that only faith and submission to the Spirit of God bound persons to the sect (Philos Harmoniae, 1833, p. 97).

> Now will you believe me? I'm really sincere.
> I'm not drag'd on, I'm a true volunteer.

A variety of formal sanctions of varying degrees of severity certainly existed; remonstrance and enforced confession, removal of privileges of worship and of rank, and outright expulsion. Individuals who seemed likely to be troublesome were put under special surveillance and, if 'unsanctified attachments' were detected, the persons involved were transferred to separate societies. Members who consistently ignored regulations or questioned revealed doctrine, might be reproved by the assembled elders of their family or, in more serious cases, by the society ministry. Such individuals were urged to curb their selfishness and egotism, and frequently were warned of the special torments awaiting backsliders. If they persisted in their disobedience they were excluded from worship and might be reduced to a lower, or 'back', family or order. On showing signs of repentance the delinquent was ordered to make a full and abject confession of his sins to the elders.

Most persons who seceded from the sect appear to have left reasonably amicably after admitting that they were insufficiently strong to 'bear a full cross'. Such persons were usually refunded some portion of their dedicated property, or given a small sum in token of their service to the group. Occasionally, however, persons were expelled for persistent indiscipline, doctrinal intransigence or sexual irregularities, and were publicly anathematized and given no portion of their goods or any quittance money. When an apostasy was announced in the family meetings, a kind of condemnatory knell was chanted (cited in Andrews, 1963, p. 193).

> I'll sense the awful situation,
> Of the souls that turn away,
> They lose all hopes of their salvation,
> For them Believers cannot pray.

Despite their horror of apostasy, the Shakers were able to interpret even secession as providential, in that the removal of evil persons increased the purity of the group, and strengthened the power of the faithful to resist sin. Thus a Shaker poet (Philos Harmoniae, 1833, p. 98) stated cheerfully with reference to apostates:

> Their trumpets a-blowing 'we're all now a-going',
> Is soul-cheering music if well understood;
> 'Tis truly prophetic, that there's an emetic,
> That's purging the evil away from the good.

The authoritarianism of the Shaker elders, the ascetic regimentation of the lives of the sectarians, and their social, intellectual and moral segregation from the world, were all justified in terms of the theology and mission of the sect, and together reinforced a coherent and all-pervasive normative system which for several decades engendered a high degree of commitment from the individual members.

The Shakers believed that only by the exercise of unremitting discipline and self-control could they increase their spirituality and so perfect and extend their societies. Order and discipline were at once the basis and the fruits of their utopian vision of the world transformed by the Holy Spirit and their efforts into the celibate Kingdom of God. Asceticism, isolation and authoritarianism were legitimized and had crucial significance as long as their utopian faith persisted.

Shaker worship

To single out Shaker religious services, songs and dances as the components of the worship of the sect is, in a sense, to make an artificial distinction, in that each Shaker was urged to conduct himself as an agent and instrument of God in every aspect of his life. However, the religious services of the sect were of special significance; they did not simply express the Shakers' devotion to God, but they were also regarded as bringing the group of worshippers into direct contact with the Holy Spirit, and so endowing them with the power to resist temptation, and to overthrow the corruption of the world (Youngs, 1808, p. 584):

> It is not merely the external performance of the present worship of
> God, by which any are justified, but the same being given by the
> special gift and revelation of God, according to promise, it is therefore
> a medium through which the faithful receive the anointing power of
> the Holy Ghost, which operates effectually to the destruction of the
> nature of sin.

During the lifetime of Ann Lee, the worship of the group was informal, largely unstructured and relatively spontaneous. The sectarians sang, danced and shouted until they fell into ecstatic trances and received prophetic revelations or humbler gifts from the Holy Spirit – glossalalia and such other physical manifestations as whirling and jumping. The 'services' in this period were undisciplined and near-hysterical, and the songs of the sect were probably versions of English and American revival hymns. Interested persons were encouraged to participate in these meetings, and if they exhibited any of the typical physical manifestations, these were hailed as signs of spiritual struggle and of ripeness for conversion.

A considerable measure of discipline appears to have been imposed on the early spontaneous and individualistic forms of worship in the years 1785 to 1792, when the Shakers temporarily ceased their evangelism and sought to absorb the converts made after the New Lebanon revival. The formalization of Shaker worship was most marked in the Sunday meetings which were open to the public. The private family meetings, which were held several times each week, were less decorous and restrained, and in these meetings 'promiscuous', or individualistic, dancing and other gifts regularly occurred.

The first formal Shaker dance was developed between 1785 and 1788, and in the first decades of the nineteenth century all aspects of the group's worship were further regulated and codified. New dances were introduced in 1817 and 1822, and the symbolic gestures involved in these were so complicated that they had to be practised repeatedly before being publicly performed. Three collections of the hymns of the group were published, and from 1820 to 1825, a system of musical notation peculiar to the sect was developed.

Although the overall pattern from 1792 to 1830 was one of increasing formalization and elaboration of ritual, this pattern was frequently broken and, in times of external religious revival, when large numbers of converts were drawn to the sect, its meetings were characterized by a high degree of excitement and frequent, seemingly uncontrollable, physical manifestations.

Such phenomena were, predictably, most common in those societies in the immediate vicinity of the revivals, but the excitement was contagious. Thus, the old-established northern societies experienced a 'sympathetic revival' in 1807, shortly after the western societies had been founded. The societies also underwent periodic internal, purificatory 'revivals', during which gifts of inspiration condemning laxity, frivolity and backsliding were common.

The practice and performance of the complicated dances and marches had an obvious recreational function for the sectarians, and the Shaker theologians were concerned to justify dancing as an act of worship. They insisted that man's duty was to devote all his faculties to the praise of God, and cited scriptural precedent for the practice.

The symbolic functions of the dances appear to have been clearly understood by the sectarians. The close-order 'marching' expressed the unity and discipline of the group, and the proximity but physical separation of the lines of male and female dancers represented the group's maintenance of celibacy in the face of temptation. More plainly still, the hymns or chants of the sect emphasized the Shaker virtues, especially the need to conquer all manifestations of selfishness (Philos Harmoniae, 1833, p. 31):

> There is but one enemy I have to kill,
> That old wicked rebel whose name is Self-will;
> This root of all evil shall get the death-blow,
> And truly I'm bound to fight no other foe;
> We'll stick to the battle and never retreat,
> Until we have trodden him under our feet;
> The war is commenced, and now we proceed,
> To mortify self and follow our lead.

'Consecrated labour'

The formal structure of the Shaker economic system; the expansion and diversification of production for consumption within and outside the societies, the methods of distribution of the goods produced, and the vicis-situdes of the Shaker economy have been described in detail in several works (Andrews, 1932, 1963; Melcher, 1941). Here, less attention will be paid to the minutiae of the sect's economic system than to the effect of the religious beliefs of the Shakers on their attitudes to work and to craftmanship.

The emphasis on the maintenance of gospel order extended into the economic activities of the Shakers. Several pages of the *Millennial Laws* were devoted to ordinances concerning every aspect of productive activity, and these regulations gave concrete expression to the ideological insistence that the believers should regard all their tasks as 'consecrated labour'; as acts of worship devoted to the glory of God.

During their first years in America, Ann Lee's small group of followers were very poor, and the sharing of goods and money was a course dictated by simple necessity. By the time of the New Lebanon revival, the Shakers had established themselves on a somewhat more secure economic footing, but the majority of the converts made in the years 1779 to 1784 either supported themselves, or were attached to the households of wealthy sympathizers where they performed domestic and agricultural tasks in exchange for their keep.

The formal communitarianism consciously institutionalized by Joseph Meacham provided a means of isolating converts from the hostility and temptations of the external society, and economic communism and agricultural self-sufficiency helped to intensify this isolation. In the economic sphere, as in others, selections from Ann Lee's diverse prophecies and strictures were used to legitimate social arrangements which were instituted after her death.

The Shakers regarded communism as the only system of production and distribution appropriate to life in the 'resurrection state'. Communistic labour was thought to demonstrate the essential properties of the Shaker Church, and to inculcate and reinforce the Shaker virtues. Communism was seen as a living demonstration of the bonds of love existing between believers, and manual labour was thought to promote humility, as well as providing the means to demonstrate Shaker charity and to cater for the thousands of converts who were confidently expected to flock to the Shaker communities.

The Shakers regarded themselves as God's stewards and pioneers, and their labour as an act of worship and of reclamation. To fertilize the soil of the communities was to improve land which, in an especially intimate way, belonged to God, and so was in some small part a furtherance of God's plan. As all labour was a sacrament, so none was considered menial, and all individuals, including the elders and ministry, were obliged to spend some part of their time in manual labour.

The original communities gathered after the New Lebanon revival were initially almost purely agricultural. Each community was established around a nucleus of land dedicated by the wealthiest convert in the district, and contiguous land was purchased with money brought in by other converts and with the assistance of funds donated by the established societies.

As indicated, the dualistic authority structure was extended into the economic sphere by the appointment in each family of two deacons and two trustees of each sex. Each deacon was responsible to the elders for specific departments of labour, which originally provided directly for the needs of the family. The trustees were responsible for the overall planning of the economic activities of the family and were its legal representatives, responsible for its financial transactions and condition. Each family had a central store where goods produced within the family were collected and from which externally produced goods were distributed.

Formally, each family was economically independent; in practice there was considerable occupational specialization and mutual aid between families of the same society and, less frequently, between different societies. Because of the small size of each family group, and the wide range of demands engendered within it, individual work assignments varied frequently, although some of the more skilled members seem to have practised their trades on a full-time basis, and the gradual expansion of non-agricultural activities made such specialization increasingly common.

The agricultural basis of the Shaker economy was soon supplemented by various craft industries and, from the time of the gathering of the societies, such agriculturally derived products as seeds, brooms and herbal preparations were sold to the external society, either by local merchants on a commission basis, or by Shaker pedlars who developed regular routes and markets for their wares. During the first three decades of the nineteenth century, the range of manufactured goods produced by the sect expanded greatly, and this expansion was paralleled by a more systematic and large-scale external sale of goods.

As the craft and manufacturing industries of the sect expanded, the Shakers sought to demonstrate their honesty in their dealings with outsiders, and strove to make their products concrete embodiments of the principles of order and unity. Unity was demonstrated by the anonymous production of largely standardized goods. Once a functional and harmonious design had been developed, the Shaker craftsmen adhered to it, scorning variation for its own sake as frivolous and unseemly. Purity was expressed in the quality of the goods produced. First-class materials were used and slipshod workmanship was not tolerated. The production of non-essential articles for consumption within the societies or for sale was prohibited, and the asceticism of the sectarians led them to reject ornamentation, which was thought to be closely associated with individuality and sensuality.

Insistence on standardization of production and the avoidance of ornamentation, together with the excellent craftsmanship of many of the Shakers, led to the gradual development of distinctive styles of dwelling houses and furniture. The sacralization of labour, and the associated emphasis on the utility and efficiency of its products, together with the desire not only to be separate from the world, but to excel it in every way, was productive of much ingenuity, and many improvements and inventions are credited to the sect (Andrews, 1963, pp. 113–15).

The necessity for sober, diligent labour was stressed in the group's basic theological works, and the *Millennial Laws* warned that drones and sluggards (among others) would 'in no wise pass unpunished, in the final settlement with souls' (cited in Andrews, 1963, p. 287). The hymns of the group reiterated these teachings and urged unremitting labour as a safeguard against temptation (Philos Harmoniae, 1833, p. 34):

> For while I am faithful to do what is right,
> And have not a moment to spare;
> I'm guarded about by the angels of light,
> And satan can never come there.
>
> O what a great privilege I do enjoy!
> Good Elders to teach what is just,
> And always a plenty of righteous employ,
> Sufficient to mortify lust.

The Shakers were successful in establishing the quality of their products and the honesty of their dealings. As a result, the demand for their products expanded rapidly in the early years of the nineteenth century, and the capital which accrued from the profits of manufactures and from the property of converts was largely invested in land, which provided the basis for new communities and new centres for missionary activity.

The large, well-tended estates of the Shakers contrasted very favourably with the small single-family farms which surrounded them, and provided impressive support for the sect's utopian beliefs. In the first decades of the nineteenth century, the Shakers were convinced that they had established the Kingdom of God on earth, and confidently expected the expansion of this Kingdom, despite the opposition of a sinful world. The coming transformation and regeneration of the earth and its people was compared to the growth of a harvest from seeds of corn; it would be the slow-ripening product of much labour. The year of the gathering of the societies was seen by the Shakers as (Youngs, 1808, p. 520):

> the commencement of all the blessedness spoken of by all the prophets, and beyond this no given period of prophecy extends, as thenceforward unto the end, in conformity to the beginning, all things will be fulfilled, pertaining to the salvation of mankind and all the glory and blessedness of the latter day.

Social composition

The Shakers sought converts enthusiastically and ardently. Each accession of new members vindicated the utopianism of the sect, and the establishment of each new society was seen as a distinct step towards the conversion of the earth into the Kingdom of God. The sectarians' beliefs permitted a wide range of interpretation. When evangelism was successful, there was much excitement in the group and the members expected a rapid transformation of the world. When recruitment dwindled, there was much disappointment which the elders attempted to counter by emphasizing the corruption of the world and the magnitude of the task of the sect. In 1823, when the extremely rapid expansion that occurred in the first years of the nineteenth century had been followed by a decade of more gradual growth, the Shakers insisted that (Green and Wells, 1823, p. xiv):

> The smallness of the work is no discouragement to us, nor any
> disparagement to its first founders. It is indeed a work of too much
> purity to find a rapid increase among the inhabitants of a sinful world,
> who are so far lost and sunk in their carnal corruptions.

The Shakers were reluctant to give precise statements of their numbers, and justified this reluctance by biblical references, but, despite the inadequacy of the data, the broad pattern of the expansion of the sect can be discerned. Between 1776 and 1779, the years of isolation at Niskeyuna, no converts were made. From 1779 to 1784, the year of the death of Ann Lee after her missionary journeys, approximately a thousand converts were attracted to the sect. From 1785 to 1797, the Shaker testimony was withdrawn from the world while the societies were gathered, and from 1797 to 1805, a steady stream of converts was drawn from religious revivals, especially in the south-west. By the end of the eighteenth century, eleven separate communities had been established, and in 1803 there were thirteen or fourteen hundred members in the societies.

By 1812, after the establishment of societies in Kentucky and Ohio, there were more than 3,000 persons in the sect. In 1823, the Shakers themselves revealed that they had 4,100 members (Green and Wells, 1823, pp. 75–6), and by the mid eighteen thirties, the establishment of several additional societies in Kentucky and Ohio had swollen the numbers of the sect to more than 5,000. A peak of something less than 6,000 members was reached in the decade 1840 to 1850, at which time eighteen separate societies existed.

The expansion of the Shakers into Kentucky and Ohio was based on the converts they drew from the subjects of the Great Kentucky Revival of 1799 to 1806. Revivals of varying magnitude had been endemic in the American colonies since 1734, when the preaching of Jonathan Edwards gave rise to the series of revivals known as the 'Great Awakening'. Revival services and preaching, and the physical responses evoked by this preaching (trances, convulsions and fits), while apparently spontaneous, had become informally institutionalized in the frontier and backwoods areas among a population who led hard and dangerous lives, and whose independent and egalitarian values contrasted with the deterministic élitism of the Calvinist denominations.

Revivalist preachers of the period proclaimed the possibility of attaining salvation through repentance and reformation, and stressed the horrors of the damnation which would be the lot of the unregenerate. Their preaching was intensely emotional, frequently coloured by millennial imagery or prophecies, and was calculated to arouse great apprehension in their audience who, while possibly not active members of any religious organization, were accustomed to conceptualize in religious terms.

The areas which became the State of Kentucky (in 1792) and the State of Tennessee (in 1796) were populated in the second half of the eighteenth century by settlers of predominantly Scots-Irish descent and Presbyterian religion. At the beginning of the nineteenth century life in these frontier areas was still primitive and hard. From 1797 to 1799, a revival, which had originated in the Carolinas, gathered momentum in Kentucky, especially in Logan and Christian counties, and reached a climax with huge campfire meetings in 1800 and 1801. The Presbyterians appear to have been the most seriously affected denomination, but members of the Methodist and Baptist Churches were also influenced, and from 1801 to 1806 the revival spread into Tennessee and Ohio.

Richard McNemar, a Presbyterian preacher who subsequently joined the Shakers, wrote an account of the development of the revival (1807) and of the secession of his group of 'New Lights' from the Presbyterian Church. McNemar and the other revival preachers challenged and rejected the orthodox Calvinist doctrine of limited election and predestination, and insisted more optimistically and more democratically that salvation was potentially open to all. The New Lights believed that all those persons who sought to discover the light of God in themselves would be saved, and taught that every man should be free to worship God in the way he thought most suitable.

In 1803 the New Lights renounced the jurisdiction of the Presbyterian Synod of Kentucky, and constituted themselves into the 'Presbytery of Springfield', a body which was more colloquially known as the 'Schismatics'. The Schismatics believed themselves to be direct recipients of the grace of God. Physical manifestations of religious excitement – rolling on the ground, 'the jerks' and 'the barks' – were encouraged as outward signs of grace. After a time some measure of restraint appears to have been imposed on the antinomianism inherent in their theological position, and the group gradually developed from 'individual manifestations' of possession by the Holy Spirit to acceptance of 'praising God in the dance'.

Shaker missionaries, dispatched from New Lebanon, arrived in Kentucky early in 1805, and encountered the New Lights just as their extreme enthusiasm was waning and their millennial expectations were being replaced by doubts and uncertainty. McNemar himself had reached a point of despair where he 'could see nothing in the past work as a foundation to build upon' (McNemar, 1807, p. 87).

The Shakers skilfully exploited these doubts and fears, and preached the necessity of the Schismatics making a full confession and embracing celibacy and communitarianism if they did not want to lose 'the extraordinary effusions of the Spirit they had been under' (McNemar, 1808, p. 83).

McNemar and Dunlavy, the leaders of the Schismatics, both joined the Shakers, as did many of their followers. In 1807 the Presbytery of Spring-field was dissolved, and in 1811 McNemar journeyed to New Lebanon to be interviewed by Lucy Wright, who had become leader of the sect after Meacham's death in 1796. Between 1811 and 1826, to the accompaniment of much persecution, six societies were founded in Kentucky and Ohio, and a seventh, short-lived, society was also established in Indiana.

No successful societies were founded by the sect after 1826, but the numbers of the group were augmented in the next two decades by recruits from later, smaller revivals, by individual converts, and by a few of the disappointed followers of Robert Owen. In the eighteen forties, the last large wave of recruits was drawn from persons who had given credence to the millennial prophecies of William Miller.

It is difficult to come to any firm conclusions regarding the social position, age and sex of the early converts to the Shaker faith, but some inferences can be made. Revivalistic fervour reached its greatest peak in isolated frontier regions, where the population was predominantly youthful and engaged in subsistence agriculture. Most of the converts to the sect in the last decades of the eighteenth and first decades of the nineteenth centuries, appear to have been independent farmers or the sons and daughters of farmers. Presumably, a large proportion of the converts to the sect were young persons, whose lack of family and property ties would have facilitated their abandonment of the world, but this assertion cannot be substantiated.

The mass of the membership were probably barely literate, though well versed in knowledge of scripture, but such men as Meacham, Dunlavy and McNemar were well-educated and had been substantial farmers. It seems likely that the sexual dualism of the sect exerted a greater appeal to women than to men, but this cannot be demonstrated for the period of the Shakers' expansion, although in the second half of the nineteenth century women converts were definitely in the majority.

Undoubtedly most of those persons who were converted to Shakerism during periods of religious revival and who became full members of the sect despite persecution, family disruption and financial sacrifice, were motivated by religious belief, and ardently hoped for the transformation of the world into a place of order, harmony and purity. However, without casting any aspersions on the sincerity of these converts, it is possible to speculate on the attraction of the sect for persons with certain common life experiences and personality traits.

Sectarian groups frequently bear the impress of the character of their founder throughout their development, and this character, infused through the particular theological and cultural emphases of the group, may exert an attraction for certain types of individual or social groups rather than others. Such differential attraction is likely to be an important influence on the evolution of the sect. In the case of the Shakers, it seems likely that the sanctification of celibacy, and abhorrence of sensuality in any form, would have had an especial appeal to persons whose own sexuality was undeveloped, or whose sexual experiences had been unsatisfactory or wounding.

The emphasis on obedience and humility probably appealed to submissive rather than to aggressive personalities. Several observers and commentators concluded that the sect appealed to timorous and socially inadequate persons, and that membership was sought by many individuals whose domestic and financial situation was precarious. Thus Senator Robert Wickliffe, speaking in defence of the Shakers before the Senate of Kentucky in 1831, urged his opponent to visit the Shaker communities and 'there see how many human beings have found shelter from the blighting effects of your divorce laws' (Wickliffe, 1832, p. 26).

The existence of such differential recruitment during the period of the sect's expansion can only be a matter of conjecture, but it seems likely that, as the novelty of the Shakers' doctrines declined, and the country surrounding their societies became more settled and civilized, the societies increasingly attracted persons seeking security and refuge, rather than theological certainty and ascetic activism. An increasing proportion of submissive and complaisant members may in part explain the slow atrophy of the culture of the sect, and the drift towards accommodation to the world which took place in the second half of the nineteenth century.

Relations with the external society

The relationship between a sect and the society in which it exists is a reciprocal one. The attitude which the sectarians adopt to the external society is primarily dictated by their religious beliefs, and this attitude largely determines the reception which is accorded to the sect by the world. In turn, the world's response to the sect, be it tolerant, indifferent, or hostile, may strengthen or modify the sect's original attitude to the external society. Thus, a sect which vigorously anathematizes all worldly institutions and values is likely to encounter extreme hostility and severe persecution, which may lead the sectarians to abandon their original witness and to adopt a retreatist position, seeking to ignore the world and cultivate their own spirituality.

When such a change occurs, or when tolerance or indifference leads a sect to a gradual *rapprochement* with the world, there is likely to be a change in doctrinal emphasis and exegesis. Those doctrines which previously legitimated active proselytization and condemnation of the world are likely to be less emphasized (or may be interpreted figuratively rather than literally) and the self-conception of the sect may change from being the vessel of the wrath of God to being a gathered remnant or, perhaps, a beacon to guide the slow progress of mankind.

Joseph Meacham appears to have been primarily responsible for refining the Shakers' utopianism out of the relatively simple, admonitory, apocalyptic conversionism of Ann Lee. After her death and the short ministry of James Whittaker, the Shakers strove to balance introversionism against conversionism, and sought to attract ever-increasing numbers of converts while maintaining and strengthening the internal order of the societies. Similarly, in relation to their economic activities and the demands of the state, the Shakers attempted to develop means of regularizing these matters without diminishing the vigour of their condemnation of the 'stained and degraded' world of generation.

For the fifty years after the New Lebanon revival (with the exception of the years 1785 to 1797 when the first societies were gathered) the Shakers were engaged in intense evangelistic activity. They did not simply 'wrestle' with and instruct interested visitors, but actively sought out centres of revivalistic activity and dispatched missionaries to them. As a result of evangelical experiences and concerns, the doctrines of the sect were systematized and greatly elaborated.

The Shaker missionaries, who were always chosen from among the most learned and trusted members of the sect, insisted that release from sin and the eventual attainment of salvation could only be found in the Shaker communities, and they inveighed against marriage and the depravity of all other religious systems. The violence of their testimonies, coupled with their success in winning converts from the orthodox denominations, aroused much hostility and violent persecution. In each area where Shaker missionaries were active they were mobbed and accused variously of carnality, treachery and breaking up families to gain land. McNemar (1808, p. 104) summarized the extreme and varied charges which were levied against the sect after the Kentucky revival:

> And according as the wind of fancy blew, so it was a fact, credible at least among the Christ-ians [*sic*], that the Shakers castrated all their males, and consequently exposed their necks to the gallows; or divested of all modesty, stripped and danced naked in their night meetings, blew out the candles, and went into a promiscuous debauch. And what was still more shocking – the fruits of their unlawful embraces, they concealed by the horrid crime of murder.

In some states, legislation specifically designed to penalize the Shakers was enacted (and was subsequently repealed) and the written covenant of 1795 was modified five times in the next forty years, each time being strengthened in the light of experience gained in prior legal proceedings. The associated question of 'settlements' made to seceders was also regularized and formalized. Settlements of cash or property were made only after seceders had signed a discharge acknowledging that the settlement was made by the Shakers as an act of generosity, and not because of any legal obligation.

The theological systematization and the successive revisions of the membership covenant which took place in the first three decades of the nineteenth century, were undertaken respectively to facilitate proselytization, and as defensive measures to protect the societies from the hostility of the world. In this same period, the Shakers were forced to compromise with the demands of the state with regard to taxes, military service and education.

The Shakers did not vote and, at least in the period here being discussed, they held themselves aloof from political concerns. Members were forbidden to discuss political events and were largely insulated from knowledge of them. The affairs of the world were thought to be inherently corrupt and degenerate and unworthy of the attention of believers. The sect's attitude to politics in this period can be well illustrated by James Whittaker's admonishment of some members who expressed sympathy with Shay's rebellion (Green and Wells, 1823, p. 47):

> They that give way to a party spirit, and are influenced by the division and contentions of the world, . . . have no part with me. . . . The spirit of party is the spirit of the world, and whoever indulges it, and unites with one evil spirit against another, is off from christian ground.

Despite their aloofness from politics, the Shakers compromised their separatist and pacifist principles to the extent of paying whatever taxes were demanded of them. Joseph Meacham appears to have been the initial advocate of this conciliatory policy and, as a result, the societies paid their local taxes even when they did not benefit from them.

Until their pacifism was legislatively recognized in the several states in which societies were established, they also paid militia taxes and sums in lieu of the military service of their members. By 1833, these cumulative compromises had been rationalized in scriptural terms, and the position of the sect was summarized in one of the group's hymns (Philos Harmoniae, 1833, p. 31):

> I've listed for Christ, I have taken the oath,
> If Caesar should call me, I cannot serve both,
> I'll follow my captain, his call is divine;
> If Caesar should sue me, I'll pay him his fine.

The attitude of the sect to worldly knowledge, and implicitly to education, has already been indicated in the discussion of social control and of the associated isolation of the members from external influences. In the years after the gathering the societies paid their education taxes to the neighbouring communities, and instructed the children of converts at their own expense, but as the relations between the societies and the surrounding population improved, a proportion of the sum raised by local education taxes was returned to the sect, and the Shakers established their own schools.

The children in the societies were either attached to the church order, or were gathered into separate 'school orders'. They were bound like apprentices to the society by their parents or legal guardian, and the Shakers promised to board and educate them until maturity, when they were given a free choice to leave or remain in the society. The education given was rudimentary, but was probably comparable to that in secular rural schools of the period; reading, writing and good manners were taught by the Lancastrian monitorial system. The curriculum was slightly expanded in later years, but the emphasis remained squarely on practical knowledge and the acquisition of manual skills. Classical knowledge was shunned and even the learning of French was condemned as likely to encourage sensuality.

Summary

In any discussion of changes in the religious teachings and associated social attitudes of a sect, it is difficult to avoid giving the impression that all these changes came about as the result of the deliberate action of the sectarians. In reality, most sects are endowed with a distinctive body of doctrine at the time of their emergence, and these doctrines remain largely unchanged throughout the life of the sect.

The changes which do occur in the teachings and social attitudes of a sect usually come about by a slow, and largely unconscious, process of shifting emphases and cumulative modifications of exegesis in response to external and internal exigencies, and to less dramatic changes in the external society, and in the social position and composition of the sectarians. Typically, these attitudinal and ideological changes are only recognized and justified a considerable time after they first become manifest in the group.

In a utopian sect, the rationale of the group – the religiously inspired attempt to establish and promulgate communities – involves a direct, conscious translation of religious imperatives into social realities. However, these imperatives are likely to reflect the doctrinal emphases which predominated in the original, pre-utopian, group, and their translation is fraught with much ambiguity and permits of much subtle variation.

In the case of the Shakers, Ann Lee's charisma was sufficient to win her the leadership of the Wardley group, and to inspire a handful of followers to accompany her to America. The early Shakers were united by their admiration for Ann Lee and their abhorrence of sexuality into an informal, largely unstructured fellowship. They believed that celibacy was the only means to salvation; in the continuance of revelation manifested in ecstatic prophecy, and condemned the world's toleration and condonation of sexual relations.

Ann Lee and her first followers appear to have expected the imminent, apocalyptic inauguration of a world-wide celibate society. The hardships and isolation suffered by the group in its first years in America led to a somewhat more gradualistic interpretation of the sect's mission, and this gradualism was subsequently elaborated into full-blown religious utopianism.

It was left to the American, Joseph Meacham, to outline the system of historical exegesis which established the Shakers as heirs to the 'lesser light' of all those groups who had revealed some part of God's will to the world. Meacham insisted that the Shaker societies were the nuclei of God's Kingdom on earth, and that they were destined to spread throughout the earth. Their expansion was, however, made dependent upon the spirituality and deliberate evangelical efforts of the sectarians. The Shakers were to establish and maintain their societies as standing examples of the perfection of the regenerate life, and were to labour to intensify their spirituality and to extend their societies.

Concomitantly with the development of the Shakers' utopianism, the social implications of their teachings were explored and, during the years of the gathering, the original unstructured charismatic fellowship was replaced by a hierarchical, dualistic, authoritarian organizational system presided over by a self-recruiting ministry, and based on formally organized communism. Communism and communitarianism were originally adopted as expedients, but they were consonant with the early Shakers' implicit perfectionism and utopianism. As the utopian element was increasingly stressed, so the establishment of communistic communities was endowed with ideological significance and became the primary goal of the sect.

The Shakers' attempt to transcend, not just the spirituality of persons outside the sect but all the institutions of the world (which were dismissed as tainted with the corruption arising from sexuality), resulted in the establishment of a distinctive Shaker culture. The religious, social and productive activities of the members were all integrated and legitimated by the value system of the group and, in turn, this value system was reinforced by every aspect of group activity.

The attitude of the early Shakers to the world was basically one of aversion and contempt. They were concerned to construct societies which, in their purity and harmony, would contrast in every way with the external society and, consequently, the sectarians had no interest in social reform. For the utopian, as for the secular or religious revolutionary, institutional change is pointless, as the whole basis of society is inherently corrupt. To the early Shakers, political parties and reformist groups were simply divisions in the forces of corruption.

In the years of denunciatory evangelism, and in the period of confident utopianism when the societies were expanding rapidly (the first three decades of the nineteenth century), the Shakers had little or no interest in the specific social questions and reformist proposals which were to preoccupy some of the later leaders of the sect.

As indicated, the Shakers rejected the Calvinist doctrines of predestination and limited election, and insisted on the universality of the possibility of salvation. This tenet, in conjunction with the Shakers' eagerness for converts and their positive estimation of 'simplicity', promoted several attempts to convert neighbouring Indian tribes. Further, the Shakers condemned slave-holding as an abomination introduced to the 'Christian' Church by the Emperor Constantine but, in the first decades of the nineteenth century, when the Shakers cited their attitudes to the Indians or slavery, they did so to demonstrate their divergence from the world, and not in the context of proposals for piecemeal reform.

In the first quarter of the nineteenth century, the original violence of the sectarians' denunciations of the world was somewhat muted. Ann Lee's diatribes against marriage and carnality had been so vehement as to infuriate many of the persons who heard her testimony, but in their major theological works the Shakers' views were presented more temperately. Thus Green and Wells discussed marriage in quite an urbane fashion, but still insisted that matrimony was incompatible with regeneration and hence with salvation (1823, p. 163):

> We consider matrimony to be a civil institution, and as such, it is both useful and necessary for mankind in their natural state; but it does not belong to the true followers of Christ; and for that reason they have nothing to do with it.

Vehement denunciations of the world were most frequent prior to the gathering of the societies in 1788, and subsequently in periods when the sectarians experienced elation or despair; when successful evangelism seemed to promise a rapid transformation of the world, or when persecution appeared to threaten the very continuance of the Shakers' testimony.

The amount of persecution experienced by the sect varied directly with the vehemence of their preaching and the success of their proselytizing, although even when the societies had apparently established peaceful relations with their neighbours, local hostility was sometimes aroused by the accounts of apostates or, in wartime, by the sect's pacifism. The Shakers interpreted persecution as a demonstration of the wickedness of the world and as a proof of the power of their testimony, and attributed any misfortune that befell their persecutors to God's wrath. They regarded their communities as being divinely protected and boasted that (Philos Harmoniae, 1833, p. 54):

> No sin can ever enter here,
> Nor sinners rear a steeple;

> 'Tis kept by God's peculiar care,
> For his peculiar people.

Despite their conviction of divine protection, the Shaker leaders were also aware that the establishment and maintenance of their communities depended on the tolerance of the external society. Accordingly, they sought to cultivate this necessary minimum tolerance, and to refute any accusations which might have led to violent persecution or to governmental suppression of the communities.

The conflicting pressures of theological conviction and expediency led the Shakers into a complicated and ambivalent relationship with the external society, and they occasionally proclaimed their loyalty and gratitude to the American nation, while more consistently condemning its basic institutions. This ambivalence can be illustrated by a quotation from a 'colloquoy' in which the Shakers praised American political institutions, while sneering at the spiritual condition of the population (Philos Harmoniae, 1833, p. 121):

> Now free toleration to conscience is given –
> we're saved from the terror of tyrants and kings,
> The American eagle now soars towards heaven,
> And bears us aloft on its virtuous wings.

However,

> Americans boast of their high independence,
> And what a great vic'try their forefathers won;
> But still we perceive that their wretched descendants
> Are press'd and enslav'd, after all that's been done.

Another poem expressed the Shakers' hatred for worldly persons who frequently ridiculed their self-sacrifice and ignored God's message. With a marked absence of humility or compassion, the Shakers dwelt on the fate which would befall all those who spurned their teachings (Philos Harmoniae, 1833, p. 88):

> Alive in the flesh they are forcibly launched,
> into a hot lake without bottom or shore: –
> Their worm dieth not, and the fire is not quenched,
> O what a sad fix for the beast and the whore.
> Alive in the midst of unquenchable fire!
> their enmity strong, and their torment as great!
> The grand dissolution, 'tis said they desire,
> and seek after death, but alas its too late.

Outwardly, in the course of the first three decades of the nineteenth century, the relations between the Shaker communities and the external society became more amicable. In this period the total membership of the sect expanded steadily, the individual communities prospered, the legal basis of the communism of the group was successfully defended and strengthened and the doctrines of the sect were systematized and made public in successive, impressively documented theological works.

Numerical expansion, prosperity and success against their opponents all served to strengthen the confidence of the members that they were living in the resurrection state, and that their selfless asceticism would merit magnificent heavenly rewards. Elkins (1853, p. 131) summarized the confident utopianism of the sectarians who believed themselves to possess the only key to salvation, and to be ushering in the last age of man – God's final dispensation for the earth:

All the events of which earth has been the theatre, have each contributed, by a providential guidance, to pave the way for them. The law and the prophets, the priest and the psalmist, typified, prophesied and sang of them. Emperors and kings, rulers and serfs have ignorantly aided on that progressive scheme, which has, at length, opened the last Apocalyptic seal, for them. Even the creation, was designed for the purpose, that all mankind might, eventually, enjoy those incalculable blessings, which God, in His mercy, has conferred on them.

Chapter 3

The Shakers – internal revival and decline, 1835–1905

In any sect, no matter how intense the emphasis on unity of thought and action, different individuals are likely to vary greatly in the degree of their faith and conviction, and this variation will affect their commitment to the goals of the sect, and may even influence their understanding of these goals. The existence of internal conflicts, and of divergent or conflicting patterns of motivation and goal interpretations, may have a profound influence on the development of the group, even though such conflicts and divergences may be unrecognized or unacknowledged by the sectarians themselves. For this reason, any summary estimation of the nature and degree of consensus and conviction existing in a sect at a particular stage of its development may, if unqualified, present an oversimplified picture of the empirical reality.

The description of the predominant mood of the Shakers, in the second and third decades of the nineteenth century, as one of confident utopianism, does not imply that all members of the group shared equally in this confidence, or that the confidence was unwavering and unambiguous. In fact, the successful institutionalization of communitarianism, and the very numerical expansion of the sect which engendered confidence, also created problems of internal control and of the maintenance of commitment which increased in severity throughout the middle decades of the nineteenth century.

Before proceeding to the analytic discussion of the internal revival, and of the subsequent cultural and numerical decline of the Shakers, three unequal time periods must be distinguished. First, the decade of the internal revival, a period in which there occurred limited, but significant, changes in the doctrines and worship of the sect. Second, the years from the end of the revival to the American Civil War, a period of seeming quiescence and stability. Third, the last four decades of the nineteenth century, when the numbers and vitality of the group declined rapidly.

In each area where societies were established, the initial converts experienced much hardship and persecution, and their success in surmounting these difficulties strengthened their faith in the 'overcoming power' of the Shaker gospel. Once the societies were made economically viable, and their relations with the world had become more amicable, the ministers and elders were faced with the task of maintaining the discipline and utopian fervour of the sectarians. This task was complicated by the need to socialize successive waves of converts who experienced the sect as a *de facto* institution, and whose faith and commitment lacked stimulation from direct contact with the early leaders of the group, or participation in the founding of the societies. It should be remembered that the early Shaker doctrinal works, which gave expression to the utopianism of the sect, were written by some of the most senior and trusted members of the group, and that the enthusiasm, faith and intellectuality of these theologians probably differed greatly from that of the ordinary members.

It appears that many of the persons converted in the second and third decades of the nineteenth century were, at least partially, motivated by a desire for economic security, and that the fervour of many of those who were impelled to join the sect by force of religious conviction was greatly dampened by the non-fulfilment of their utopian hopes, and by the dogmatic authoritarianism of the elders. Those persons who joined the sect seeking refuge and security tended to be indifferent to the spiritual aspects of the Shaker life, and probably sought to ingratiate themselves with their elders by strict observance of regulations, and the cultivation of the required patterns of behaviour and comportment. Many of those converts whose hopes for a speedy transformation of the world were disappointed, and whose doubts and speculations were countered by sharp injunctions to 'keep in the gift and follow your lead', left the sect. Despite the Shakers' concern to conceal internal discord, an increasing incidence of behavioural ritualism, intellectual scepticism and indiscipline can be inferred from the scanty evidence which is available for the early years of the nineteenth century.

In 1816 Lucy Wright announced that she had received a revelation which commanded the believers to engage in a 'work of purification' as they had 'lapsed into a lukewarm state'. This directive was accompanied by a prophecy that, once the societies were purified, they would receive an influx of new members (White and Taylor, 1905, p. 136). In 1827 a group of Owenite converts, members of the Pleasant Hill, Kentucky, Society, had the temerity to ask for a voice in the selection of their elders, and there was another period of 'revival' in the societies.

Such revivals reflected the sense of urgency which accompanied the Shakers' utopianism, and implicitly indicated the tensions inherent in their mission; the desire to fulfil God's commandments immediately, and the fear that, unless success was quickly achieved, the Divine Spirit would be withdrawn from the group. Elkins (1853, p. 125) shrewdly commented;

> Like all zealous men, they wish their ideal of probation, of renovation, and of the great work of the regeneration of the human race, accomplished in the twinkling of an eye. If it fails to be done under their immediate observation, they fear the work will be relinquished.

The deliberate stimulation of 'revivals' served to rekindle the flagging enthusiasm of the sectarians, by demonstrating the continued presence of the Holy Spirit within the group, and its power to overcome evil. These revivals were prefaced by admonitory and exhortatory prophecies. The members were urged to prepare themselves for a great advance towards the attainment of their goal; an advance which could only be achieved when all sinful and degenerate tendencies had been purged from the sect. This technique of periodic internal revival was developed during the ministry of Lucy Wright (who succeeded Meacham after his death in 1796, and who died in 1821), but it reached a climax in the decade 1837 to 1847, the period of the sustained spiritualistic revival which the Shakers called 'Mother Ann's Work'.

Religious teachings

The doctrines of the Shakers remained fundamentally unchanged throughout the life of the sect; the changes which did occur in the teachings of the sect, or rather of informal groups within the sect, took the form of cumulative modifications of the original broad doctrinal statements, and of the elevation to central importance of previously disregarded or unemphasized prophecies. The elaboration of the basic doctrines of the group, in particular the spiritualistic development of the doctrine of continuing revelation, served to legitimize the views of those sectarians who, in the second half of the nineteenth century, advanced an essentially reformist conception of the mission of the sect. The shifting emphases of prophetic exegesis also appear as attempts to explain the lack of evangelical success in the middle decades of the nineteenth century, and the group's numerical decline after the American Civil War.

The initial manifestations of 'Mother Ann's Work' occurred in August of 1837, at Watervliet, New York, where some children reportedly received spiritual communications, and experienced physical seizures. These visitations spread to the adolescent and adult members of the society and, shortly afterwards, the Ministry of the sect pronounced them to be genuine expressions of the presence of the Holy Spirit. The original phenomena appear to have occurred spontaneously, but it is significant that they first spread in the 'gathering orders' of the societies, among persons who had recently experienced the strains and excitements of conversion, and who were still, at least partially, in contact with the outside world.

Indubitably, the manifestations were influenced by external events, especially the economic crisis of 1837 which inaugurated a period of severe depression which lasted until 1844. This slump, which terminated a period of particularly rapid expansion of the manufacturing economy of New York State, produced a crisis of confidence in American society at large, and led to the virtual abandonment of the optimistic programmes (or perhaps better, crusades) for social reform which had been undertaken in the previous decade. The economic disturbances produced much social unrest in the manufacturing cities, and this unrest found expression in anti-Catholicism and associated nativistic movements. In the rural areas, which for some time remained centres of enthusiastic revivalist activity, many persons interpreted the disturbances as presaging the millennium, and some gave credence to the millennial prophecies of William Miller.

The Ministry of the sect appear to have actively fostered the expectation of further, more significant and comprehensive, gifts of the Spirit; and physical seizures and trance states spread rapidly through the societies. Glossalalia occurred frequently in the first months of 1838, and in April of that year, Philemon Stewart, a member of the New Lebanon society, received a revelation from 'Mother' Ann Lee. Stewart was the pre-eminent medium, or in the Shaker term, 'instrument', of the sect, but as the revival progressed, messages and revelations of varying degrees of generality and importance were received by instruments in the subordinate societies.

From the commencement of the revival, the ministries maintained a high degree of control over the manifestations, and sought to prevent self-aggrandizement by the instruments, and to check the spread of false revelations or of gifts which were conducive to disorder. The most important instruments worked in close conjunction with the ministries and, as early as 1840, the Central Ministry insisted that all spiritual communications should be written down and examined by the society ministries before being announced to the assembled members. This right and duty of the ministries to censor spiritual communications was duly confirmed by revelation from Ann Lee, who disclosed that she had given her servants 'spiritual spectacles' in order that they might be able to detect communications from evil spirits (Andrews, 1963, p. 174). The visits of the more important spirits were announced in advance by the instruments, and prior to these visits the members fasted and performed purificatory rituals.

Throughout the period of the revival, the instruments and ordinary members received a wide variety of spiritual communications and gifts, most of which were preceded by physical seizures. The instruments were attended by 'scribes' who made verbatim reports of their revelations, and who also attended the society and family meetings to record the various gifts which were received.

The spiritual phenomena can be grouped in several categories: physical seizures and trances unaccompanied by verbal revelations or with attendant glossalalia; pronouncements directed to the whole society or sect, purportedly from the spirits of leaders of the sect or, via intermediary angels, from the deity himself; revelations of new rituals or songs for the group; 'gifts', in the ordinary sense of the word, for individual members, and messages to individuals and to the whole sect from the spirits of persons other than past leaders of the sect. At this point, only the revelations which were directed to the sect as a whole will be discussed.

These major messages were received by the most important instruments in the years 1838 to 1844. The earliest took the form of communications from the 'heavenly parents' of the sect, Christ and Ann Lee, and were subsequently reinforced by the spirits of deceased elders. From 1842, a more important series of messages was received from the most august of all the communicants – the spirit representing the female aspect of God, 'Holy Mother Wisdom'.

The most significant spiritual communications were edited under the supervision of the Ministry, and were published in two books attributed to the instruments who received the revelations (Stewart, 1843; Bates, 1849). Of these two collections, Stewart's attracted the most attention, but Bates's revelations contained more illuminating strictures and prophecies. Stewart's revelations primarily consisted of a comprehensive restatement of the theology and history of the group. The Shakers were instructed by the spirits to send copies of the work to 500 'rulers of men' and other notables (only the King of Sweden acknowledged receipt of the work), and a curse was pronounced on any person who presumed to alter or erase any detail of the book. Readers were assured that the revelations were not 'the invention of the people called Shakers, whose religion is so universally despised throughout the earth' (Stewart, 1843, p. 161) but were the direct words of God to his earthly subjects.

Bates's book was a more sustained and coherent work. It included a reiteration of Shaker theology, and a justification of its tenets and of the principles governing life in the societies. One complete section was devoted to communications reproving God's people on earth, and a number of prophetic promises were scattered through the work; the fulfilment of these promises being conditional upon the purification of the sect, and the rededication of the members to the task of establishing the Kingdom of God on earth.

The importance of a completely frank confession of sins as an indispensable preliminary for entry to the regenerate life was stressed, and great emphasis was placed on the belief that the sect was the only road to salvation (Bates, 1849, p. 128):

> Hide ye nothing from my witnesses, let your deeds be never so foul in my sight; for this is the fountain which I have opened in this day, for the cleansing and purifying of the children of men; the only door of hope which is, or ever will be opened to man.

The communications in which the spirits reproved delinquent members of the sect indicate the spread of laxity and insubordination, and a decline in the prevalence of the virtues of humility and purity in the group in the years prior to the revival. The spirits insisted that the duty of all believers was to obey their superiors humbly and unquestioningly (Bates, 1849, p. 385):

souls cannot be born of me, and find entrance into my kingdom of peace and rest, unless they first become as little children, knowing nothing of themselves, but relying wholly upon the parental care and instructions of those who are anointed and appointed as fathers and mothers in Israel. . . .

More explicitly, the spirits condemned 'jars and discords' among believers; the concealment of sins from the elders and malicious gossip about these sins, and the tendency of some members to avoid work and of others to take a selfish pride in the products of their labour. Holy Mother Wisdom also inveighed against the even greater sins of masturbation and homosexuality, and warned backsliders and the disobedient of the eternity of torment which awaited them.

In return for the restoration of the unity and purity of the sect, the spirits promised that renewed evangelical activities would be rewarded by large numbers of converts. Two prophecies, considered together, provide a clear demonstration of the dual ideological commitment of a utopian sect to evangelism and the maintenance of internal purity by means of separation from the world. In the context of a discussion of the erroneous nature of apocalyptic millennial expectations, the Shakers were warned to guard against impatience, and not to expect a rapid transformation of the world (Bates, 1849, p. 261):

Nation shall rise against nation, and kingdom against kingdom . . . , but the end is not yet. For the gospel of the kingdom must first be preached to all nations before the elect can be gathered from the uttermost parts of the earth.

Evangelism was enjoined by the spirit, but the condition of the success of evangelism was also clearly stated (Bates, 1849, p. 8):

And, saith the Lord, Great shall be the ingathering of souls into Zion, when my people have become righteous, and are able to show forth a righteousness, an exceeding righteousness, which will far surpass all other righteousness which was ever made manifest in the children of men.

The series of communications from Holy Mother Wisdom, which occurred throughout 1842 and early 1843, represented the peak of the revival, and by 1845 the excitement of the Shakers had declined sufficiently for the Sunday society meetings, which had been closed in 1842, to again be opened to the public. According to the sectarians the spirits finally departed for the world in 1847, and there manifested themselves to the Fox sisters and others in crude and unsophisticated forms appropriate to the rudimentary spiritual development and comprehension of non-believers (White and Taylor, 1905, p. 237).

The long period of internal revival can be understood as an attempt by the

Shaker leaders to counteract the religious indifference and indiscipline which had increased in the second and third decades of the nineteenth century. Such reactions appear to have been most marked among the younger members, who were effectively debarred by the hierarchical structure of the group from rapid attainment of positions of power and prestige. Further, the rigidity of Shaker discipline, and the insistence that every aspect of life be performed as a religious service, appears to have resulted in the development of a class of 'hand-minded' members, who valued mechanical skills above spiritual qualities (Melcher, 1941, p. 140). During the internal revival the Shaker leaders attempted to explain the slow progress of the group towards its goal of transforming the earth into the ideal society by reference to external and internal factors. They emphasized the extreme degeneracy of the world which rendered the task of the Shakers more difficult, but which would make its ultimate completion still more glorious, and they castigated all manifestations of laxity and indiscipline in the group, insisting that only when all evil had been driven from the group, would the blessing, and hence the power of God, be accorded to its missionary activities.

The spiritual communications appear as attempts to revitalize the doctrines, worship and mission of the sect by demonstrating their continuing relevance, and by endowing them, in a peculiarly immediate and personal form, with supreme, divine, authority. The self-esteem of the Shakers was bolstered by testimonies from the spirits of religious leaders, political notables and other famous men who had seen the error of their earthly ways, and had embraced Shakerism in the spirit world. This restatement and revivification of the doctrines and regulations of the sect was accompanied by changes in its ritual which, together with the implications of the employment of the mediums as instruments of direct social control, will be discussed below. At this point it is appropriate to consider the modification of the doctrine of continuing revelation which was the theological legacy of the internal revival.

The theological justification of reformation

The Shakers believed that they were distinct from all other religious groups in that the spirit of God was continually active in their midst, inspiring the decisions of their leaders, and endowing the members with the power to overcome temptation and personal weakness, and so to establish and expand their societies despite the scorn and opposition of the world. Belief in continuing revelation legitimated the authority of the leaders of the sect who were believed to be closest to the source of such revelation.

During the revival, physical manifestations of religious excitation became much more frequent and the most important revelations were vouchsafed, not to the leaders of the sect, but to the instruments of the various societies who were ordinary members. The instruments insisted that the leaders of the group had in no way influenced their communications, and the spirits themselves forbade the members to doubt the authenticity of the revelations because of the low status of their recipients. The spirits stated that, as the wisdom of man could never comprehend the things of God, so the innocent 'Babes of Zion had been chosen to reveal His ways' (Bates, 1849, p. 34).

This change in the recipients of spiritual communications did not involve any repudiation of the conception that the ministers and elders were the most enlightened members of the group. In the revival period while the locus of revelation changed, the locus of authority did not; but the conception (implicit in the idea of continuing revelation) of the nature of the relationship between the heavens and earth was greatly elaborated.

The early Shakers were less concerned with explaining the mechanism and nature of divine inspiration than with promulgating the message which they believed God had entrusted to them. Their understanding of the nature of revelation was relatively simple; they believed that the spirit of God flowed directly into their communities and endowed them with the power to transform the world. They said little regarding the spiritual world, beyond the fact that the distinction of the sexes persisted there, and, more vaguely still, that the natural world was 'a figure' of the spiritual world.

By the period of the internal revival, the early enthusiastic expectations of the sectarians had been largely replaced by a more cautious and gradualistic conception of the mode of fulfilment of the task of the sect, and by a more emphatic insistence on the priority of the establishment of internal order and purity. God's gift of the power of the Holy Spirit, or rather of that degree of the power of the Spirit which would eventually enable the Shakers to expand their communities throughout the world, was seen increasingly as being conditional upon the Shakers' worthiness to receive this power.

During the revival, this conception of the conditional nature of divine assistance was made more explicit. The Shakers came to conceive of themselves as being at once observed and guided, not just by God, but by the spirits of past members of the sect. The medium, Paulina Bates, provided the clearest statement of the relationship between heaven and earth, or more precisely, between the heavens and the earthly 'new heavens', the Shaker communities (Bates, 1849, p. 366):

> The light which is established in the heavens or invisible world, is
> closely connected with the light which is established on earth; and they
> who walk in the light which is manifest on earth, are compassed about
> by those who walk in the same light, although in the invisible world.

This quotation contains the nucleus of the theory of spiritual 'correspondence' and spiritual guidance, which was developed in the middle decades of the nineteenth century by the New Lebanon elder, Frederick Evans. Evans was born in England in 1808, and in 1820 he emigrated to America with his elder brother George. The two brothers campaigned for a variety of reformist measures which included limitation of landholding, the abolition of monopolies and imprisonment for debt and, more peripherally, female emancipation and the establishment of Sunday postal services.

Frederick Evans appears to have become dissatisfied with such piecemeal ventures, and according to his autobiographical account (1869) his sympathies with the Owenite and Fourierist communitarian experiments led him, in 1828, to join a communistic community at Massilon, Ohio, which dissolved two months after his arrival. Undaunted by this failure, he travelled to England in 1829, returned to America in 1830, and was planning a new community with other persons who had participated in the Massilon experiment, when, in June of 1830, he visited the Shakers at New Lebanon. He was quickly converted after having several spiritual experiences and, perhaps more important, after finding that in this religious group 'all the principles of materialistic socialism were in practical operation' (Evans, 1869, p. 37).

Evans rose fairly rapidly in the Shaker hierarchy until, by 1843, he was the chief elder of the New Lebanon novitiate. From his formal position as the external representative of the leading society of the group (a position which he retained until his death in 1893) Evans gradually became the publicist and informal spokesman of the whole sect. By 1870, Evans had successfully taken advantage of the weakness and apathy of the formal leaders of the sect, the New Lebanon Ministry, and had so consolidated his position as spokesman of the sect that he appeared, at least to persons in the world, as the *de facto* leader of the group.

Evans's pamphlets, books and articles in the sect's periodical document the development of his spiritualistic justification of reformism, and also his increasing independence and confidence in his security from ministerial reproof. Thus, in his first works, Evans was concerned to demonstrate the essential congruity of his spiritualistic conceptions with the established canon of Shaker theology. Later, his writings became more idiosyncratic, and his advocacy of reformism more explicit and radical, until finally he argued that the revelations which had guided the earlier leaders of the sect should be regarded as largely superseded.

In two pamphlets (1853a and b) Evans provided a restatement of the theology of the group, and laid especial emphasis on the importance of the continuance of revelation through spiritual communications. He emphasized that true revelation always taught men self-denial, and, conversely, revelation which encouraged egoistic or licentious behaviour stemmed from evil spirits. Further, Evans drew a distinction between a sect and a church, a distinction which formed the basis for his later, more explicit, proposals for reconciliation with the world (Evans, 1853a, p. 115):

A sect looks back; a Church looks forward. The highest aspirations of the former never ascend above the measure of its founders, while those of the latter reach to God, by an endless progression, through the means of continual revelation, or intercourse with the spirit world, in the Divine order.

On the basis of this distinction, Evans argued that the Shakers should be progressive and should seek to ally themselves with all worldly reformist groups to whom, in significant contrast to the early Shaker theologians, he attributed some measure of the Divine Spirit. Further, Evans elaborated, in markedly Swedenborgian terms, his conception of the continuing, reciprocal, relationship between the church of God on earth and the spiritual world (Evans, 1853b, p. 10):

It is therefore an unchangeable law, that a union between intelligences
in these two spheres can only occur by those in the natural sphere
becoming abstracted from earthly things, and their spiritual senses being
developed – or by those in the spirit sphere clothing themselves with
material elements whereby they can be discerned by mortals with their
natural senses, as were the angels who appeared to Abraham and Lot.

In his biography (published sixteen years later) Evans provided a comprehensive and unified statement of Shaker spiritualist theology, and explicitly linked this theology to the advocacy of worldly reform. He argued for the abandonment of the utopian attempt to transcend the world in isolation from it, insisting instead that the Shakers should seek to exert a beneficent influence on the world, and should be an inspiration to mankind. The following passage (1869, p. 8) illustrates Evans's conception of the role which he felt the Shakers should play in relation to the world:

the Shaker Order is the source and medium of spiritual religious light
to the world; the seedbed of radical truths; the fountain of progressive
ideas. For 'in Christ are hid all the treasures of wisdom and knowledge',
with which to bless and redeem the race from every form of evil, and
from every cause of human misery and suffering, unto God.

Interestingly, in connection with the genesis of his spiritualistic conceptions, in the same work Evans made the unlikely claim that the illiterate Ann Lee had said that Emanuel Swedenborg was 'her John the Baptist'. Evans also proposed that there should be two orders in American society: the Republican order, the embodiment of perfect civil government; and the superior Shaker order, the perfect spiritual government. Evans categorically asserted that the establishment of these dual orders would result in the abolition of war and most other causes of human misery.

From 1871 until his death in 1893, Evans promulgated his opinions through the sect's monthly periodical, which was published continuously (under a bewildering variety of titles) from January 1871 until December 1899. Evans edited this journal in the period from January 1873 to December

1875, and was its chief contributor, the subsequent editors being largely sympathetic to his reformist views. Evans's concern to establish the continuing relevance of Shakerism for reformers became more intense as the numbers of the sect declined rapidly after 1870 and, correspondingly, his interpretation of the theology of the sect became more liberal.

In marked contrast to the dogmatic authoritarianism of the early Shaker theologians, who had insisted that unity of belief was fundamental for the maintenance and expansion of the group, Evans argued that religious belief was essentially an individual matter, and that declarations of faith and conviction made by a member of the sect should be regarded as an expression of his or her own theology or creed, and not necessarily as expressing beliefs shared by all the sectarians.

Evans was staunchly opposed to biblical literalism and, in regard to his own conversion, he stated that he had accepted Ann Lee's revelations on their logical merits, but 'was sorry that they were so bibleish' (Evans, 1869, p. 48). He inveighed against static conceptions of the theology of the group and argued that men's 'spiritual sensibilities' were subject to evolution and so rejected the 'guiding light' of the early Shaker leaders as being inadequate and inappropriate for believers in the latter part of the nineteenth century (*Shaker and Shakeress*, December 1873, p. 89):

> As Believers in the second manifestation of Christ, we have heretofore assumed, in our writings, that our spiritual order was the new heaven; and that our community of goods was the new earth. This was true, but not the whole truth.

During the last three decades of the nineteenth century, Evans and his associates repeatedly prophesied that large numbers of converts would flock to the sect but, as the spokesman of the group, Evans faced the acute problem of explaining the reality of continuing numerical decline. He qualified his more optimistic predictions by citing a prophecy (attributed to Joseph Meacham) which, by placing the development of the group in a wider historical context, permitted an interpretation of its decline as a temporary phenomena which presaged a period of expansion.

Briefly, Meacham had claimed on an unspecified date to have had a vision of the full establishment of the Shakers as the perfect church of God on earth, and had announced that this final state would be attained only after seven different dispensations or 'travels' had been passed through. This meant (White and Taylor, 1905, p. 104)

> that seven periods would elapse, each introduced by a fresh opening of the Gospel with new and broader revelations of truth. He claimed to see all the particulars of the first travel of Believers for sixty years, intimating that then there would be an important change. The end of the sixty years marked the period of transition when the government

and leadership passed from the first generation to the second. He
further said that the full and perfect work, as he saw it, could not be
accomplished for several hundred years.

In the context of this prophecy, Evans urged the Shakers not to be down-
hearted at the apparent lack of success of the sect, and reminded them of the
vast and progressive nature of their task. He interpreted Meacham's prophecy
not simply as foretelling seven waves of expansion and retrenchment of the
sect, but as legitimizing seven separate Shakers testimonies against worldly
evils.

The first of these testimonies, that against lust, had been borne by the
previous members of the group. The task of Evans and of his contemporaries was to maintain this testimony, but more especially, to bear witness
against the other categories of evil which beset mankind: perverted physiology – habits which stimulated lust and disease; selfish agriculture and
perverted commerce which together produced class distinctions; perverted
literature which diverted the minds of men away from God and from the
evils which beset them; and, more vaguely still, the prostitution of spiritual-
ism and of religion.

In summary, Evans and his associates elevated the basic, and originally
unsophisticated, belief in continuing inspiration into a theological legiti-
mation of reformism, and of alignment with the world. They urged that
the Shakers, as the most spiritually advanced group on earth, should
endeavour to promote a gradual reform of earthly conditions. They should
seek converts among the most enlightened members of reformist groups
while invigorating these groups with their gospel and by the example of
their way of life. The reformist members of the Shakers conceived the sect
to be a beacon which would cast the light of divine approval on every
aspect of man's struggle for self-improvement and which, by its very
existence, would inspire and strengthen every attempt to ameliorate the
condition of man.

The conservative reaction to reformism

In the thirty years prior to his death in 1893, Evans's advocacy of a wide
range of reforms, coupled with his evangelical tours and general appeals for
members, won much publicity for the group. His external influence is
unquestionable; what is much more difficult to gauge is the extent to which
his ideas were accepted by the Shakers themselves. Evans and his followers
virtually monopolized the group's periodical, but it seems likely that their
intellectualism and reformist sympathies were alien to many members of the
group, the majority of whom, in the latter decades of the nineteenth century,
were elderly women, who were probably more concerned with economic
security and routine religious observance than with doctrinal revitalization

and the piecemeal reform of the world. This question will be discussed at greater length below; more germane to the immediate discussion is the fact that Evans's increasingly liberal theology, and his associated advocacy of alignment with worldly reformist groups, did not pass totally unchallenged.

The chief spokesman of the body of intellectual conservative opinion was Harvey Eads, who was born in the sect in 1808 (his parents were converted shortly before his birth) and who died one year before Evans, in 1892. Eads's work consisted of an exhaustive restatement of the orthodox theology of the sect. Its significance lay in its emphases rather than in its originality. Eads reiterated the Shakers' claim to be the sole representatives of Christ on earth, and insisted that there were no real Christians outside the sect. He issued an uncompromising invitation and warning to his readers, and stated that, only by forfeiting the whole life of the world, 'wife included', could an individual hope to attain eternal salvation (Eads, 1879, p. 63).

In contrast to Evans's liberal theological statements, Eads made no attempt to disguise those aspects of Shaker eschatology which were likely to prove unpalatable to progressive thinkers. He emphasized that, while those persons who had lived before the Shakers, or who were unacquainted with their message, would be offered the chance of salvation in the spiritual world, those who finally rejected the gospel would be subject to eternal torment. Eads's analysis of scripture was markedly more literal than that of Evans. Whereas Evans had enthusiastically accepted the theory of biological evolution, and indeed had drawn analogies from this theory to support reformist proposals, Eads presented an ingenious solution to the problem of reconciling biblical exegesis with scientific evidence. He declared his acceptance of the orthodox date of the Creation, 'which is so lustily berated by the scientific evolutionists', as being the date at which man was created in God's image. Before this time man had existed, lacking a soul, as simply another animal species.

Eads countered Evans's doctrinal liberalism by theological restatement and reassertion. He urged the Shakers to cultivate anew the virtues of unity and purity in order that they might, in God's own time, be endowed with a further degree of the power of the Holy Spirit. Eads and the other conservatives insisted that the Shakers should become more isolated from the world. They should withdraw into their communities in order to re-establish that degree of purity of life and unity of action which would ensure the continued presence and power of the Holy Spirit within the group. Separation from the world and re-entrenchment of the communal values of the sect were held by this group to be the preconditions of any future numerical expansion, but in Eads's writings, the possibility of expansion, and more particularly of the total transformation of the world, was scarcely discussed. The emphasis of Eads's work was separatist and devotional. The conservatives among the Shakers conceived the sect to be an especially enlightened group, and their task to be the preservation of their own

purity and exclusiveness, and the dedication of every aspect of their lives to
the praise of God.

The divergence of opinion between the progressive and conservative
Shakers was not only manifested in opposed theological statements, but was
occasionally expressed in more personal and astringent terms. Thus, when
in April 1873 Evans inaugurated his editorship of the sect's periodical with a
catholic appeal to all classes of reformers (religious and non-religious,
communitarian and non-communitarian), he provoked expressions of
extreme disapproval from those elders who believed him to have abandoned
'the light' of the early Shakers. Two years later Evans combined condemnation of the more restrictive aspects of authoritarian conservatism with an
appeal for greater tolerance of new ideas. He insisted that 'true' conservatism
and radicalism were reconcilable, and inveighed against his opponents in a
manner which typically mingled scientific and religious concepts (*Shaker
and Shakeress*, April 1875, p. 25):

> This idea of sufficiency, carried out, would turn back the wheels of time
> and progress for two thousand years, and teach a savage life. Under its
> rod of iron we would not dare to say what we know to be true –
> because of self-adulated conservatism. Evolution is the key word of
> progress – the forerunner of the 'good time coming'. Her legitimate
> children are additions to genuine revelation.

The conservative reply to this criticism came some months later from one
Reynolds, who was a member of the Union Village, Ohio, society, the
chief elder of which was Eads. Reynolds's reply was cutting, and revealed the
devotional emphasis of the conservative thinkers; their insistence that the
sectarians should isolate themselves in the societies, the earthly dwelling
places of the Spirit of God, in order to cultivate their purity and unity.
Sarcastically, Reynolds charged the reformers as a group, and implicitly
Evans himself, with neglecting the true task of the Shakers (*Shaker and
Shakeress*, September 1875, p. 68):

> We have been told, that in other worlds, man's employ will largely
> consist in praising God. But what time will Egotists find for such
> employ. Habits are stubborn things. His penchant for self-glorification
> will go with him. Let us get out of our miserable selves into community
> Heaven, and find an element in community praise.

Reynolds praised the selflessness and devotion of the elders and ordinary
members who resisted the allure and flattery of the world, and lived retired
and ascetic lives (*Shaker and Shakeress*, September 1875, p. 65):

> There are reasons for believing, that in Community life the real
> worthies . . . are but little known. They counsel in secret, and point
> where Wisdom directs – where success will result; And when the

seekers of self-praise are lost in forgetfulness, shall not these remain a blessing and a praise to our sacred cause.

The above passages illustrate the extent of the ideological divergence between the progressive and conservative wings of Shaker opinion, and provide some indication of the hostility which existed between them. (Another conservative elder, Henry Blinn, is reported to have spoken scornfully and often of 'the Gospel according to St Frederick'.) The members of each group regarded the others as selfish, arrogant and perverse, and as leading the sect into a course which would result in its further decline and eventual extinction.

Evans's writings were directed externally. He attempted to attract converts to the sect by demonstrating that the Shakers were the earthly vanguard of divine reform. Eads's writings were directed internally. He sought to regenerate the faith of the members and to strengthen their convictions that their lives were directly inspired by the Spirit of God. Both men were unsuccessful. Evans failed to attract any significant number of converts to the group, or halt the drift of younger members away from the sect, and Eads failed to counteract the ritualism and laxity which became increasingly apparent among the ageing members.

Evans's and Eads's contrasting interpretations of the mission of the sect, and of its associated relations with the world, can be described respectively as reformist and introversionist. Each position represented the elevation to central importance of one aspect of the dual commitment involved in the earlier utopian faith of the Shakers. Both positions were developed and formally expounded in the years after the internal revival, when every aspect of life in the Shaker communities first stagnated, and then became moribund. Both interpretations of the role of the sect or, more accurately, the programmes of action proposed on the basis of these interpretations, failed to check or counter the cultural and numerical decline of the group, the empirical details of which will be examined after brief consideration of the last significant Shaker theological work, which was published in 1905, by which date the Shakers were facing the clear possibility of extinction.

White and Taylor's work combined a summary of the theology and history of the group with appeals for members and arguments in favour of consolidating the remaining societies. The authoresses sought to explain the decline of the sect, and proclaimed its imminent expansion and resurgence. They revealed a previously unmentioned vision, which had been received by one Daniel Morton in 1827 after he had fasted for three days. Morton had announced that (White and Taylor, 1905, p. 369):

At the present time, the Church is in great peace and prosperity, and it seems as if nothing could disturb her tranquillity. But a change will come over her, many will prove unfaithful and drop out of her ranks. Sorrow and adversity will visit her, and desolation and defection will be such

that even the most devoted and faithful will begin to forebode the utter
annihilation of the Church. But this destruction will not take place,
for after she has reached the lowest level of her adversity she will arise
and move to a higher culmination of glory than at any previous
period – to the highest reachable in that day.

On the basis of this prophecy, White and Taylor sought to rally the
remaining Shakers to fight against despair, and urged them to make ready for
the new members who, when God so willed, would be sent to them. In
conformity with the fundamental doctrine of continuing inspiration and
spiritual guidance, White and Taylor expressed their conviction that the
next cycle of progress of the sect was imminent, and held out to the members
the sublime possibility that in this coming cycle an individual even greater in
divine endowments than Ann Lee might arise.

Accordingly the gradualistic optimism which characterized the beliefs
of the sectarians found final and rather touching expression in the last of the
many natural analogies which the Shakers used to support their arguments and
to rationalize the vicissitudes of the group (White and Taylor, 1905, p. 389):

> Progression is the law of life. Always at the passing of the old and the
> coming of the new is a period of apparent decline, as between the
> harvest of one year and the leafage of the next.

Ministerial passivity and its consequences

The formal communitarian structure institutionalized by Joseph Meacham –
the rigid hierarchical system of orders and families each ruled by elders
responsible to the society ministry and presided over by the self-appointed
Ministry of New Lebanon – remained unchanged throughout the life of the
sect. But after 1835, within this structure, there were gradual cumulative
changes in virtually every aspect of the life of the sectarians.

The effects of the internal revival were threefold. It purged the sect of
many disgruntled or lukewarm members whose discontents were crystallized by the increased asceticism of life in the intervals between periods of
intense religious excitation, and by the surveillance and condemnation to
which they were subject. It strengthened the faith and self-esteem of those
members of the group who accepted the spiritual communications and gifts
as genuine manifestations of the divine spirit, and to some extent it resanctified the authority exercised by the ministers and elders of the group.

However, the austerities of the revival period were not followed by the
prophesied increase in numbers and, in subsequent decades, there was a
qualitative and quantitative change in the nature of the authority exercised
by the central Ministry. The Ministry continued, throughout the whole of
the period under discussion, as a self-appointed body, and as the unchallenged formal leaders of the sect, but they gradually relaxed the original

vigilance of their supervision of the subordinate ministries. Especially after the Civil War, the Ministry laid an increasing emphasis on the devotional and exemplary, rather than on the activist and authoritarian, components of their role. This change was probably, in part, brought about by the failure of Shakers' evangelism after the revival, a failure which sapped the confidence of the leaders who seem, in addition, to have been weak and indecisive personalities.

The increasing passivity of the Ministry facilitated Evans's gradual establishment of himself as the representative of the sect to the outside world although, as indicated, he appears to have accumulated informal power and influence very slowly and cautiously. The reluctance of the Shaker Ministry to employ the powers vested in their office and, presumably, their lack of confidence in their ability to subdue Evans and his associates, resulted in an informal ideological bifurcation of the group. On the one hand were the self styled 'progressives', who were probably few in number but whose influence was enhanced by their virtual monopoly of the periodical of the sect. Opposing them was the conservative group, whose views were probably more representative of the majority of the ageing sectarians, and whose primary spokesman was Harvey Eads.

Despite this ideological conflict, no schism occurred in the sect, presumably in part because the leaders of both factions were concerned to maintain its dwindling numbers. Perhaps more important in preventing the developing of a schism, was the inaction of the central Ministry which, by 1875, exercised only a minimal amount of control over the wider affairs of the sect. The fact that the Ministry refused to reprove Evans and his followers, probably prevented the articulation of a clear-cut reformist position, and the energies of the members of this group were dissipated in the proclamation of their allegiance to, and especially enlightened comprehension of, a varied range of progressive causes and proposals.

Ministerial inaction may also have prevented the articulate members of the conservative majority from engaging in more vehement and more systematic denunciations of the progressives, but the essence of the conservative ideological position, the insistence on separatism and the cultivation of community virtues, also inhibited their spokesmen's use of the periodical which was, at least theoretically, directed towards the external society. Consequently, the periodical was largely controlled by the progressives, and was presented by them as a forum for debate, but participation in such debate was generally frowned upon by the conservatives as being destructive of unity.

Social control

The internal revival has been interpreted as an attempt to check the indiscipline which became manifest after the successful institutionalization of communitarianism. The ministers and elders sought to accomplish two things: to counter potential challenges to their authority, and to quicken the faith of those members whose initial expectant ardour had been dulled by the unremitting ascetic regulation of every aspect of life, and by the failure of the sect to make any significant progress towards its goal of the transformation of the world.

During the revival period two types of messages conveyed spiritual condemnation and approbation to the Shakers: general communications to the societies or the sect as a whole, and those directed to individuals. In the general communications, the spirits itemized the sins which had beset the Church of God on earth; sensuality, factionalism, selfishness, disobedience and apathy, and messages from apostates and reprobates warned delinquents of the danger of invoking the wrath of God, and of the excruciating torment which they were suffering in hell. The spirits lavished praise on all faithful members of the societies, and dwelt on the rewards which they would receive as compensation for their selflessness and fidelity.

The messages further served to enhance the self-esteem of the sectarians by recapitulating the Shaker interpretation of history as an interplay between the forces of good and evil which had culminated in the emergence of the sect. Thus, Columbus was held by the spirits to have been the servant of God in that he discovered the 'wilderness of America' in which Ann Lee's message won acceptance. The communications also detailed the testimonies and tributes of great men who had embraced Shakerism in the spiritual world. Among these were George Washington; William Penn; the Emperor Nero, who repented bitterly of his sins; Mahomet, who confessed his false doctrines; Alexander the Great, who was described as 'humbled', and Napoleon Bonaparte, from whose conversion the moral was drawn that kings and princes must all come to mingle with the dust of the earth.

Spiritual communications addressed to individuals appear to have increased in number as the revival progressed. A member might be inspired to praise the elders of his society in the course of a religious meeting, and later, in conformity with the ruling of the Ministry, such 'gifts' were first censored and then written down and presented to the individual concerned. More significant than these relatively spontaneous communications, was the introduction in 1841 of a form of routinized, public, spiritual evaluation of the conduct of the ordinary members of the societies.

In this ritual (or ordeal) each member was summoned before an instrument and the elders and ministry of his society. The chief elder of the individual's family then provided a short assessment of his character and spiritual condition, and the instrument, as the mouthpiece of a spirit, usually Holy Mother Wisdom, passed judgment. In most instances, where the individual was adjudged to be doing his best to live up to 'the light accorded him', his commendation followed a set pattern. The virtues of some members were noted with special praise, but in other cases the spirits violently and explicitly castigated offenders (one female member of the Canterbury New Hampshire Society was accused of 'gratifying her lusts' with a cleaver) and, very occasionally, the individual was denounced and expelled from the sect.

Presumably, most of those persons who were condemned by the instruments, but not immediately expelled, left the sect shortly afterwards. To them, the process of spiritual examination must have appeared as the culminating instance of the leaders' arbitrary authoritarianism, and readiness to impose on the gullibility of the ordinary sectarians. In the case of the faithful members, who accepted the communications as outpourings of the Divine Spirit, direct and personal praise from the female aspect of the deity must have provided an incentive and positive sanction of the greatest magnitude, especially when combined with promises of successful evangelism once the sect had been purified.

The employment of spiritual communications to sanctify and legitimate the social arrangements of the sect and to pronounce judgment on the conduct of the members, was a method of social control whose exercise was confined almost entirely to the decade of Mother Ann's Work, but the development of this technique did not represent such a great departure from previous Shaker practice as it might at first appear. Prior to the revival the Ministry had claimed that one of the gifts conferred on them, as the persons closest to God on earth, was the capacity to detect evil; not simply evil doing, but also evil thinking, and, as shown, in the period of the revival, the Ministry further claimed the ability to pronounce revelations and gifts to be true or false.

The system of spiritual examination provides an example of the way in which inspiration was routinized and made subject to ministerial control as the revival developed; apparently, the close relationships between the ministers and the mediums did not prevent some of the latter from regarding themselves as something more than 'simple and innocent' vessels of the spirit, and from challenging ministerial authority. Many of the mediums subsequently left the societies and, in or around 1874, Evans told a journalist (Nordhoff, 1875, p. 158):

> That the mediums in the societies had given much trouble because they imagined themselves reformers, whereas they were only the mouthpieces of spirits, and oftenest themselves of a low order of mind. They had to teach the mediums much, after the spirits ceased to use them.

In the following decades, the indiscipline of the former instruments, together with a more objective assessment of some of the spiritual communications and the non-fulfilment of the inspired prophecies, combined to produce a reaction against the 'excesses' of the revival. This reaction was particularly strong among the progressive members of the sect, who were concerned to win the good opinion and intellectual approval of the world. The two published collections of spiritual communications were withdrawn

66

from circulation, and when Nordhoff visited the sectarians he was told by Evans that the volumes should be burnt, but commented that the books were available to visitors and were probably still revered by some of the sectarians.

The internal revival appears to have been immediately successful in that it resulted in the departure of many troublesome members from the sect, and resanctified the authority structure and social arrangements of the group. Further, it temporarily regenerated the enthusiasm of those members who accepted the manifestations as genuine. However, the explicit nature of the revealed prophecies, and their unequivocal attribution to divine sources, heightened the disappointment felt by the sectarians when the prophesied events did not come to pass, and engendered a crisis of confidence in the sect as a whole; a crisis which was evidenced by the slow atrophy and decay of every aspect of the life of the sect after the Civil War.

The Civil War caused widespread disruption of the affairs of the sect and, for a time, Shaker pacifism aroused much animosity in the external society, but persecution soon died away and its bracing and unifying effects were short-lived. In the era of reconstruction which followed the Civil War, the membership and vitality of the sect declined rapidly. At this point it is necessary to provide some indication of the incidence of indiscipline in the sect, and of the more subtle but pervasive relaxation of behavioural regulations which indicated the spread of despondency among the sectarians, and their rejection of asceticism and associated desire for more of the comforts and conveniences of the world.

Mother Ann's Work was followed by a period of tranquillity and apparent stability. In the decade prior to the Civil War, the few converts who were made joined the group not in an atmosphere of revivalistic excitement, but more soberly and deliberately, after having gained some knowledge of the advantages and disadvantages of life in the societies. The majority of the post-revival converts were mature women, whose conversions were probably as much influenced by economic exigencies as by religious conviction. Prior to the Civil War, the persons who seceded from the sect seem to have left amicably, and there is little record of internal disruption in this period.

Immediately after the Civil War, there was a marked increase in indiscipline, particularly in the southern societies, and it can be inferred, although not demonstrated, that the more violent malcontents were persons who had joined the sect during the war period, seeking refuge from economic or familial disruption. Be this as it may, the records of the southern societies reveal a high incidence of indiscipline and of occasional, seemingly totally disproportionate, irrational violence.

For instance, the 1869 journal of the ministry of the South Union, Kentucky, society recorded that Hugh Relner, a member of the junior order, on being refused the keys to the piano room, broke down the door of the room with an axe and severely wounded an elder who remonstrated with him (Neal, 1947, pp. 248–9). Two years earlier, in the same society, another junior member had attacked an elder with an axe and had then eloped with one of the junior sisters. The same record detailed less violent, but perhaps more significant, instances of disobedience in the society, including the cardinal sin of questioning the authority of 'the lead'; in this case Harvey Eads, whose appeals for greater discipline and uniformity of behaviour have already been cited. In 1875, Reuben Wise openly accused Eads of covertly investigating his conduct and, a year later, two members flatly refused Eads's order, or 'gift', that they should move from the West to the Centre family of the society.

Outright challenges to the authority of the ministers of the societies appear to have been frequent only in the years immediately after the Civil War, and presumably were followed by the expulsion or voluntary departure of the delinquents. In the latter decades of the nineteenth century, the remaining members of the sect were predominantly elderly, committed, unworldly individuals, members of the church order who were primarily concerned with maintaining the threatened fabric of their community life and worship. Religious disappointment and doubts were manifested among this 'residual' membership, not in violently assertive ways, but in a gradual decline in their hostility to the external society, and a disregard of those regulations which seemed unnecessarily restrictive or rigorous.

Such a rejection of asceticism, which implied a despairing abandonment of the ideals and mission of the sect, was evidenced by numerous small attitudinal and behavioural changes. Meat eating and smoking had been largely prohibited in the revival period, but these practices gradually won tacit acceptance, and after 1874 the Shakers recognized and celebrated American national holidays.

Nordhoff reported that each male sectarian had a sister especially assigned to him to care for his clothes, an arrangement indicative of an ageing and sedate membership, but one which, earlier in the life of the sect, would have been violently denounced as conducive to 'particular attachments'. The informal relaxation of behavioural regulations increased as the decline of the sect became more marked, and, with the deaths of Eads and Evans in 1892 and 1893 respectively, the likelihood of any future expansion of the sect must have appeared small, even to the most devoted of believers.

White and Taylor betrayed their objective realization of the extent of the decline of the sect, and of the possibility of its demise, even as they insisted that, consequent upon the consolidation and renewed evangelical efforts of the members, the group might rise to greater significance than ever before. The contradictory emphases of their work illustrate the dilemma of the spokesmen of all declining social movements, who seek to establish the achievements of their group and so to vindicate the efforts of its members without, in so doing, admitting, and thereby hastening, the inevitability of its decline. Thus White and Taylor seemingly approved, or at least tacitly endorsed, the increased reconciliation of the sect with the world, and remarked that (1905, p. 280):

> With the passing of the years, and the change of attitude of outside Christians, the absolute crucifixion of all natural ties and affections is no longer deemed necessary.

However, later in their work they appealed against 'ritualism' and 'concentration on niceties of dress', and condemned smoking and meat eating. They combined these appeals for renewed asceticism with the assertion that, in view of the materialism and economic and social disruption of the external society, the prospects for an expansion of the group were great. In more far-reaching preparation for this predicted increase in members, and for the phoenix-like resurrection of the sect, White and Taylor urged the regroupment of the sectarians, and the consolidation of their resources. This last appeal illustrates the persistence of organizational structure in a sect which was dependent for survival on recruits from the external society, and whose members had been unable or unwilling to effect an ideological and organizational transformation sufficient to attract such converts (White and Taylor, 1905, p. 404):

> Fifteen societies, separate, each from each, families within each society forming still smaller integrate [*sic*] particles, can no longer hold their own in domestic, business, and spiritual efficiency. For the future of this noble inheritance for the love of Truth, we should unite our forces.

Shaker worship

It has been shown that the initial manifestations of Mother Ann's Work were hailed by the Shaker Ministry as presaging further, more important, 'promptings of the spirit', and that, consequently, physical symptoms of religious excitation spread rapidly throughout the societies, and culminated in the first major spiritual communications delivered by Stewart in 1838. 'Promiscuous gifts', which had been an expected part of the early religious services of the sect, continued to occur throughout the revival and, in addition, new songs, dances and rituals were developed. The general atmosphere of excitement which characterized Shaker services during the revival, and more specifically the revealed 'eccentric' songs and dances, gave rise to much ridicule of the group by the 'world's people', and as a result the Sunday society meetings were closed to the public.

The Shakers' contempt for worldly institutions and persons was given full expression during the period of Mother Ann's Work in the spiritual testimonies and revelations, and by the resuscitation of such earlier songs as the hymn 'Gospel Relation' – which appears also to have been known, more colloquially and directly, as the 'Fleshly-kindred' song. This hymn, which was accompanied by vigorous gestures and facial contortions, celebrated the bonds of love which united the Shakers, and emphasized their hatred of the world (cited in Andrews, 1940, p. 20):

> Of all the relation that ever I see,
> My old fleshly kindred are furthest from me,
> So bad and so ugly, so hateful they feel,
> To see them and hate them increases my zeal.
> O how ugly they look!
> How ugly they look!
> How nasty they feel!

The complicated marches and dances, introduced by written revelation, gave more restrained symbolic expression to the unity of the sectarians in the face of persecution and mockery. In addition to such formal performances, and to individual dancing and outbursts of glossalalia, the services of the sect were enlivened by such mimes as 'Shooting the Devil', in which the members arrayed themselves like a file of riflemen, fired a symbolic volley at the devil, and then rushed violently about the meeting room to drive all vestiges of evil from it.

In 1842, after Holy Mother Wisdom had counselled with the Ministry, and the believers had purified themselves by fasting, several new rituals were revealed. Among these were the 'Midnight Cry', an annual ceremony in which every room in every building of the societies was exorcized by a company of mediums; and the 'Cleaning Gift' in which, again annually, a band of vocalists and mediums passed through the buildings of the societies pantomiming the action of cleaning the rooms, and singing a hymn which promised the destruction of evil spirits. In more literal conformity with Mother Ann's practical teachings, this symbolic activity was followed by an actual scouring of the buildings of the society. The final important ritual innovation of 1842 was the establishment of twice-yearly 'love-feasts', on which occasions the believers repaired to a specially designated plot of land, and there danced, sang hymns and received 'spiritual' or imaginary 'gifts'. The whole ceremony culminated in a spiritual feast which, after the exertions of worship, was consumed voraciously with much thankfulness and merriment.

At the individual level, actual and symbolic expression was given to the ideals which governed the conduct of the sectarians; the instruments stressed that the Shakers should strive to repress their selfishness, and were to look humbly and thankfully to their elders for guidance. Holy Mother Wisdom emphasized that 'a childlike spirit' was to be the standard of greatness in the sect, and many of the imaginary gifts received by the Shakers during the course of the love-feasts and other religious services – drums, gaudy items of clothing, sweetmeats – were appropriate to children. Similarly, the revealed songs frequently stated that the believers were united in being 'Mother's Little Children'.

This positive estimation of simplicity and ingenuousness was clearly reflected in the words and sentiments of the songs and statements delivered by the spirits of 'primitive' peoples (Hottentots, Siberians, Laplanders, and others) who were uniformly represented as being eager for the Shaker message, and grateful for the attention of the sectarians. The most numerous categories of such communications were those from American Indian and Negro spirits which were delivered in an appropriate dialect, and in which the spirits expressed their gratitude to the 'Whity Mudder', Ann Lee, for having shown them the way of truth. One example of an 'Indian song' is enough to illustrate the genre (cited in Andrews, 1940, pp. 72–3):

Me Indian come / Me come here stay / Me tanke de white man / He show me de way / He tell me to dig up / And fess all me sin / Dat make me look pretty / All Whity and clean.

The religious excitement and enthusiasm of the sectarians had so declined by late 1845 that the Sunday general meetings of the society were reopened to the public. The Midnight Cry and the Cleaning Gift rituals were performed until 1850, and, for several decades after this date, spiritual communications and revelations were reported in the meetings of the sect, and newly composed songs were routinely attributed to inspiration. However, the close of Mother Ann's Work marked the end of significant innovation in Shaker worship.

After the Civil War the services of the group became increasingly formal and ritualized, and the sacral aspect of the sectarians' lives, like every other, was gradually modified by the adoption of worldly practices, and in deference to external opinion. The several hymnals published by the group in the post-war period contained few songs which expressed open hostility to the world or which were, to use the Shakers' own term, 'eccentric' in content. The acquisition of musical instruments to accompany the services of the group was sanctioned by the Ministry in 1870, and in the same year classes in music were instituted at New Lebanon.

In 1870, a day was appointed on which every member of the sect prayed for its preservation and expansion, but this effort, which indicates the desperation and devotional concerns of the Ministry, was unsuccessful. A year later there was a minor recrudescence of spiritual 'manifestations', and a wave of excitement passed through the societies. This excitement was apparently stimulated by the depression of the American economy, which generated hopes that the promised numbers of converts would flock to Zion, and was heightened by the coincidence of this depression with the impending centenary of the sect's establishment in America.

Neither the depression nor the centenary produced any significant increase in the numbers of the group, and on the day of the centenary, the journalist of the South Union, Kentucky, society (the membership of which had fallen, through death and desertion, by sixty-four to a total of two hundred in the year 1872–3) could only record that (cited in Neal, 1947, p. 238):

This day 100 years since our blessed Mother Ann Lee and her little company landed in America bringing with them tidings of everlasting gospel to all who were hungering and thirsting after righteousness – It is hoped that in 100 years more the gospel will have spread to the ends of the earth.

Despite this pious hope, the membership of the sect continued to decline in the last decades of the nineteenth century and, as the number of persons in each society dwindled, so the society meeting houses were closed, and the ageing sectarians held their services in the family assembly rooms. The services of the group were finally closed to the public in 1902. After this date the Shaker dances were rarely performed, these relatively strenuous 'exercises' being replaced by silent prayer and meditation.

The Shaker economy

The revivalistic emphasis on purification extended into the sect's economic system, and led to the prohibition of some industries and, temporarily, to a stricter regulation of every aspect of economic activity. The conception that all forms of labour were consecrated, and that the performance and products of labour should be appropriate to its sacramental quality, was also re-emphasized. A whole section of the 1845 edition of the *Millennial Laws*, by far the longest of those concerning the various 'lots of care' or positions of trust in the societies, was devoted to regulations delimiting the powers and defining the duties and obligations of deacons and trustees. The trustees were reminded that all things made and bought by the societies should be 'plain and decent', and conformity with this principle was unequivocally set above economic advantage, the trustees being forbidden to buy 'articles which are needlessly adorned because they are a little cheaper'. The insidious influence of worldly standards of beauty and ornament in the pre-revival period was evidenced by the devotion of another entire section of the *Millennial Laws* to the prohibition of 'superfluities', which included such items as embroidered handkerchiefs and silver pencils, which tended to 'feed the pride and vanity of man'.

A passage from the New Lebanon Ministry Sisters' Journal (cited in Andrews, E. D. and F., 1937, p. 19) for 1840, indicates that the reaffirmation of the idea that the products of the societies should symbolize the twin principles of unity and purity was not confined to written strictures:

> David Rawley has been employed for several days in taking out Brass knobs and putting in their stead wood knobs or buttons. This is because brass ones are considered superfluous, thro spiritul communication.

Further, the tendency of some members to scorn manual labour and, conversely, the spirit of pride in economic activity, were both condemned by Holy Mother Wisdom. The spirit insisted that, even when the gospel had spread to all the world, 'the new man [will] cultivate the earth by the sweat of his brow' (Bates, 1849, p. 165). It was not the amount of labour done, but the spirit in which it was performed, that merited praise.

After the revival, the economy of the sect was to some extent rationalized. The chair-making industry, which had been scattered throughout the eighteen societies and which had encountered increasingly severe competition from outside manufacturers, was concentrated in a single factory-type establishment at New Lebanon, and the societies practically ceased the production of woollen goods, which they could buy more cheaply from the world. External competition in manufactured goods, and the separatist emphasis of the revival years, redirected the attention of the sectarians to agricultural production. In the south-west, the societies' landholdings were expanded and unified, and this agricultural emphasis, in conjunction with the predominance of women in the group and the secession of many young members, led to a steady increase in the employment of hired help; a practice which inevitably tended to reduce the separation of the believers from the world.

The Civil War imposed a direct financial burden on the southern societies, which had declined most markedly in the pre-war period. Not without expedient considerations, the southern Shakers extended hospitality to the troops of both armies, and, although the societies suffered relatively little damage from regular troops, they lost heavily from arson, especially in the immediate post-war years. The Ministry of the South Union, Kentucky, society alone calculated that they had spent 100,000 dollars in aiding the soldiers of both armies. In addition, this society suffered four serious fires, which were attributed to the envy and malice of deserters or of returning members of the defeated Confederate Army.

After the Civil War, the trends which had been apparent in the pre-war years became still more pronounced. The sectarians became increasingly dependent on hired help to cultivate their estates, and by the eighteen seventies, a large part of the land belonging to the societies was leased to outsiders. In this decade land was sold by some of the more rapidly declining societies, a move which bespoke a total abandonment of any hope of an immediate expansion of the sect. Many of the more strenuous craft industries were abandoned or their production confined solely to that of goods for use within the societies, and seeds and patent medicines, in the preparation of which the available female labour could be used, became increasingly important items in the Shakers' trade with the world.

The relaxation of ministerial control over the societies, and the consequent relative autonomy of the society trustees, resulted in several cases of embezzlement. More frequently, ignorance and financial naïvety gave rise to imprudent investments which inflicted severe financial losses on individual families or societies. More important still, throughout the second half of the nineteenth century, the distinctive aesthetic and economic standards of the sect were eroded by contact with the external society. The extent of the Shakers' departure from their earlier principles can be illustrated by brief consideration of the *Shaker Almanac* for 1886. This publication (which was virtually identical with those distributed by secular commercial enterprises in the same period) contained advertisements for Shaker nostrums, accounts of near-miraculous cures effected by these, and a calendar and meteorological predictions.

Each monthly calendar was accompanied by a lithographic portrait and an adulatory biography of one of the 'money makers of America', who included Cornelius Vanderbilt and the speculator Jay Gould. Jokes concerning the foibles of Negroes and Irishmen were printed at the bottom of the pages, and, in complete contravention of the principle of the anonymity of labour, an advertisement for 'Shaker Extract of Roots' was accompanied by a large picture of 'Alonzo Hollister, the famous Shaker chemist', at work in his laboratory. On the last page of the *Almanac* readers were urged to have faith in all the properties of the advertised remedies for 'the Shakers could not be induced to prostitute their good name'.

Social composition

The predominant mood of the Shakers at the close of the long period of internal revival was one of expectation; corrupt practices and persons had been driven from the sect, new heights of ascetic virtuosity had been attained, and the members looked with confidence for the 'hungry souls' in the world outside, of whom Holy Mother Wisdom had stated (Bates, 1849, p. 72):

> when they are ready to famish, will they hear of Zion, and the fullness thereof. Then will they say. Let us arise and go and buy of this bread, that we perish not.

The confidence of the Shakers must have been greatly increased by the influx of some of the disappointed followers of William Miller to the communities, especially those in the west, in the years 1844 to 1846. However, this accession of perhaps three hundred members, although temporarily heartening, probably did little more than restore the numbers of the sect to their pre-revival level, and, after 1846, no further mass conversions were made. As the failure of evangelism became apparent, and the prophecies announced during the revival remained unfulfilled, doubts arose concerning, not only the validity of the spiritual communications, but also, more important, the value of continued asceticism and separation from the world, and of the very conception of the mission of the sect which justified this ascetic separation.

Faced with this situation, Evans insisted that the sect should stand as a beacon of encouragement and hope for all mankind. It should guide the progress of reformers by providing them with an example of true Christian community of goods and purity of life. The group should extend its sympathy and divine influence to every attempt to ameliorate the condition of mankind, and should draw converts from among the more spiritually minded members of reformist groups. The catholicism of Evans's appeals for members, as well as his easy subsumption of science as a form of religion, can be demonstrated by a quotation from his editorial column in the sect's periodical (*Shaker and Shakeress*, January 1873, p. 1):

> we invite all progressive minds and classes, all truth loving, religious
> persons, from the most scientific rationalist to the revivalist, to take the
> Shaker and Shakeress, and thereby help us to inaugurate the blessed
> era of universal virtue, wherein civil governments and all society
> organizations shall, by their organic laws, do as we would individually
> be done by.

Throughout his writings, Evans asserted his conviction that the decline of the sect was but temporary and that, in the near future, many men would become aware of the 'radical' testimony of the Shakers, and of their divinely appointed position as the vanguard of reform. Thus, in 1859, he expressed his confidence that the action of spiritual forces on the world would 'agitate the religious elements' and would produce revivals on a grand scale (Evans, 1859, p. 17). Despite this confident statement, which he reiterated some fifteen years later to the journalist Nordhoff, Evans became increasingly concerned about the future of the sect. His efforts to attract converts became more desperate as the decline became more marked, and occasionally he appealed for members in ways which laid stress on the material advantages of life in the group. The following advertisement was inserted in several New York newspapers and reprinted in the sect's periodical (*Shaker and Shakeress*, February 1874, p. 9):

> Men, women and children can find a comfortable home for life, where
> want never comes, with the Shakers, by embracing the true faith and
> living pure lives. Particulars can be learned by writing to the Shakers,
> Mount Lebanon, New York.

Evans attributed the stagnation and decline of the sect to its continued separation from the world, and to the timidity and short-sightedness of the advocates of this separation – those members who refused to accept the validity of the progressive 'new testimonies' which the spirits had announced or had made evident, to the most enlightened members of the sect. Eads explained the decline of the sect as the result of internal disunity, and also as a consequence of the increasing corruption of the world. He insisted that the Shakers should not seek the approval of the world, but should stand witness to the 'one right way' revealed by God to man. He guardedly admitted that there was 'not much increase' in the sect's numbers, and also laid his hopes for expansion on a fresh upsurge of external religious revivals.

Like Evans (but in exaggerated form) White and Taylor combined optimistic but vague exegetical assertions with more direct and materialistic appeals for members. While in one part of their work they expressed their conviction that the surviving Shakers would shortly become the leaders of a 'world movement', elsewhere they offered lifelong security from want to all those who would join them in their struggle against 'modern combinations, competitions and trade rivalries'.

The Shakers' reluctance to reveal their numbers persisted in the period under discussion, and increased as the decline of the sect accelerated. In 1875 when, in a quarter of a century, the membership of the group had halved, Evans would only admit 'that the societies had not increased in recent years, and some had decreased' (Nordhoff, 1875, p. 158). The broad pattern of decline can be revealed by a few figures. From 1823, when the Shakers themselves announced that they had 4,100 members, the membership rose to a peak of upwards of 5,500 in the eighteen fifties. In 1860, the Eighth Census of the United States revealed the sect to have 5,200 members. After the Civil War the decline became more marked, the total membership in 1874 being 2,400. By 1891 there were 1,700 members in the society, a total which had fallen to between thirteen and fourteen hundred by 1900, and to approximately one thousand in 1910.

In the period of the expansion of the sect, converts were primarily drawn from among the disappointed subjects of religious revivals, and the Shakers believed that revivals were instigated by the Spirit of God to furnish them with converts. The failure of Shaker evangelism dates approximately from 1846, in which year the last converted Millerites were absorbed into the societies. By this date, the economy of the north-eastern States had recovered from the severe depression of 1837, and thereafter expanded rapidly. The growth of industrialization, and the drift of population to the larger manufacturing cities engendered by this expansion, removed, or ameliorated, the conditions of frontier isolation, physical hardship and extreme poverty which had been important in the perpetuation of endemic revivalism in the remoter regions of New York State since the middle decades of the eighteenth century.

The change in the primary location and type of revival activity in the United States in the eighteen thirties and forties, and the concomitant changes in attitudes to social reform, will be further discussed below. Here it is sufficient to state that, after 1846, the absence of widespread intensive rural revivals, and the consequent failure of Shaker evangelical activities, engendered a mood of profound disillusionment in the sect and an overall decline in active proselytization.

The later missionary activities of the sect were educative and restrained in tone rather than, as previously, emotional and declamatory. This change of emphasis was closely related to the ideological bifurcation of the sect.

Consonant with their advocacy of increased separation from the world, Eads and his followers confined their evangelical activities to the instruction of those few 'self-controllers' who, whether prompted by the Spirit of God, or by economic necessity and social dislocation, individually applied for admission to the sect. Conversely, as indicated, Evans and his associates directed their appeals to all 'progressive' thinkers and groups and, in the sect's periodical, sought to provide a continuing demonstration of the wide-ranging sympathies and enlightened views of the sect.

In addition to publication of their views, the reform-oriented members of the sect undertook a number of missionary journeys within the United States and overseas. Immediate success crowned the efforts of two representatives of the Shakers who travelled by invitation to Sweden in 1869, and returned with fifty-four converts; but most of these recruits left the societies shortly after their arrival, and the Shakers subsequently admitted their disappointment with this venture. Evans visited Britain in 1871 and 1887, and each time spoke to enthusiastic audiences, but the two journeys produced only a handful of adult converts in addition to several children who were consigned to the care of the sect.

Children had been adopted by the Shakers throughout their history, either directly from institutions, or after being entrusted, or in some cases abandoned, to the care of the sect by their parents or guardians. After the revival, few of these children remained in the sect upon attaining maturity and, consequently, the Shakers became increasingly reluctant to undertake the fruitless expense involved in adoption. Evans stated categorically to Nordhoff that the Shakers preferred to convert mature persons who had had some experience of the rigours of the world; but children were occasionally adopted until the end of the nineteenth century.

Although detailed statistical evidence is unavailable, it can safely be inferred that, after the period of revival, the average age of the Shakers gradually increased. The revival was instigated to combat the indiscipline which was primarily manifested among the more youthful members, and presumably many of those persons who were expelled or voluntarily left the sect during the revival, were young persons. In 1875 Evans, who as has been shown was inclined to minimize the setbacks suffered by the group, stated that, during the Civil War period, 'a great many of our younger people went into the army' and that few returned (Nordhoff, 1875, p. 159), and in the second half of the nineteenth century, the individuals who joined the sect were predominantly mature or elderly women.

The predominance of women among the Shakers was noted by some early observers, and in the southern societies women were twice as numerous as men in the pre-Civil War period (Neal, 1947, p. 163). Nordhoff's summary of the statistical details of the sect in 1874, revealed that, of the total population of 2,415, 531 persons were under the age of twenty-one. At this date, there were 695 adult males and 1,189 adult females in the sect; figures which reveal an overall, and an adult ratio of males to females of very slightly more than one to two. Taking into account the greater tendency for males to leave the societies, the increasing preponderance of females among the few recruits, and the greater life expectancy of women, it seems certain that the proportion of women in the sect increased as the nineteenth century drew to a close.

As mentioned earlier, the southern societies declined sooner than those in the north. Their initial converts had been made among the subjects of the Great Kentucky revival and, with continuing revivals in the frontier areas of Kentucky, Indiana and Ohio, the societies in these territories expanded steadily until 1823. In that year the Union Village, Ohio, society reached a peak membership of 600, rivalling that of New Lebanon, and South Union, Kentucky, attained its maximum of approximately 350. The enthusiasm of many of the western converts appears to have been short-lived and, as the frontier moved steadily westward, the societies lost a large proportion of their membership – the seceders being primarily younger males.

By 1830 the membership of Union Village had fallen to 500. Thereafter it declined slowly to something less than 400 in 1852, and extremely rapidly in the next decade to a mere 100 members in 1862. The pattern of decline of the Kentucky societies was similar, but less pronounced. Both societies apparently lost a large number of younger members in the 1825 land rush to the newly opened Missouri territory, and by 1850, despite the fact that its policy regarding the adoption of children was the most liberal of all the societies, the total population of South Union had fallen to approximately 270.

Many persons left the southern societies during the Civil War and, after the war, continued numerical decline and financial losses combined to heighten the general apathy and listlessness of the southern Shakers. In 1868, concern regarding the spiritual condition of the Kentucky societies prompted the Ministry of the sect to recommend that the two societies be regrouped into a Bishopric, with Eads as the chief elder. This partial consolidation and reorganization of the societies did little to quicken the faith of the southern members, who appear to have accepted the devotional emphasis of Eads's theological writings, but to have largely ignored his insistence that introversionism should be accompanied by renewed asceticism.

The northern communities generally maintained their numbers until the end of the Civil War, but, from the eighteen seventies, they too declined rapidly. A few converts still sought refuge in the moribund sect, but by the end of the nineteenth century the decline was such that several families, and three societies, Tyringham (Massachusetts), North Union (Ohio) and Groveland (New York), had been closed.

From the end of the Civil War, despite Evans's insistence that the Shakers were the persons best qualified to guide the counsels of leaders of nations, the world, which once had accorded the Shaker testimony the compliment of persecution, regarded the sect as anachronistic and dying. That this opinion was tacitly shared by the sectarians themselves, is evidenced by the historical and apologetic tone of their later writings, and their last significant authors' (White and Taylor, 1905, p. 395) insistence that, despite the transience of all earthly arrangements, and the inevitable decay of institutions:

> Essential Shakerism can never die, for it holds within itself principles which the developed life of humanity demands to have embodied in practical daily living.

Relations with the external society

The preceding discussion of the theological and institutional concomitants of the stagnation and decline of the sect has indicated, or intimated, many aspects of the changes in the reciprocal relationships between the Shakers and the external society. At this point, it is necessary only to summarize the overall pattern of these changes, and briefly to consider the Shakers' attitudes to certain significant problems and issues.

In the last chapter it was shown that, in the decades prior to the internal revival, direct expressions of the sectarians' hostility to the world were expediently suppressed, and that correspondingly, the persecution suffered by the group greatly diminished. In the period of the revival, the ascetic regulation of the lives of the sectarians, and their associated separation from the world, was greatly intensified, and the members again gave unrestrained expression to their contempt and hostility for worldly persons and institutions. Thus, in the last year of the revival, a recent convert jubilantly proclaimed that the divine origin of the Shakers' testimony against lust was evidenced by the distress and disruption which it caused to the families of their converts, and asserted that (anon., 1847, p. 52):

> Unlike all other religious societies, the same persecuting spirit which existed against them at the first, still continues, and no more prospects [sic] of becoming popular with the world now, than there was then.

The Shakers withdrew into their communities the better to prepare themselves to launch a new attack on the world, and at the end of the revival, fortified by the conviction that the Spirit of God dwelt in their midst and by divine assurances of success, they recommenced their evangelistic activities. The confidence with which they sought converts heightened their bewilderment and despair when their missionary activities met with little success. Evangelical failure led many to repudiate the authority of the leaders of the sect and, eventually, to secede, while the members who remained in the group gradually relinquished their hopes of transforming the world.

In the middle decades of the nineteenth century, in the absence of any positive guidance from the formal leaders of the sect, the majority of the sectarians concerned themselves increasingly with the practical affairs of the societies, and with their individual salvation in the world to come, rather than with collective action to establish the Kingdom of God on earth. In this period, and more markedly after the Civil War, the sectarians slowly accommodated themselves, ideologically and behaviourally, to the external society, and the distinctive culture of the sect was gradually eroded by contact with worldly practices and values.

As the Shakers accommodated themselves to the world, so the hostility of the world to the group declined. Early in the life of the sect, each point of contact with the world generated tensions between the sect and the external society, and the Shakers necessarily developed mechanisms and procedures to counter the hostility of the world, and in part to obviate its causes. Thus, by the third decade of the nineteenth century, the covenant of the group had been modified in the light of successive legal proceedings, and the Shakers had succumbed to the demands of the world to the extent of paying their civic and federal taxes, including militia and defence levies. Such compromises of their pacifist and separatist principles removed many of the sources of earlier hostility, and, after the revival, few legal suits were brought against the societies, and the sectarians suffered little persecution.

This latter statement must be qualified in that the abolitionist sympathies and pacifism of the group engendered considerable hostility prior to, and during, the Civil War. Opposition to slavery had been part of the teachings of the early theologians, and, from the first gathering of the societies, there had been a few coloured members in the northern communities. In the south Negroes were settled in 'black families', and slaves belonging to novices were usually freed when their masters became full members of the sect. During the revival the societies received many communications from Negro spirits, and Holy Mother Wisdom herself condemned the institution of slavery, and the treatment of the Indians as 'wild beasts', and added rhetorically (Bates, 1849, pp. 106–7):

> Am I as man, that I should have respect to persons? Am I as man, that
> I should have respect to colors? Have I not created all, and placed upon
> them the color which seemed good in my sight.

Such strictures and prophecies were later cited by Evans to establish the long-standing nature of Shaker abolitionist sympathies but, in the period of the revival, the Shakers were more concerned to demonstrate their divergence from the world than to reform it. In the decade before the Civil War, the slavery question became of ever greater significance, but despite promptings from the southern societies the Ministry of the sect, passive in this as in nearly all matters, issued no directive concerning the rejection or acceptance of monies derived from the sale of inherited slaves, or from the profits of their labour.

With the outbreak of the Civil War, the pacifism of the sect increased the hostility of many of the neighbours of the communities, but the Shakers' exemption from military services was later confirmed by President Lincoln, after he had received a deputation headed by Frederick Evans (see White and Taylor, 1905, pp. 180 ff.). The persecution suffered by the sectarians in the Civil War period was relatively mild, and overall the sect's relationships with the world became increasingly amicable throughout the nineteenth century.

The degree of tolerance of the sect exhibited by persons in the external society varied directly with two factors, which were themselves closely interrelated: the lack of success of the Shakers' evangelistic activities, and their increasing accommodation to the world. From the time of the gathering of the societies, until a decade after the end of the Kentucky revival, the Shakers had engaged in persistent and successful evangelism. In this period, the anxiety and outrage of the families of converts, and the anger of revivalistic preachers and other ministers of religion, combined to generate intense hostility to the sect.

With the failure of Shaker evangelism, the world's attitude to the sect changed. The sectarians were no longer regarded as seeking to ensnare the young or disrupt families, but as providing a place of refuge for inadequate and helpless individuals. They were looked upon not as dangerous, but as eccentric, not as fanatical, but as misguidedly zealous, and gradually the honesty, diligence and charitable activities of the sectarians won them some measure of condescending approval from the world. The attitude of many of the neighbours of the Shakers can be illustrated by the words attributed to John Morgan, a Confederate guerrilla leader, who had grown up in the vicinity of the Pleasant Hill, Kentucky, society, and who forbade his troops to plunder the Shaker communities. He described the sectarians as 'a harmless, inoffensive people; that took no part with either side, injured no man and had no desire to do so . . .' (cited in Fry, 1939, p. 30).

When persecution virtually ceased after the Civil War, the sectarians were forced to come to terms with the facts of evangelical failure, institutional stagnation and of their partial acceptance by the world. The reaction of the ordinary members to the situation of the sect has been discussed above, but the attempts by the Shaker intellectuals to diagnose the causes of stagnation of the group and to indicate appropriate courses of action for the sectarians, must be examined in more detail.

The opinions of Eads and the other conservative intellectuals merit only slight further discussion. Eads insisted that the Shakers had betrayed their inspiration by becoming too friendly with the world. He advocated that they should, as far as possible, sever their connections with the external society. They should retreat behind the bulwark of their covenant into the security of the societies, and there should maintain their testimony against lust, and cultivate their spirituality, trusting to God to perpetuate His Church on earth. Eads roundly condemned the institutions of the world, and his denunciation of marriage had something of the vehemence of the early Shaker theologians. Thus, he stated that 'legal prostitution' (or marriage) was almost as odious in the sight of God as the illegal form, and in this context asked rhetorically whether the demoralization of a man who kept a brandy barrel at home was in any way different from that of a man who drank in different saloons (1879, pp. 50–1).

Evans and the other reform-oriented Shakers sought converts less in terms of their religious convictions than of their possession of progressive views. The catholic nature of Evans's interests and of his appeals for converts has already been discussed, but the significant fact is that his attempts to demonstrate the relevance of Shakerism to 'all classes of reformers', were confined to general statements. Evans insisted that the Shakers were, by divine commission, the vanguard of reform, but neither he nor his associates offered worldly reformers anything more than sympathy and encouragement.

In their writings the reformers vigorously condemned worldly abuses; they specified the reforms which they desired and jubilantly reported all progressive legislation and movements, but they offered no concrete programmes of action to implement reform. Not surprisingly, in view of the intensely pragmatic intellectual climate of the United States in the late nineteenth century, they drew few converts from the wide spectrum of reformist movements. The world in general, and 'persons of liberal sympathies' in particular, persisted in regarding the Shakers as anachronistic and irrelevant, and looked on the progressive sectarians as misguided in their continued allegiance to the group.

No attempt will be made to discuss the entire range of social movements with which Evans and his associates individually or collectively identified themselves – they included women's suffrage, temperance, the abolition of capital punishment, pure food legislation, eugenics and the abolition of novel reading. However, it is necessary to mention the culmination of Evans's thought – his advocacy of a total reorganization of American society under Shaker guidance. The examination of this proposal involves very brief consideration of three closely related topics: the modification of the original Shaker testimony against lust, the pragmatic justification of this modification and Evans's increasingly favourable attitude towards the ideals and political principles of American society.

The force of the testimony of the early Shakers, and the hostility which they encountered, was derived largely from their uncompromising denunciation of every aspect of sexuality, and from their condemnation of the institution of marriage as a blasphemous sacralization of lust. The early Shakers and the later conservatives insisted that sexuality was the tap-root of all sin, and emphasized that, in whatever form it was manifested, lust remained lust. In partial contrast, Evans and his associates insisted that the demonstration of the virtues of the celibate life was but the first part of the

Shakers' testimony against the evils of the world, and, concomitantly with the progressives' reconciliation with the world, their attitude to marriage changed.

The reformist members of the sect granted the legitimacy of marriage as an institution for the world, and accepted the legitimacy of sexual relations within marriage, provided that such relations were entered into solely for procreative purposes (Evans, 1859, pp. 59–60). As the reformers' acceptance of the institution of marriage and of limited sexual relations within marriage became more explicit, they were forced to rejustify their continued celibacy, and they did so both in orthodox and in pragmatic terms. Evans and his associates emphasized that celibacy was necessary for the development of full spiritual awareness, and indeed, for the full development of more mundane faculties. In addition, they argued that only the widespread adoption of celibacy would prevent world-wide overpopulation and its attendant miseries.

Evans first extensively adduced Malthusian arguments to support Shaker celibacy, and to demonstrate the sectarians' concern for worldly problems, in his autobiography. In this work, he insisted that the government of the United States should, 'as the most important of all its functions', enforce the word of God and prohibit all sexual relations except those for purposes of procreation. Without further comment, he asserted that such action would put an end to war, and would inaugurate an era of prosperity and social improvement (Evans, 1869, pp. 80 ff.). Similarly, during his first evangelical journey to England, Evans spoke, in a somewhat less exalted fashion, of the 'Shaker remedy for the population problem', and urged all persons who were concerned about the condition of society, and who felt themselves 'elected' to be true Christians, to gather in the Shaker societies.

The reformers' tolerance of marriage, and their Malthusian justifications of celibacy, were obviously closely related to their evangelical concerns, but more broadly, these changes in doctrine and social teachings were accompanied by an increasingly favourable attitude to the institutions of the external society. It has been shown that the early Shakers tempered their contempt for the world with assertions of their gratitude and loyalty to the government of the United States, but the writings of the progressive Shakers went far beyond such expedient protestations, and expressed the conception that the destinies of Shakerism and American society were interdependent, and that both were blessed and guided by God.

The ideals of American society were seen as a condition of the existence of the Shaker Church which, in turn, was held to encapsulate these ideals in their highest form. The Shaker reformers subscribed to the conception, widespread in North America in the second half of the nineteenth century, that the manifest destiny of the United States was to transform the ideals and institutions of other, more backward, nations and races.

In his later writings, Evans advocated a total reorganization of American

society, a reorganization which he believed would result in a gradual abolition of all worldly evils. He urged that American society, and eventually the
world, should be organized in three orders: the Shaker or 'Resurrection'
order, the Republican or 'Platonic' order, and the residual mass of mankind –
the order of Generation. In addition to his earlier unusually specific, if
scarcely practicable, recommendation that the President of the United States
should ban all sexual relations other than those for purposes of procreation,
Evans proposed that the Shaker principle of sexual dualism should be extended
to all administrative positions in American society, and that the incumbency
of these positions should be restricted to celibates. The members of the highest,
Shaker, order would exert a beneficent influence upon the rest of mankind
by virtue of their spirituality and, increasing in numbers as mankind became
more enlightened, would (Evans, 1877, p. 9):

> by drawing millions of men and women up into the Christ heavens,
> even while yet in the body . . . become the normal regulator of the
> otherwise unlimited principle of generation in the production of human
> beings.

The practical details of the government and administration of the world
were to be entrusted to the members of the second, Platonic, order who
(Evans, 1877, p. 10):

> shall be selected from a class of men and women who, on the natural
> plane, have risen into an intellectual condition in which celibacy is an
> inevitable necessity. I call this the Platonic order, which will intervene
> between the normal order of propagation and the Shakers.

Evans appears to have believed that indulgence in sexual relations had a
deleterious effect on the physical and mental powers of the participants, and
insisted that the task of rearing children was a sufficient burden for the mass
of mankind. He allowed that talented individuals might usefully contribute
to the administration of society once they had discharged their parental
duties, but emphasized that 'breeding' men and women should not sit on
governmental bodies 'lest their energies fail, and their wisdom be turned into
foolishness' (Evans, 1877, p. 12).

It is unnecessary to discuss the apogee of Evans's thought at further length.
The minor details of his last proposals varied, but all his programmes for
reform were alike in that, despite the optative mood and exalted tone of
their pronouncement, no indication was provided of the methods by which
the proposed reforms could be implemented.

Evans's proposals for the reconstruction of American society attracted
little attention, and won few converts for the sect. After his death in 1893,
the Shakers abandoned any real hope of influencing worldly governments,
and confined themselves to more modest reformist interests. Thus, White
and Taylor described the sect as a 'centre of good influences', and mentioned

that one member of the group was secretary to an anti-vivisection society. The resignation and passivity of the sectarians at the beginning of the nineteenth century can be illustrated by a quotation which reveals a conception of the sect's relation to the world more akin to that of a monastic order, than to that of the early members of the group, who had hoped to mortify, and eventually destroy, the world with the 'consuming fire' of their testimony. White and Taylor (1905, pp. 302–3) indicated that the Shaker regarded himself as:

> harvested from the world for a special life, and does not grudge that other men, not so called, should live in their order the common life of nature.

Summary

In the previous chapter, the origins of the Shakers' religious utopianism, and the institutionalization of their communitarianism were discussed. This chapter has dealt with the circumstances, and the ideological, institutional and behavioural consequences of the disconfirmation and eventual abandonment of the utopian faith of the sect. In the course of this discussion considerable significance has been attached to the failure of Shaker evangelism in the period after the internal revival, and, before concluding the specific analysis of the development of the Shakers, the social background of this failure must be briefly examined.

The Shakers' espousal of celibacy rendered them peculiarly dependent on successful evangelism. In most sects new members are recruited from the external society, and also internally from among the children of the sectarians, but the possibility of internal recruitment was not open to the Shakers. This statement must be qualified in that children were occasionally adopted, but few of these children remained in the group after they had attained maturity, and the Shakers do not appear to have considered wholesale recruitment by adoption to be a feasible, or desirable, alternative to evangelism.

Until the period of Mother Ann's Work, the majority of converts to Shakerism were drawn from among the subjects of rural religious revivals, and the Shakers themselves acknowledged that their decline was due to the absence, or the lessened intensity, of such revivals after 1850. Writing with specific reference to western New York State, Cross (1950) has described how decades of intensive revivalistic activity, which culminated in Charles Finney's evangelical tours in 1826 and 1831, in combination with the expansion and fluctuation of the economy of the State, generated an intellectual and religious mood which he, and writers of the period, termed 'ultraism'. This term denoted a state of mind in which every manifestation of religious fervour and moral concern was interpreted as a work of the Holy Spirit, and as presaging the imminent collapse of sin before the power of the Spirit.

Cross indicated that such exalted excitement and expectation was a near to impossible state of mind, and that the generalized moral concern of many of the subjects of the revivals eventually found expression in the condemnation of specific social evils, each of which was interpreted as hindering the progress of the Spirit of God, and thus delaying the 'final revival of spirituality' which would usher in the millennium. In this emotionally charged intellectual climate which was, in less extreme forms, duplicated in each area of intensive revivalistic activity, the Shakers' utopian promise (itself refined in the revivalistic crucible) of personal salvation through active participation in the construction of the Kingdom of God, won them many converts.

Religious and reformist ultraism reached its peak in the boom year of 1836, and collapsed with the depression of 1837, the year in which the first spiritual manifestations occurred among the Shakers. As a result of the depression, the donations and church subscriptions which had supported the revivalistic preachers were greatly reduced, and the economic crisis directed the attention of reformers to more specific problems of unemployment and poverty, and threw new light on the social causes of these problems.

Even before the economic depression, there had been growing dissatisfaction among the members of reformist movements, some of whom at least had gradually come to realize that such evils as intemperance and prostitution had their roots in the very structure of society, and were not simply the results of individual corruption and perversity. Many reformers had become aware of their inability to abolish social problems simply by condemning them, and with specific reference to abolitionism, Cross commented (1950, p. 224):

> What more could be done, after all, by religious enthusiasm than to record a mass conviction of the sinfulness of slavery and urge its remedy at the earliest moment?

In consequence, after 1837, many reformers, chastened by the non-attainment of their goals and by the non-arrival of the millennium, turned to more limited reforms, and gradually developed an activist, but more modest conception of the mode and possibility of the implementation of social change and improvements.

The American economy did not fully recover from the depression until 1844. After this date it expanded rapidly, particularly in the north-eastern states (the main theatre of the Shakers' evangelical activities) where population increase and general prosperity largely removed the earlier conditions of 'backwoods' poverty and isolation. As the rural areas of these states became more settled and prosperous, they ceased to be regarded as mission territories, and, from the middle of the nineteenth century, evangelical and reformist groups increasingly focused their attentions on the cities, where the middle classes anxiously faced new, or newly realized, problems associated with industrial poverty, overcrowding and the assimilation of immigrants.

In 1845 the Shakers emerged, filled with evangelistic zeal, from their period of self-imposed purificatory retreat, but their hopes of rapid expansion were quickly disappointed. Few revivals occurred in the rural districts adjacent to the societies, and those which did occur did not generate the same widespread millennial expectancy, the disconfirmation of which had earlier led many persons to embrace Shakerism. Moreover, many of the societies of the sect had been in existence for upwards of fifty years, and the Shaker teachings had lost much of their novelty.

The impact of evangelical failure was severe. The leaders lost their confidence and thereafter exerted only a minimum of ideological and administrative control, while the disappointment of the ordinary members led those who remained in the sect to question, implicitly or explicitly, the relevance of continued asceticism, and to a greater preoccupation with devotional concerns or with the practical affairs of their societies.

The doubts of the sectarians in the post-revival period were heightened by the generally tolerant attitude of the world towards the sect. Gradually, the neighbours of the societies ceased to perceive the Shakers as a threat and, reciprocally, the tolerance of the world facilitated and encouraged closer relations between the sectarians and the external society. The extent and rapidity of the behavioural and attitudinal changes engendered by the lack of evangelistic success should not be exaggerated. The Shakers did not immediately abandon their utopian faith and become totally reconciled with the world, but very slowly repeated evangelical failure, the absence of revivals, and the secession of the young, weakened the faith and increased the despair of the sectarians, and concomitantly every aspect of life in the societies was permeated by worldly values.

In ideological terms, in the second half of the nineteenth century the beliefs of the sect became more gradualistic, and the distinctive religious vision of the Shakers more attenuated. The conception of a celibate, communistic world under the direct guidance of the Spirit of God was increasingly regarded as a remote ideal, rather than as a spur to immediate collective action and individual self-denial.

After the Civil War, the facts of numerical decline and institutional stagnation became unmistakable, and the theologians of the sect sought to diagnose and remedy the evils which had beset the group. The resultant informal ideological bifurcation of the group developed from the twin, largely incompatible, components of religious utopianism – separatism and evangelism. The conservatives urged that the Shakers should concentrate on the cultivation of their communal and personal spirituality, relying on God and the example of their ascetic renunciation of the world to draw sufficient converts to 'keep up the institution'. The reform-oriented members sought to win converts and respect for the sect by demonstrating the enlightened comprehension of the sectarians, and the progressive nature of their sevenfold testimony against worldly evils. However, while Evans and his associates asserted the relevance of Shakerism to all reformers, and emphasized the long-standing nature of their concern with reform, their complete failure to suggest practical means for the implementation of their proposals bore the hallmarks of the earlier, and totally discredited, ultraist approach to social reform.

The general intellectual mood of late nineteenth-century America, and in particular of the members of reform-oriented social movements, was imbued with the conception that the United States stood in the vanguard of evolution and of earthly progress; but this rationalistic perfectionism was intensely pragmatic and activist. God was on the side of America, and American institutions were inspired by the Divine Spirit, but the expansion of these institutions, and the removal of all social evils, was held to be dependent on the deliberate action of men. In such an intellectual climate, Evans's claims and appeals, coming from the spokesman of a rapidly declining, celibate and rural sect, appeared unrealistic and irrelevant, and were accordingly ignored.

The contradictory emphases of White and Taylor's work bespoke a realization of the possibility of the extinction of the sect, and an understandable reluctance to admit this possibility. White and Taylor combined immediate exhortation on the basis of optimistic exegesis, with an evolutionary relativization of the history of the sect and of its inspiration. Thus they suggested that, in a future 'dispensation', God's will for mankind might be made known in more advanced revelations than those which had guided the Shakers.

Evidently concerned to vindicate the efforts and sacrifices of the sectarians, they summarized their achievements, and in these passages emphasized the importance of the fact that the Shakers had provided a demonstration of the brotherhood of man, and of the viability of economic communism. In the last Shaker writings, with the abandonment of the utopian vision of a total transformation of the world, the communitarian organization of the group, which had originally been adopted as an expedient, was adduced as the most important fruit of Shakerism, and as a justification of all the Shakers' endeavours.

Chapter 4

The Perfectionists of Oneida –
origins and incipient communitarianism,
1831–1848

The founder and leader of the Oneida Community throughout the four decades of its existence as a communistic group was John Humphrey Noyes, who was born of prosperous and influential parents at Brattleboro, Vermont, in 1811. In this year, his father, John Noyes, a teacher turned merchant, was elected to the Vermont legislature, and from 1815 to 1817 was a member of the federal House of Representatives. In 1821, John Noyes retired and sought a place to settle in order to devote himself to the education of his children. His highly religious wife, Polly Noyes, sought divine guidance on the subject for three months, and finally felt inspired to suggest that the family remove to Putney, Vermont, which was a local centre of revivalistic activity, and the home of several friends of the family.

In 1826, John Humphrey Noyes entered Dartmouth College, and on graduating, studied law at Chesterfield, New Hampshire. In this year, the religious excitement generated by the first wave of revivals conducted by Charles Finney and his associates reached a peak, but left Noyes unmoved, and in his adolescence he regarded religion with a considerable measure of cynicism. In 1831, the year of Finney's Rochester revival, Noyes, at the request of his mother, attended a four day 'protracted' revival meeting at Putney. Initially he was unmoved, but after the meeting suffered a feverish cold which led him to think of death, and to humble himself before God.

Noyes embraced religion with the vigour with which he had previously rejected it, and appears to have shared fully in the millennial expectations of the period. His earlier consciousness of the short-lived nature of revivalistic conversions in no way damped his enthusiasm, and, regarding himself as having been brought to the truth by the providential administration of suffering, he determined to be a 'young convert' forever (Noyes, 1848, p. 2).

Noyes immediately abandoned all thoughts of a legal career, and, after a preparatory study of Hebrew, entered Andover Theological Seminary in November, 1831. His immediate reaction to Andover was one of disappointment at the 'unhallowed levity' of his fellow students, but, after a few months in which he distinguished himself by his application to biblical studies, he was invited to join 'The Brethren', an informal student society. The members of this group were drawn from among the more dedicated students who strove to improve their spiritual condition by especially intensive study, and by a practice which was later elaborated by Noyes into the primary method of social control in the Oneida Community: the systematic employment of personal criticism (Noyes, 1848, p. 4):

> One of the weekly exercises of this society was, a frank criticism of each other's character, for the purpose of improvement . . . the member whose turn it was . . . to submit to criticism, held his peace, while the other members, one by one, told him his faults in the plainest way possible.

Despite his membership in this informal élite, Noyes's dissatisfaction with Andover persisted and, at the end of a year, attracted by the doctrinal studies conducted by Nathaniel Taylor, and following what he took to be clear divine guidance revealed by bibliomancy, he transferred to the Yale Theological College at New Haven. Here he became deeply involved with the nascent abolitionist movement, and participated in various charitable and religious attempts to improve the condition of the coloured community. In 1833 he was instrumental in the formation of the New Haven Anti-Slavery Society, and was also prominent in the development of the inter-denominational 'Free Church'.

Doctrinally, the New Haven Free Church can be characterized as 'Perfectionist', in the radical sense that the members laid great emphasis on the ideal of perfection as being attainable in this life, and, more important, as being a guide and standard for Christian conduct. However, in the period under discussion, the term 'Perfectionist' was applied to a wide spectrum of doctrinal positions and religious groupings. The latter ranged from the liberal members of the Calvinistic denominations, through the revival-oriented Free Churches, to the most extreme groups of 'Come-outers', several of which evinced antinomian and quasi-communistic tendencies.

Concomitant with the development of revivalistic activity and techniques from the time of the Great Awakening, some of the theologians of the Congregational and Presbyterian Churches had gradually modified the harshness of Calvinistic theology by rejecting the doctrine of total human depravity, and, correspondingly, emphasizing human free will. This movement culminated in the work of Nathaniel Taylor who taught that, while men might suffer from sinful motives, their free will consisted in their ability to choose between good and evil motives, and that Christian perfection, the development of an entirely unselfish love for God, was theoretically attainable in man's earthly existence. Similarly, the evangelist Charles Finney, who became the chief spokesman of Oberlin Perfectionism, taught that perfection was attainable in this life, and that it consisted in an entire surrender of the human will to that of God.

Any attempt to distinguish between the Free Churches and the more extreme Perfectionist groups is inevitably artificial, as the doctrinal positions of these groups were closely interrelated, and as there was a considerable interchange of members between the two categories of groups. However, this reservation having been made, the Free Churches can be broadly described as composed of persons who had adopted the ideal of Christian perfection as the cardinal, if rarely attainable, goal of their spiritual endeavours, and the most radical groups as consisting of persons who either professed to have attained perfection, or who expected its early attainment.

The most pejorative connotations of the term Perfectionist were reserved by the orthodox for the members of those informal associations which espoused the more radical forms of the doctrine of perfection. The most numerous, and least extreme, of these groups consisted of the followers of James Latourette. Latourette left the Methodist Church in 1828, and in New York City formed a group which was devoted to the attainment of perfect holiness, and to the performance of 'miracles' of conversion and regeneration by the power of prayer. Latourette's followers differed little from the members of the Free Churches except in so far as their attempt to recapture the spirit of early Methodism, and their associated repudiation of formalism, led them to reject fixed religious services and the appointment of ministers or pastors.

Smaller groups, practising informal communism and living in expectation of the final revival which would abolish sin, and all the social abuses which were the manifestations of sin, were scattered throughout New York State and New England. Of these groups, perhaps the most extreme were the Perfectionists of Massachusetts, who displayed marked antinomian tendencies and who, as will be shown below, were concerned to give practical demonstrations of their immunity to temptation and their contempt for legalistic restrictions.

The development of 'New Haven Perfectionism'

At New Haven, Noyes's theological opinions gradually became more unorthodox. From the time of his conversion, he had been an enthusiastic student of the Bible and, in 1833, concluded from such study that the second coming of Christ was not a future event, but that it had occurred at about the time of the destruction of Jerusalem in AD 70. According to his own account, this conviction led Noyes (1848, p. 9) to doubt all established theological authorities, and to conclude that, as the second coming was past,

> human nature under divine culture, was gradually ascending
> heavenward, not only before, but much more after the incarnation of
> Christ, – that at the end of the apostolic age, 'this world' and 'the world
> to come' flowed together, and the true Christian dispensation was
> ushered in by the glories of the Second Advent.

In August 1833, Noyes received his licence to preach, and for several weeks of his final year at Yale officiated as pastor at the Presbyterian Church in North Salem, New York. Here he had more direct contact with 'dead orthodoxy', and was appalled at what he took to be the narrow-mindedness of the presbytery. On his return to New Haven, he read a paper to the assembled seminary in which he argued that persecution was the primary test of faith, and was reproved by Nathaniel Taylor, who pointed out that ministers of the churches were not persecuted in Connecticut.

Noyes appears to have suffered this rebuke without comment or retort, but he advanced an increasingly radical interpretation of Christian perfection and sanctification. Convinced that the second coming was past, Noyes concluded that he was living in the age of the fulfilment of Christ's prophecies, and hence that perfect holiness and sinlessness were not only attainable in this life, but that only persons who could lay claim to such perfection were truly Christians. The radical implications of this conception caused Noyes much anguish, and led him to doubt his own sanity, but, again resorting to bibliomancy, his eye fell on the comforting line 'the Holy Ghost is with thee' and, convinced that he was in direct communication with God and under his guidance, he resolved to make public his revolutionary theological opinions.

Consequently, on 19 February 1834, Noyes preached a sermon at the Free Church on the subject 'He that committeth sin is of the devil'. He insisted that this text should be understood literally, realizing that he was exposing himself to an *argumentum ad hominem*. That evening, after suffering some doubts, Noyes was further convinced that he was acting under the guidance of the Holy Spirit (Noyes, 1848, p. 18):

> Three times in quick succession a stream of eternal love gushed through
> my heart and rolled back again to its source. . . . All fear and doubt
> and condemnation passed away. I knew that my heart was clean, and
> that the Father and the Son had come and made it their abode.

The next day, Noyes received the expected challenge from a fellow student and, on being asked if he himself did not commit sin, replied that he did not. Most of Noyes's acquaintances and associates appear to have regarded him as deranged, but he won a few followers among the members of the Free Church, including James Boyle who had been appointed pastor of the church at Noyes's recommendation. Noyes became romantically attached to the first of his followers, Abigail Merwin, who quickly professed her personal holiness and freedom from sin. In April 1834, when it was seen that Noyes persisted in his heresy, his licence to preach was revoked, and he joyfully interpreted this revocation, and his loss of reputation, as being tantamount to martyrdom.

Three months later, Noyes travelled to New York to attend the 'anniversary meetings' of the Congregational clergy, and also to visit James Latourette, who was regarded as the informal leader of the scattered groups of Perfectionists in the state. Latourette gave Noyes an attentive hearing, but was not impressed by his teachings, and warned him that the antinomianism implicit in his theology might 'beget carelessness' (Noyes, 1848, p. 32). After this interview, Noyes stayed on alone in New York to write a tract, and suffered a period of profound doubt and depression in which his faith in his own inspiration was shaken, and in which he became convinced of the existence of the devil as a personal and uncreated spirit of evil.

According to his own account, he was unable to eat or sleep, and at first was prey to fantasies and hallucinations. He initially looked for the literal appearance of Christ in the sky, but slowly came to realize that Christ would come to earth, not cataclysmically, but in a 'gradual spiritual operation'. Subsequently, his faith was restored to him, and he was fortified by the knowledge of his own sinlessness, and by the conviction that 'hell has done its worst; and yet I live' (Noyes, 1848, p. 45).

In this period, Noyes wandered aimlessly through the slums of Manhattan, preached in taverns and in the streets and, once his conviction of his freedom from sin was restored, drank 'ardent spirits' in order to reprove the spirit of legality that he felt still hovered over him. At the end of about three weeks of such exertions, Noyes became ill and returned to New Haven, leaving his bills in New York to be paid by a fellow Perfectionist. His own accounts of his experiences in New York were magnified by rumour, and, as a result, family pressure was exerted on Abigail Merwin, who withdrew from the Free Church.

After a short recuperation at Putney, Noyes returned to New Haven in August 1834 and, in collaboration with James Boyle, launched a monthly periodical, *The Perfectionist*, in the first six issues of which he elaborated and defended his theological position. After six months, he left Boyle in charge of the periodical, and travelled to visit a group of Perfectionists at Brimfield, Massachusetts, but was appalled by the antinomian licence, or licentiousness, which he found there.

The Massachusetts Perfectionists cultivated freedom of manners between the sexes in order to demonstrate their contempt for legalism and their superiority to sexual temptation. Some days after his arrival at Brimfield, Noyes was given a 'kiss of fellowship' by one of the 'sisters', and was thrown into great consternation by this. Later that evening, in the solitude of his room he received what he believed to be 'orders to withdraw' from the Holy Ghost and, without more ado, set off in a snowstorm on a sixty-mile march to Putney. After Noyes's flight, two of the 'sisters' in the same house entered the bedroom of one of the 'brothers', in order to demonstrate their immunity to carnal impulses. Whether sexual intercourse, or merely 'bundling', took place is uncertain, but much of the blame for the affair was very unjustly attributed to Noyes. The events at Brimfield convinced Noyes of the dangers of antinomianism, and led him to emphasize that discipline and order were inevitable concomitants of true Christianity.

In the following two years, Noyes's ideas further developed in reaction to what he deemed to be the errors and excesses of his fellow Perfectionists. In this period, the course of his wanderings was determined by a combination of financial and evangelical concerns, and by his frustrated passion for Abigail Merwin, whose parents had forbidden her to see him.

In the summer of 1835, Noyes preached with very little success to his neighbours at Putney, and in the course of this year, quarrelled with his family, who thought him mad, and with his chief Perfectionist associates: Charles Weld, James Boyle and Theophilus Gates. Noyes rejected Weld, who had introduced him to many influential Perfectionists, as being patronizing, and appears to have been particularly piqued by the fact that, under God, Weld arrogated to himself supreme authority in the coming Kingdom of God on earth. James Boyle, Noyes's earliest and closest associate, had fallen under the influence of Gates, who can best be described as a religious anarchist, who staunchly opposed every aspect of organization and discipline in religious bodies.

Noyes was influenced by Gates for a time, but as a result of his Brimfield experience, he repudiated Gates after the latter had attacked the apostle Paul as authoritarian. By the end of 1836, depressed by his failure to win widespread support for his teachings, and by the 'death-like spread of antinomianism' among the Perfectionists, he returned to Putney where he established the 'Putney Bible School', which was chiefly devoted to the instruction of his family. Subsequently, in February 1837, Noyes's mother, his sisters Harriet and Charlotte, and his fourteen-year-old brother, George, made a profession of their freedom from sin and dedication to Christ.

As shown above, Noyes's religious ideas, in part, developed in reaction to other varieties of perfectionism, and became more radical and idiosyncratic as he found himself rejected by many of the persons whom he felt were ripe for conversion, as well as by Abigail Merwin who married another man early in 1837. In March of that year, Noyes travelled to New York to visit the abolitionist William Lloyd Garrison, and to read him a manifesto or personal declaration of his independence from the government of the United States. This declaration was later published by Garrison, without attribution, in his periodical. Noyes's letter took the form of a parody of the American Declaration of Independence, and combined vehement denunciations of American institutions with prophetic assertions. Noyes asserted the title of Christ to the 'throne of the world', and renounced his allegiance to the American Government, of which he stated (*The Liberator*, October 1837, p. 158):

When I wish to form a true conception of the government of the United States, (using a personified representation) I picture to myself a bloated, swaggering libertine, trampling on the Bible – its own Constitution – its treaties with the Indians – the petitions of its citizens; with one hand whipping a Negro, tied to a liberty-pole, and with the other dashing an emaciated Indian to the ground. . . . But every other country is under the same reprobate authority. I must, then, either go out of the world, or find some way to live where I am, without being a hypocrite, or a partaker in the sins of the nation.

In August 1837, Noyes travelled to Ithaca, New York, where Abigail Platt (*née* Merwin) was living, and established a periodical, *The Witness*, three numbers of which appeared before publication lapsed for more than a year. Noyes's labours on the paper ceased as a consequence of an adventitious combination of circumstances which resulted in the publication of a letter which he had written on 15 January 1837, to David Harrison, a sympathetic Perfectionist of Meriden, Connecticut. This letter passed through several hands and was eventually sent to Theophilus Gates, who had just launched a new periodical, *The Battle-Axe*, the first issue of which contained a lengthy denunciation of the institution of marriage. Gates published a part of Noyes's letter anonymously on 1 September 1837. Noyes quickly came to regard this unintended publication as providential, and on 23 September 1837, he acknowledged authorship of the letter, and was immediately engaged in a furore of controversy.

In the '*Battle-Axe* letter', Noyes gave an account of his interpretation of biblical prophecy, and indicated clearly that he conceived himself to be God's agent on earth. He asserted that (cited in G. W. Noyes, 1923, p. 306):

God is about to set a great white throne on his foot-stool, and heaven and earth, that is, all spiritual and political dynasties, will flee away from the face of him who shall sit thereon. The second resurrection and the second judgment are at the door. . . . Between this present time and the establishment of God's kingdom over the earth lies a chaos of confusion, tribulation and war such as must attend the destruction of the fashion of this world and the introduction of the will of God as it is done in heaven. God has set me to cast up a highway across this chaos, and I am gathering out the stones and grading the track as fast as possible.

This passage generated less outrage than that in which Noyes outlined the sexual relationships which he believed prevailed in the spiritual world, and which would prevail on earth once the Kingdom of Heaven was established there (cited in Dixon, 1868, vol. 2, p. 55):

When the will of God is done on earth as it is in heaven, there will be no marriage. The marriage-supper of the Lamb, is a feast at which every dish is free to every guest. Exclusiveness, jealousy, quarrelling, have no place there, for the same reason as that which forbids the guests at a thanksgiving dinner to claim each his separate dish, and quarrel with the rest for his rights. In a holy community there is no more reason why sexual intercourse should be restrained by law, than why eating and drinking should be; and there is as little occasion for shame in the one case as in the other.

On the day on which Gates published the *Battle-Axe* letter, Noyes received eighty dollars, the exact sum of his indebtedness at Ithaca, sent 'by inspiration' by a female admirer, Harriet Holton. The receipt of this sum enabled him to leave Ithaca and, returning once more to Putney, he commenced to defend the views he had outlined in his letter to Harrison. Early in 1838, Abigail Platt left her husband and Noyes immediately wrote to her, but received a discouraging reply. On returning to Ithaca in March 1838, he found further letters from Harriet Holton, who rapidly replaced Abigail Platt in his affection, or at least in his estimation.

In April 1838, Noyes replied to an antagonistic article in the journal of the New York Magdalen Society (which was dedicated to the reformation of prostitutes) and, while repeating his claim that monogamous marriage did not exist in heaven, and would not exist in a regenerated world, sought to repudiate accusations of general licentiousness by emphasizing that the heavenly state had not yet been established on earth. Two months later, he wrote to Harriet Holton proposing marriage, and cited at length the advantages of the match, which, in addition to promoting their mutual happiness, would win him 'freedom from reproach', and increase their individual usefulness to God. Harriet accepted his proposal, and in her letter of acceptance stated that she agreed with Noyes that marriage would not limit the range of their affections. Further, she indicated that she had previously considered celibacy to be the most virtuous state, and this remark drew a sharp reply from Noyes (cited in Parker, 1935, pp. 63–4):

> I know not how far you may have imbibed the spirit of Shakerism; but I will say frankly, that there may be no mistake between us, that so far from regarding the act of sexual enjoyment as in itself unholy, I am sure that there is no sacrifice except that of the heart, that is more acceptable to God.

A short time later, the couple married at Chesterfield, New Hampshire, and then returned to Putney where Noyes resumed his task of strengthening the convictions of his few followers and of elaborating and promulgating his radical religious doctrines.

Noyes's religious teachings – an ultraist gospel and mission

In the three weeks of his 'New York experience' in the summer of 1834, Noyes tentatively explored the implications of his theological position, and, after rejecting his millennial expectations of the Advent as fantasies, developed a somewhat more gradualistic conception of God's plan for the redemption of mankind. In this period also, he appears to have begun to regard himself as God's sole agent on earth who, after suffering temptations analogous to those of Christ, was commissioned to announce the true Christian message and so pave the way for the inauguration of the Kingdom of Heaven on earth. On his return to New Haven, Noyes began to promulgate his doctrines in *The Perfectionist*. For a time he was influenced by the anti-authoritarianism of Gates, but his Brimfield experience, and his ungratified appetite for power, led him to emphasize the need for order and subordination even among the regenerate, and to elaborate his earlier defensive statement that the attainment of freedom from sin did not preclude 'room for improvement'.

During the period of his collaboration with James Boyle, Noyes appears to have believed that the simple announcement of his doctrinal system would be sufficient to attract large numbers of converts to the 'gospel of holiness', but, after his flight from Brimfield, he encountered much opposition and experienced a variety of personal and ideological rejections which led him to an increasingly radical and idiosyncratic doctrinal position. Noyes's reputation had suffered considerably from his exalted accounts of his repudiation of the 'spirit of legalism' in New York, and, despite his subsequent rejection of antinomianism, Noyes's opponents were largely successful in attributing the blame for the scandal at Brimfield to his teachings and example. As a result, by 1836, many of the more moderate Perfectionists and, for a time at least, his family, had come to regard Noyes as, if not a deliberate evil-doer, at least deranged.

Rejection and isolation served only to heighten Noyes's conception of himself as the sole possessor of an understanding of true Christianity, and his growing conviction that he was God's lieutenant led him to break with all those Perfectionists who, explicitly or implicitly, denied his commission. Early in 1837, his more mundane hopes and expectations were finally dashed by the estranged Abigail Platt's cool reception of his approaches, and in this same period, the disappointment of their millennial expectations, and the onset of the economic depression, led even the more enthusiastic Perfectionists to concentrate on limited and practical, rather than on general and moral, reforms. This dual frustration of his romantic and evangelistic hopes appears to have prompted Noyes's wistful depiction of the sexual relationships which would prevail in the Kingdom of Heaven, and also his violent denunciation of the corruption of the institutions and of the inhabitants of the United States and of the world.

Despite the vigour of his diatribes against sexual restrictions and worldly institutions, the only immediate result of Noyes's testimony was the final estrangement of many of his sympathizers, and a further increase in the moral and theological opposition to his system of 'New Haven Perfectionism'. As has been shown, Noyes admitted to Harriet Holton that marriage would, to some extent, protect him from further calumny, and after his marriage, he resolved to concentrate on the intensive instruction of a few followers as a necessary preliminary to the more widespread promulgation of his gospel.

In the decade after his return to Putney in 1838, he elaborated a complex theological system which was given full expression in *The Berean* (1847), the work which was the 'bible' of the Oneida Community – the theological fundament of its social teachings and practices. As Noyes elaborated his distinctive religious ideas, his conception of his mission changed. He came to believe that his task was to establish the Kingdom of Heaven on earth as a demonstration of the practicability and perfection of the regenerate life. The circumstances of this ideological transition will be examined after consideration of Noyes's fully developed theological system.

At Andover, Noyes had distinguished himself by the intensity of his scriptural studies, and, in *The Berean*, he emphasized that any person who professed to respect Christ's message should also respect the Bible as the vehicle by which that message had been conveyed to mankind. Somewhat tautologously, he cited scriptural references in order to establish the credibility of the Bible, and then proceeded to denounce those persons who denied the validity and relevance of scripture. He condemned alike the Catholics, for having denied the mass of the population access to the recorded word of God, and the 'infidel' rationalists, whose teachings had given rise to the French Revolution, the horrors of which Noyes believed had providentially generated a reaction against atheism and in favour of the Bible.

Turning to his contemporaries, Noyes poured scorn on the members of the temperance and abolitionist movements who had perverted the sense of those passages of scripture which appeared to sanction the abuses they condemned. He cited the 'finding' of phrenologists that modern men lacked the capacity for veneration, and accused American reformers of being particularly deficient in that faculty. More generally, Noyes commented regretfully that the scriptural message that Christ was absolute monarch of all men found little favour among the American people, whose political institutions taught them that subordination (even to the word of God) was a disgrace.

After having demonstrated his commitment to 'bible religion', Noyes discussed the means by which the Bible might be interpreted. He admitted that learning was necessary for such interpretation, but emphasized that learning alone was insufficient, and that only guidance by the Holy Spirit could bring an individual to a true understanding of scripture (Noyes, 1847, p. 42):

> uninspired men, with all their resources, are utterly incompetent to
> interpret those parts of scripture which are concerned with the 'deep
> things of God'; and . . . the Paraclete, instead of the Church as the
> Papists hold, or the philologists as Protestants hold, is the ultimate
> arbiter of biblical interpretation.

In this manner, Noyes implicitly laid claim to personal divine inspiration, and further emphasized that social reforms and schemes of improvement could only succeed if they were based on a true understanding of the Bible, and were undertaken in direct response to the promptings of the 'indwelling' Spirit of God.

In his autobiographical *Confessions* (1848) Noyes indicated that he regarded the spiritual torment he suffered during his three-week sojourn in New York as a 'God-arranged test', and that in this period he was convinced of the personal existence of the devil. In more formal theological terms he asserted in *The Berean* that the ultimate cause of all evil was the existence of an uncreated evil being, and that the universe was 'manifestly created' to serve as a theatre of action for uncreated good and evil (Noyes, 1847, p. 104).

Noyes agreed with the Calvinist denominations in that he believed that God had created the world and foreordained everything that happened in it, but he differed from orthodoxy in his conception of the nature of evil. He believed that while God had not created the devil, He had deliberately allowed the devil to enter the world and foresaw the results of his actions in the world. Noyes argued that, although God had thus, in a sense, decreed the actions and movements of the devil in the world, He was not responsible for these evil actions, as He had not decreed either the existence or the wickedness of the devil. The eventual outcome of the divine plan would be the destruction of Satan, and the redemption of the world.

By this ingenious (and admittedly Manichean) solution to the problem of theodicy, Noyes established the ultimate benevolence of God, but he expressed agreement with the Calvinists who regarded the mass of mankind as being under the influence of the devil, and some men as being totally depraved. The latter, who were fit only for damnation, he described as the 'seed of Satan', but, in terms which betrayed the influence of Charles Finney, and more especially of his teacher at New Haven, Nathaniel Taylor, Noyes argued that all men were free moral agents and could choose between good and evil. Illustrating his discussion by an interpretation of the Parable of the Sower, he stated that while the 'seed of Satan' were disposed by their spiritual nature to commit evil, they still chose freely to do wrong, and so could with justice be punished for their transgressions.

According to his own account, while at New Haven in 1833, Noyes was struck by a verse in the Revelation of St John (21:22) which seemed to him to indicate that the second coming of Christ would occur within a generation of Christ's ministry on earth. Noyes immediately read the entire New Testament ten times over, paying especial attention to all those passages pertaining to the second coming of Christ, and was thereby convinced that this event had occurred in the past, and that the second coming was 'an event in the spiritual and not in the natural world', which took place immediately after the destruction of Jerusalem in AD 70 (Noyes, 1847, p. 288).

Noyes held that at the second coming of Christ in the spiritual world, there occurred the first resurrection and the first judgment, which he was at pains to distinguish from the 'final and general judgment' which was yet to come. The first resurrection and judgment was that of the Jews, the first harvest, who for two thousand years had been subject to divine discipline. Noyes emphasized that the Jews would remain especially beloved by God, and prophesied their restoration to Zion and the humiliation of all those Gentiles who had trodden the Jews underfoot. He further indicated that the Gentiles were indebted to the Jews for having given them the Bible, and for having kept civilization alive in the dark ages of Catholic apostasy. Consequently, enlightened Gentiles should acknowledge the birthright of the Jewish people and should seek to lead them to the truth by modesty.

At the second coming, the Primitive Church was established in the spiritual world, its members having been among the subjects of the first resurrection. Noyes rejected as counterfeit the claim of the Catholic Church that the Papacy stood in direct line of apostolic succession (Noyes, 1847, p. 297):

> we lay the axe at the root of that accursed tree of spurious Christianity, which has overshadowed and blasted the earth through these eighteen hundred years.

In a curious but characteristic vein of theological pragmatism, Noyes outlined the practical implications of his teachings, and sought to show the 'good purposes' which would be effected by their espousal and promulgation. Announcement of his teachings would increase faith in the word of God, as they showed Christ's promises to have been fulfilled; they drew men's attention to their relation to the Primitive Church, and they demonstrated the falsity of the claims of all those persons, among them Ann Lee, Swedenborg and William Miller, who predicted a future millennium, or made themselves agents of it.

Having stated that the first resurrection and judgment had occurred shortly after the destruction of Jerusalem, Noyes attempted to establish the date of the final judgment of mankind. As has been shown, he believed that the judgment of the Jews took place after they had been subject to the Mosaic Law for two thousand years, and he therefore asserted that, as the 'Gentile crop' had been maturing for almost the same time, the 'Gentile harvest' was near. Elsewhere in *The Berean* Noyes referred to his own teachings in a way which indicated a more definite conception of the time of the occurrence of the final judgment (Noyes, 1847, pp. 384–5):

> The second resurrection will take place within the lifetime of a generation from the period of the second ministration of true Christian regeneration. In our view, the redevelopment of the gospel of salvation from all sin by the resurrection of Christ, is the recommencement of the process which in the apostolic age ended in the second advent and the first resurrection. If this is true, we are now in the 'beginning of the end'.

Noyes insisted that a great expansion of the influence of the Spirit of God on earth was imminent; an expansion which would result in the conversion of all those who were capable of regeneration. He indicated that the completed Church of God on earth would consist of five parts, one of which, the Jewish and Gentile members of the Primitive Church, was already gathered in the spiritual world. The other groups, the Gentiles, the Jews, the Mohammedans and the Pagans, would successively be gathered into the church and, once the harvest was completed, the final resurrection and judgment would take place, and all those 'sinners unto death' who had deliberately rejected the grace of God would be subjected to eternal torment.

The eschatological conceptions which Noyes presented in *The Berean* were accompanied by a detailed interpretation of human religious development. This system of historical exegesis served to demonstrate the benevolence of God, and the progressive nature of the divine plan for the destruction of the devil and the regeneration of mankind. Moreover, it legitimized Noyes's conception of himself as being divinely appointed to restore knowledge of true Christianity to the world, and thus to usher in the final phase of human history – the dispensation of the 'fullness of times'.

The period of history from the time of Adam to that of Moses, Noyes interpreted as being an era of sensuality and longevity, dominated by the physical faculties of mankind. The era from the time of Moses to that of Christ, was a period of moral development under the guidance of the Mosaic Law; the era from the time of Christ to the time in which Noyes wrote, he saw as one of intellectual development, which was distinguished by advances in scientific knowledge rather than in morality and spirituality. Thus, the three preliminary periods of human development were past, and the fourth and last, the period of rapid development of spiritual knowledge which would culminate in the regeneration of mankind, was approaching. Indeed, Noyes believed that this final period had commenced with his appreciation of the true nature of the second coming, and hence, that modern man was living in the time of fulfilment of prophecy.

Having outlined the past and future development of mankind, and established himself as the harbinger of the final dispensation, Noyes examined, first, the meaning of Christ's ministry on earth, and second, the history of the Christian era, in order to demonstrate the way in which Christ's message was perverted and obscured until, under divine guidance, he had discovered its true meaning.

The death and resurrection of Christ opened the way for the attainment and maintenance of Christian perfection on earth. Noyes emphasized that Christ, who was sinless, did not suffer himself to be crucified as 'legal compensation' for the sins of men, but rather in order to render himself a perfect mediator between God and man. Noyes interpreted the resurrection of Christ as the first blow struck at the devil, who was the ultimate source of all corruption, death and sin (Noyes, 1847, p. 57):

Jesus Christ, by his death, entered into the vitals of the devil, and overcame him. He thus destroyed the central cause of sin. The effect of this act on them that believe, is to release them from the power of sin; and on them that believe not, to consign them with the devil to destruction.

The crucifixion and resurrection of Christ paved the way for the full operation of the 'New Covenant' between God and man, which began to take effect at the commencement of Christ's ministry on earth, but which was not fully effective until his second coming (Noyes, 1838, p. 150):

> its fulfillment gives perfect holiness, perfect security of holiness, perfect liberty, and perfect independence of human instruction . . . it is fulfilled in believers by the energy of the blood of Christ, the spirit of the living God.

The thousand years after the second coming of Christ were the millennium, a period not of the supremacy of Christ, but of 'the reign of the beast' during which, after the decline of the Primitive Church, knowledge of true Christianity was virtually extinguished.

As shown above, Noyes asserted that the Jews had been dominated first by the letter of the Mosaic Law, and then for a short time by its spirit. In the case of the Gentiles, he postulated a reverse historical process. The members of the Gentile churches first lost their 'personal acquaintance' with the Spirit of God and substituted sterile organizational forms for true spirituality. Subsequently, the Catholic Church, which had usurped the mantle of the Primitive Church, deprived its communicants of the Bible, and Christendom descended into 'the dungeon of the dark ages' (1847, pp. 53–4).

The first step upwards from this nadir of apostasy, was the Protestant Reformation, the primary achievement of which was the rescue of the Bible from the clutches of the priesthood. The Protestants restored the word of God to mankind but had not restored true pentecostal powers to the Gentile churches.

The re-establishment of true Christianity guided directly by the Spirit of God would be the fruit of the second resurrection which, on a world-wide scale at least, was yet to come. Noyes sought to substantiate his assertion that the final 'spiritual manifestation' was imminent, by adducing various 'signs of the times'. He believed that the highest attainable stage of merely intellectual development had been reached, and was manifested in an 'idolatrous enthusiasm for science'. Moreover, he indicated that in Germany, the country which had pioneered the first reformation and which, consequently, was the 'emporium of human wisdom', there was much interest in psychological and mystical theories, and more generally (Noyes, 1847, p. 54):

> Men of note in the learned and religious world, are not ashamed to indulge in speculations which once would have been classed with the hallucinations of Swedenborg and Ann Lee.

Noyes believed that as a result of Christ's ministry, resurrection, and second coming in the spiritual world, the New Covenant was fully effective. In consequence, perfect sinlessness was attainable on earth; indeed, for Noyes, perfect holiness was the only standard of true Christianity.

Noyes qualified his radical perfectionism in two ways which reflected his reaction against what he deemed to be irresponsible and erroneous perfectionist doctrines. He stressed that Christian holiness in no way precluded the possibility that the individual might err, or of 'room for improvement' in spiritual terms. He also distinguished carefully between two classes of Christians: those who had been through one conversion, 'believers', and those who had experienced a second and final conversion, the 'Sons of God'.

The first conversion was a 'voluntary' product of religious stimulation and of a desire for improvement, and typically occurred as a result of a religious revival. Noyes described persons who had experienced a first conversion as being in a state of 'spiritual puberty', by which he presumably meant that their powers were awakened but not yet fully developed or focused, and he insisted that such persons were not in a permanent relationship with God. They had no right to feel secure, as at any time they might lapse into sin.

The second conversion was 'wrought upon' the believer by the power of the Holy Ghost (Noyes, 1847, p. 220):

By this power the cross is spiritually revealed to believers, and its virtue infused into their hearts, so that they receive it not as a mere outward example, but as an assimilating energy, by which they are crucified with Christ to the world, become dead to sin, and fully subject, as Christ was, to the perfect will of God.

As a result of this incorporation, or internalization, of the Spirit of God, the subjects of the second conversion enjoyed complete freedom from selfishness and freedom from sin, and their holiness was amissible – it was perfectly secure. The regenerated man would possess a stable mind, a loving heart and an unquenchable desire for spiritual progress.

The primary characteristic of those persons who enjoyed perfect holiness was that they were free from selfishness, which Noyes saw as the barrier standing between men and the spirit of God. Contentiousness, egoism and jealousy were all incompatible with the unselfishness of the Christian. Unity was the fruit of holiness, and Noyes insisted that 'a solitary, self-absorbed spirit cannot have true faith', and compared a body of true Christians to a swarm of bees who were guided by the spirit of unity, subordination and combined labour (Noyes, 1847, p. 462).

Noyes did not confine himself to theoretical statements, but indicated that the regenerate life implied the renunciation of all selfish claims to property and to persons. A community of true believers would practise the economic communism of the Primitive Church, but would go beyond the Primitive

Church as it had been established on earth, in that it would model its social arrangements on those of the spiritual world, and would abolish family and marital ties in favour of communism of affections (Noyes, 1853, p. 29):

> We admit that the community principle of the day of Pentecost, in its actual operation at that time, extended only to goods and chattels . . . but the same spirit which abolished exclusiveness in regard to money, would abolish, if circumstances allowed full scope to it, exclusiveness in regard to women and children.

In addition to discussing the implications of unselfishness – the primary characteristic of the regenerate man – Noyes also designated several secondary characteristics or attributes of holiness. The regenerate man would enjoy in addition to total security in his freedom from sin; freedom from necessity of instruction, the implications of which will be further examined below; freedom from the law, and possession of pentecostal powers.

In *The Berean* as elsewhere, Noyes was concerned to distinguish his theological anti-legalism from licentious and unrestrained antinomianism. He insisted that the apostle Paul had no quarrel with the moral character of the 'letter-law', but was merely concerned about its ineffectiveness. Persons who had attained perfection were free from legalistic restrictions, but were placed under the guidance of the Spirit of God, and Noyes emphasized that governance by reproof and example, as well as by the 'providential administration of suffering', would be necessary even in the Kingdom of God on earth.

He rejected the necessity of observing the Sabbath, as every day and every action in the lives of true believers would necessarily be holy, and also denied the validity of the sacraments of baptism and marriage. In the case of the former, true Christian baptism was not to be attained by a single act of immersion in water, but only by 'everlasting immersion in the blood of Christ'. With regard to marriage, Noyes interpreted Paul's advocacy of marriage as a concession to expediency, and insisted that Paul had no aversion to sexual relationships as such, but merely to the tendency for exclusive relationships to distract the persons involved in them from spiritual concerns.

The discussion of the appropriate attitude of believers to the temporary institutions of worldly government was tempered with caution. Noyes stressed the fact that all wrongdoers would eventually reap divine punishment, and stated that while individual Christians should refrain from violence, such restraint was not incompatible with the employment of force by duly appointed agents of the government.

Noyes believed that, under divine guidance, he had restored the 'faith of the saints' to the world, and those who possessed this faith would necessarily possess the powers which had been manifest in the Primitive Church (Noyes, 1847, p. 50):

The age of miracles certainly is not past with God. He is as mighty as ever; and wherever his Spirit comes at all, there is superhuman, i.e. miraculous power . . . and the way is therefore open for all the primitive manifestations of divine power.

Noyes indicated that believers could expect miraculous events to become more frequent, and their powers over the 'diabolic manifestations' of disease and death to increase, as the Spirit of God flowed out over the earth in a process which would culminate in Christ's victory over the devil and the establishment of a physically and morally perfect human race. Noyes believed that his understanding of the truth contained in the Bible was divinely inspired, and that his task was to lead mankind into righteousness. He recognized that his theological system might appear to be eclectic, but insisted that he had arrived at truths which had eluded, and indeed had been obscured by, all the churches of the world.

Briefly, Noyes agreed with the Calvinist denominations in that he held that God had preordained every event which occurred in the world, including the future fate of men, but he denied that a benevolent God could create evil. To this extent, he agreed with the Universalists but, against them, insisted that those men who freely chose to do evil merited, and would receive, eternal torment. Noyes's affinity to the early perfectionism of Wesley is apparent, but he felt that Wesley had to some extent betrayed his inspiration, and had laid undue emphasis on the first conversion, seeking large numbers of converts to partial holiness, rather than concentrating on the cultivation of perfect sanctification.

Noyes's divergence from contemporary exponents of other varieties of perfectionism has already been discussed, and needs only to be briefly summarized at this point. He differed from the more moderate Perfectionists in his insistence that the holiness gained through the second conversion was totally secure, and he dismissed the followers of James Latourette as being 'little more than Methodists'. He differed from the more radical groups of Perfectionists in his insistence that even the second conversion did not preclude further spiritual development, and that even the perfectly sanctified were bound by the moral laws of God.

Holding that unity was the primary characteristic of the church of God, Noyes emphasized that authority and subordination were essential prerequisites for the task of spreading the gospel of holiness and, as the primary recipient of inspiration, he laid claim to supreme authority over believers, and to be arbiter of all subordinate inspiration. He and his followers rejected all earthly systems of government, and recognized only the authority and social arrangements of the Primitive Church which, for a short period, had been manifested in an incomplete form on earth. In the context of a scathing critique of the 'Associations' of the secular utopians, Noyes asserted that (Noyes, 1847, p. 503):

The true form of government is not a thing which remains yet to be worked out and tested. It was invented at least eighteen hundred years ago, and has been in actual operation ever since the destruction of Jerusalem.

Noyes stated that the invisible church in the spiritual world would shortly extend to earth, and there form branches which would break down the partition between heaven and earth. He offered his followers the sublime task of being 'co-workers with God', in ushering in the final reign of spiritual wisdom and power.

In *The Berean*, which was compiled between 1845 and 1847, Noyes spoke of the first sign of the coming of the Kingdom of God, the establishment of branches of the Primitive Church on earth, as a future event which he and his followers eagerly awaited. However, by 1847, Noyes was convinced that he sufficiently understood the social principles of the Kingdom of Heaven to establish them on earth, and that his followers were sufficiently 'advanced in holiness' to permit such establishment. Consequently, on 1 June 1847, the assembled believers at Putney solemnly resolved that the Kingdom of God had come to earth, and was, in nuclear form, established in their own association. They affirmed that as a body they were the earthly representatives of the Primitive Church, and at least potentially, the possessors of its pentecostal powers.

Their task was twofold; they were to make public the social and moral principles of perfect holiness, and in their organization were to institutionalize and perfect the communism of property and affections which were the basic principles of the Primitive Church as it has been developed in the spiritual world. Such a practical demonstration of the social principles of the Kingdom of God would establish the superiority of these principles, and would provide a model for the foundation of further societies, so inaugurating a process which would rapidly effect the transformation of the world. The circumstances of the development of Noyes's conception of his mission from quasi-messianic evangelism to fully developed religious utopianism, and the concomitant development of rudimentary forms of communitarianism, will be discussed below.

The Putney Association – charismatic communitarianism and ideological transformation

Noyes's utopian conception of his mission developed concomitantly with the elaboration of his theological system, and with the disappointment of his ultraist expectations. Discussion of this development, and of the formal organization of the Putney Association, is complicated by Noyes's subsequent tendency to rationalize these ideological and institutional changes, and by the secrecy which veiled the introduction of the 'social arrangements of the Kingdom of Heaven' – complex marriage and male continence. Broadly, it can be stated that until 1844, Noyes was primarily concerned to publicize his teachings as widely as possible, and that after this date his conception of his mission gradually changed, and he came to regard his task as, not simply the proclamation of the gospel of holiness and of the imminence of the Kingdom of God, but the literal establishment of a nucleus of that Kingdom on earth.

The letters published by Garrison and Gates in the autumn of 1837, gained Noyes much notoriety but few followers, and after his marriage, he retired to Putney to strengthen the convictions of those members of his family who earlier subscribed to his teachings. At Putney, he found that his mother had lost faith in his inspiration and that his sisters had so far strayed from his teachings as to have conceived the idea that holiness should be manifested in lifelong celibacy. After 'wrestling' with his mother and with the 'Shakerism' of his sisters, he succeeded in restoring their faith and set about establishing his authority more firmly, insisting that his followers should defer to him in all matters, spiritual and temporal.

Noyes's original followers consisted almost entirely of his relatives, but in 1839 and 1840, a few other residents of Putney came under his influence and, in the winter of 1840–1, he sought to distinguish his disciplined followers from other Perfectionists by constituting the 'Putney Society of Inquiry'. In 1841, when Noyes's father divided most of his estate among his children (he died later the same year) a few further converts were made, and the members of the association built a store and a chapel.

The majority of the members of what eventually came to be called the 'Putney Association' were relatively well educated and, if not wealthy, were at least in comfortable economic circumstances.

Lack of education was not a formal barrier to membership in the association, but the unemotional and intellectual character of the meetings of the group, and Noyes's early conception of his mission as primarily involving literary evangelism, would have had little attraction for uneducated persons. The numbers of the group rose slowly until 1842, when twenty-one adults, presumably the whole of the membership, signed the bull of excommunication cited below. In 1843, twenty-eight adults and nine children were supported from the common treasury and, despite defections as discipline increased, in 1847, immediately prior to the move to the Oneida Reserve, the group consisted of thirty-one adults and fourteen children.

Noyes's insistence that his followers should subordinate their wills to his stemmed from his conception of himself as the primary recipient of inspiration and grace, and, in *The Berean*, he justified his claim to authority by citing the example of the Primitive Church, the leaders of which he believed were 'commissioned to reprove, correct, exhort and watch over the church' (Noyes, 1847, p. 221). Noyes's demand for subordination generated some measure of resistance, originally from his mother who, even after her second 'submission', was occasionally refractory. In 1842 two converts, who had contracted a marriage after Noyes had forbidden them to do so, were expelled and anathematized by a 'bull of excommunication', which was reprinted by the Methodist minister who was the chief opponent of the sect in Putney (Eastman, 1847, p. 166):

> Whereas, faithful subordination is essential to the welfare of our association, and whereas John B. Lyvere and Almira Edson, by a clandestine marriage in defiance of the known will of the acknowledged head of the corporation, have committed an act of gross and deliberate insubordination, therefore . . .
>
> Resolved, That our connection with them be dissolved, and that they be requested to withdraw from the corporation.

Following this incident, a rudimentary hierarchical structure was imposed on the Putney Association. After Noyes had presented theological arguments to demonstrate the need for subordination, the assembled members voted unanimously to support the principles of total theocratic government, with Noyes as the supreme executive. Subordinate executive officers were appointed: John Skinner (a schoolteacher) as moderator of the chapel, John Miller as manager of the group's store and general finances, and George Cragin (who had been manager of the New York Magdalen Society) as assistant to Noyes in his editorial and evangelical labours.

In 1843, Noyes's brother, George, attained his majority and succeeded to the patrimony which Noyes had held in trust for him, and in February of the following year, when a decline in the income derived from the group's store threatened the continued publication of *The Perfectionist*, Noyes and the wealthier executives of the group united in financial partnership. This contract of partnership formally established the Putney Association, the members of which pledged themselves to promulgate the doctrine of holiness and, if necessary, to provide financial support for the periodical. This contract was superseded in 1845 by a 'constitution' which was also signed by the senior members of the group (reprinted in *The Circular*, December 1868, p. 306).

Noyes's authority was originally charismatic in the purest sense of the term. It rested upon his claims to divine inspiration and commission, and, in the later years at Putney, upon the manifestation of this inspiration in 'miraculous' powers of healing. He regarded himself, and was regarded by his followers, as the instrument through which the redeeming power of the Holy Spirit was to be poured out over the earth. The organization and social arrangements of the group at Putney and, subsequently, of the Oneida Community, were entirely of his devising, and were believed by his followers to be the fruits of inspiration. Despite the 'democratic' general meetings and committee structure of the Oneida Community, until the last decade of the existence of the community as a communistic group, Noyes's authority was virtually unchallenged. His major decisions were not submitted for critical discussion by the majority of the membership, but were simply communicated to them for affirmation.

After having institutionalized his ascendency over his followers in a constitutional theocracy, Noyes devoted more of his time to evangelical journeys, but in the two years after 1844 he appears to have become dissatisfied with the results of such evangelism, and gradually came to believe that the conversion of the world would be effected by the spirit of God only after a 'visible branch' of God's Kingdom had been established on earth. The precise circumstances of this ideological transformation from prophetic evangelism to utopianism are obscure, but it appears to have been closely linked to the 'liberating' effect of Noyes's development of the sexual technique of male continence, and to his growing confidence in his possession of pentecostal powers. From 1845, Noyes gradually explored the implications of his changed conception of his mission, and communicated his findings to his immediate followers, and, more obliquely and equivocally, via the periodical to his scattered sympathizers.

Noyes argued that the close and exclusive association of believers or, as he termed it, the 'Condensation of Life', would at once increase their resistance to evil and magnify their spiritual qualities and powers. He rejected the 'chimerical' ideas of advocates of 'scientific marriages', and offered a short way to the improvement of mankind (*The Spiritual Magazine*, March 1846, p. 8):

> By the unity of life to which Christ calls believers, the good elements of an innumerable multitude of characters will be condensed into one, and the perfection of the compound will be transfused through every individual.

Somewhat more concrete evidence of the direction in which Noyes's mind was tending was provided, six months later, when Noyes stated (also in the periodical) that the first resurrection, that of the Jews, had come about by 'the separation and seclusion of a chosen phalanx', and intimated that the second resurrection would come about, in and through, a similar seclusion of those persons most advanced in holiness.

As will be shown below, in 1844 and 1845 Noyes developed a technique of sexual intercourse which facilitated the institutionalization of 'community of affections' and, from the spring of 1846, he and some of the more trusted members of the group clandestinely practised 'complex marriage'. After more than a year of 'bible secretiveness', during which the new sexual arrangements were concealed from the junior members and from the world, Noyes's confidence in his inspiration was such that, at the meeting of the association on 1 June 1847, he proposed the resolution that 'the Kingdom of God has come'. Speaking to his own resolution (*The Spiritual Magazine*, July 1847, p. 65), Noyes expressed his conviction that the establishment of the Kingdom of God on earth would be a gradual and almost invisible process, and that at the time of its establishment:

> The primitive church, like the sun, will come near to us. The destruction of evil, and all the transactions of the last judgment, will be effected by a spiritual infusion from them of the light and energy of God.

Noyes cited evidence in support of his contention that the Kingdom of God was realized in their own association. The tribulations and rewards experienced by the group were those of the day of judgment, they possessed a power that could conquer death, and had abolished separate households and exclusiveness with regard to property. Noyes concluded that the Spirit of God was trying to manifest itself fully to the believers, and through them to the world, and that such a manifestation was dependent on an act of will and of dedication by the group.

The assembled members dutifully affirmed that the Kingdom was realized in their own association, and that their consequent task was to develop a perfect community as a necessary preliminary to the transformation of the world. They recognized that they would encounter opposition and persecution, but were confident that this would only stimulate their spiritual development. Their open adoption of the institutions of the Kingdom of Heaven would at once demonstrate the superiority of these institutions and ensure a continuing 'infusion' of grace to the group, and through them, to the world.

Relations with the external society

The frustrations which Noyes experienced in the years immediately after his announcement of his freedom from sin, found expression in 1837 in the letters in which he violently denounced American institutions, and proclaimed himself commissioned to announce their imminent replacement by the institutions of the Kingdom of God. Initially, Noyes believed that simple proclamation of the gospel of holiness would be sufficient to transform the world, but, as his conception of the mode of establishment of the Kingdom of God on earth became more gradualistic, and as concomitantly his utopian vision developed, so his denunciation of the world was expediently tempered.

In the later years at Putney, Noyes to some extent realized the futility of simple ultraist condemnation of sin, and gradually developed the social principles which he believed would inevitably, by virtue of their divine origin, spread throughout the earth. This change of emphasis did not imply Noyes's acceptance of the institutions of the world, but rather his increased realization of the extent and deep-rootedness of the corruption of these institutions. He stated publicly that the Kingdom of God was realized in the Putney Association only when it had developed to such an extent that it was based 'on principles opposed at every point to those of the world' (Cragin, 1850, p. 6), and when he was confident that the spiritual unity and purity of the group was such as to ensure further 'infusions' of the Holy Spirit, and so to enable the believers to withstand opposition, and commence the 'harvest of the Gentiles'.

Throughout the decade which he spent at Putney, Noyes engaged in evangelistic activity, primarily through the periodical and, intimately associated with this, in acrimonious theological debate in which he sought to demonstrate the errors of all other theological systems, and the independence and divine origins of his own teachings. His diatribes and frank espousal of totally heretical opinions infuriated his opponents, and led them to mingle slanderous accusations of immorality and licentiousness with their theological arguments, but such attacks only confirmed Noyes's conviction of his own inspiration and, for several years, do not appear to have been reflected in much overt hostility among the persons living in the vicinity of Putney. Local toleration of the Association was undoubtedly in part due to the prominence and good reputation of Noyes's family, and to the fact that most of the converts were made from among the more prestigious inhabitants of the village.

In the economic sphere there was little tension between the sect and the surrounding population, many of whom continued to patronize the 'Perfectionist store' as they had patronized that of John Miller before his conversion. At Putney, as was to be the case during the first years at Oneida, the group largely lived on its capital, the chief element of which was the divided estate of Noyes's father, and they expediently complied with the fiscal demands of the state while theologically repudiating its authority.

The relationship between the Association and its neighbours was reasonably amicable until 1846, after which time local hostility grew rapidly as knowledge of the social practices of the sect, and of the implications of their claim to possess pentecostal powers, increased. The process of informal adoption of complex marriage, the so-called 'warfare with death' waged by Noyes and his followers, and the train of events leading to the sect's removal from Putney will be examined after a brief consideration of Noyes's attitudes to other religious bodies and of his evangelical activities.

Noyes's opinions of the major denominations have already been indicated. He held them in contempt for having perverted the sense of the Bible and for their formalism and uninspired authoritarianism. He shared in the anti-Catholicism which increased in New York and New England as immigration from Ireland accelerated, and condemned the 'periodic repentance' of the Catholics as a 'horrible hypocrisy' (Noyes, 1847, p. 169). More generally, he accused the denominational clergy of 'moral imbecility', in that they urged their congregations to forsake sin while themselves confessing to be sinners.

Noyes was extremely concerned to distinguish his teachings from those of other sectarian groups, as well as from other varieties of perfectionism. He dismissed the Millerites as 'intellectual barbarians', and their leaders as ignorant frauds, and dwelt gleefully upon the falsification of their millennial prophecies in 1843 and 1844. His attitude towards the Shakers was scarcely different, at least in the period at Putney and the early years at Oneida. He condemned Ann Lee as a charlatan for claiming that she was the female incarnation of Christ, and asserted that (*The Perfectionist*, July 1844, p. 37):

> Their anti-marriage theory is based on the revelations received by Ann Lee, authenticated not by miracles, or by any other sound tests, but by her own bold assertions.

Noyes's attitudes towards reformist groups crystallized as his conception of his utopian mission developed. The transition from his early interest in abolitionism to his repudiation in *The Berean* of all forms of 'do-gooding', was by no means a smooth one. In 1838 he had been disappointed by the decline in the enthusiasm of Perfectionists, and by the fact that they had channelled what remained of their ultraist energies into the anti-slavery movement, but in 1840 Noyes himself issued a pamphlet calling for the north to unite politically against slavery. However, in the following years his rejection of reformism became more reasoned and consistent; he condemned abolitionists for having perverted the Bible and also for (*The Perfectionist*, 15 November 1843, p. 73):

> the unnecessary and false practice which is prevalent among abolitionists, of exciting sympathy for the negroes by exaggerating the merits of the race in defiance of facts.

Elsewhere, Noyes argued perceptively that while slavery would soon be overthrown in the United States, its overthrow would not be accomplished by moral influences, and that the oppression of slavery would be replaced by another, more subtle, oppression.

Noyes pitted the same arguments against the secular utopians, or 'associationists', as against the abolitionists, and insisted that the fabrication of new institutions without the guidance of the spirit of God would not produce new men, but would simply give free rein and licence to old vices. He argued that a 'change of heart' through regeneration by the 'indwelling' spirit of God must precede any successful reconstitution of society, and stated that the error of the associationists was that they sought relief 'in a change of circumstances, while it can be found only in a change of heart' (*The Perfectionist*, 15 July 1843, p. 42).

Noyes's discussions of religious bodies and reformist groups were prompted by his desire to establish the independence of his teachings in the public mind, and to exonerate himself from charges of theological plagiarism, but the main idiosyncratic elements of his teaching were developed in reaction to the foibles of the other Perfectionists, on whom he sought to impose his authority, and among whom he sought converts. In 1842, he recommended journeying among his scattered sympathizers, and in this task was assisted by George Cragin, who increasingly took on the role of perambulating evangelist among the persons 'who bear the despised name of Perfectionists'. Gradually, by dint of persistence and his indisputable powers of persuasion, Noyes won the allegiance of many of the Perfectionist groups.

In the period from 1845 to 1847, emboldened by his success in establishing his authority at Putney and elsewhere, and encouraged by his discovery of 'male continence', and by evidence of his possession of pentecostal powers, Noyes came to believe that he was empowered by God to establish the nucleus of the divine Kingdom on earth. In September 1847, the Perfectionist conferences at Lairdsville and Genoa, New York, passed resolutions expressing sympathy with Noyes's ideas as expressed in *The Perfectionist*, and pledging to hold themselves in readiness for the physical manifestation of the Kingdom of Heaven. However, by this date, the sexual arrangements of the spiritual world had been secretly established at Putney, and hostility to the group had developed rapidly as persons in the immediate vicinity of the sect came to have some knowledge of these arrangements, and of the curative methods employed by the sectarians.

'Complex marriage' and faith healing

The furore generated by the *Battle-Axe* letter was caused, not by Noyes's claim to divine commission, but by his depiction of the sexual arrangements which he believed prevailed in the spiritual world, and by his obvious desire for the establishment of comparable institutions on earth. For Noyes, communism of affections was a counterpart of communism of property and, in the resurrection state, all selfish, exclusive claims of every kind would be abolished. However, as shown above, Noyes married in the year after the publication of this letter, and justified his act by reference to the teachings of the apostle Paul, and as being consonant with the 'law of the apostasy'. Thus in 1842, when Noyes's conception of the nature and time of the second resurrection was still vague and ill defined, he stated (*The Spiritual Moralist*, 25 June 1842, p. 15):

> So with us in regard to the institution of marriage; notwithstanding we
> find many objections to it, and pronounce it imperfect and adapted
> only to a state of trial and discipline, yet we believe the new order of
> things which we anticipate, will not take its place until we have attained
> the resurrection of the body; and then only by the manifest authority
> of God.

Noyes was led to speculate further on sexual matters by his own marital experiences. In the six years after 1838, his wife became pregnant five times but, with the exception of the birth of a son, Theodore, in 1841, each of these pregnancies terminated in stillbirths. In the summer of 1844, Noyes vowed not to expose his wife to further fruitless suffering, and, after some cogitation, arrived at what he termed his 'great discovery of male continence', by which term he meant the technique of sexual intercourse referred to by later writers as *coitus reservatus*. By the adoption of this technique he escaped from his dilemma without resorting either to 'Shaker legalism', or to the technique advocated by Robert Dale Owen, *coitus interruptus*, which Noyes regarded as sinful and debilitating (Owen, 1831). He gradually realized that male continence made possible the attainment of the heavenly state of community of affections, without the complicating and embarrassing factor of issue, and it can be inferred that his excitement at this realization was heightened by his infatuation with George Cragin's wife, Mary.

In May 1846, Noyes made some tentative overtures to Mary Cragin but, presumably from fear that his motives might be misconstrued, broke these off and discussed the adoption of complex marriage 'in the quartette form' with his wife and the Cragins. Apparently the idea was enthusiastically received (Cragin who appears to have been Noyes's creature in every way, confessed his love for Noyes's wife), and in the following months, the secret of the commencement of complex marriage was revealed to the most spiritually advanced members. John Miller was initially unwilling to subordinate himself totally to Noyes, and Noyes wrote to his sister, Harriet Skinner, with regard to Miller (cited in Parker, 1935, p. 124):

> I cannot go along with him until he has decisively adopted our
> principles and has put himself wholly into my hands. He will need
> much discipline, and he has never yet shown that he knew the value of
> discipline. He will need to be instructed in regard to secretiveness and
> the law in relation to propagation before he can be safely trusted with
> liberty.

In the same letter Noyes complained that Miller was unwarrantedly availing himself of the privileges of complex marriage, and had 'embraced' Mary Cragin on the previous night. Noyes instructed Harriet to hold herself aloof from Miller, 'or at most to coquette with him' until Miller had subordinated himself. Miller's recalcitrance was quickly overcome and, five months after the commencement of complex marriage, a statement of principle was signed by the participating members, who by this instrument surrendered all individual proprietorship of persons and things, and reconfirmed their submission to Noyes's spiritual decisions. In November 1846, some measure of consolidation of households took place, presumably in the interests of the maintenance of secrecy.

In *The Berean*, Noyes confessed to believing in 'the pathology' of Christ and the apostles, and asserted that, as all physical maladies and death itself stemmed from the operations of the devil in the world, so the impact of disease and death would dwindle as the world was regenerated, and these afflictions would be abolished when the devil was finally cast out of the world by God.

Noyes rejected the orthodox claim that the age of miracles was past, and stated that wherever God's Spirit was present in some measure, so the persons influenced by that spirit would possess a corresponding measure of pentecostal power. Possession of such power, the most important manifestation of which was the power of healing, was thus at once a consequence and a yardstick of grace, and every increment of faith could be expected to give increased resistance to disease. To succumb to illness was, in a sense, to confess to lack of faith, and believers were urged to deny or suppress symptoms of illness. Thus, Noyes claimed to have cured himself of a tubercular throat infection by denying its existence and continuing his regime of vigorous public speaking (*The Spiritual Magazine*, October 1847, pp. 153–4).

Noyes's theoretical conceptions regarding the method of transmission of the curative properties of the divine spirit, appear to have been developed by the end of 1846, and were closely related to his idea that the 'condensation of life', or fusion of individuals in a group, served to increase their spiritual powers and decrease their exposure to evil influences. In *The Berean* he commented approvingly on the basic conceptions of the 'science of mesmerism', and made special reference to the idea of animal magnetism as being a 'transmissible fluid'. Elsewhere, he discussed biblical cures effected by the laying on of hands, and cited scriptural evidence to show that the curative contact, by which the spirit of God flowed from one individual to another, was not limited solely to that of hands. Pushing the logic of his position to its extreme, he asserted that (Noyes, 1853, p. 45):

> the more intimate and perfect the contact, the greater will be the effect, other things being equal. On this principle, sexual intercourse is in its nature the most perfect method of 'laying on of hands', and under proper circumstances may be the most powerful external agency of communicating life to the body, and even the Spirit of God to the mind and heart.

Persecution and departure from Putney

Noyes's account of his New York experience, the Brimfield scandals and the *Battle-Axe* letter, had together led him to be generally regarded as a prophet of licentiousness and, while he interpreted persecution as a test of faithfulness, Noyes was also concerned to refute those grosser accusations which seemed likely to threaten his evangelical activities or personal safety, Thus, in 1843, he repudiated some 'ludicrous and filthy reports', emanating from Oberlin Seminary, that the members of the Putney Association had abolished marriage in favour of unrestrained promiscuity (*The Perfectionist*, June 1843, p. 35). In the same article, Noyes blithely insisted that the faith of the members of the Association was such that slanders and persecution could not trouble them; but rumours persisted, and Noyes deemed it wise to cover the inauguration of complex marriage in a cloak of 'bible secretiveness'. Details of the new sexual arrangements were revealed only to those members of the sect who were judged sufficiently developed in faith to comprehend the sublime nature of the system, and to appreciate, in a disciplined manner, the privilege of a foretaste of heaven.

The attempt to conceal the new sexual arrangements from the junior members, and from the malicious curiosity of opponents of the group, was probably doomed to failure from the outset, and specific rumours appear to have been generated by the 'advance into community of households' in the winter and spring of 1846–7. The events which culminated in the arrest and flight of Noyes have been outlined in detail elsewhere (see Eastman, 1848); here only the major incidents in an extremely complicated, and partially obscure, sequence of events will be outlined.

In the spring of 1847, Harriet Skinner succumbed to persistent questioning by the daughters of another member, and admitted the existence of complex marriage. The girls were subsequently converted by Noyes himself, and in their enthusiasm effected the conversion of a school-fellow, Lucinda Lamb. The latter's father disapproved of her association with the sect and, after sounding the opinions of his neighbours, ignored Noyes's plea that the girl should not be separated from her religious friends, and sent her away from Putney. The opponents of the sect were enraged by what they interpreted as an attempt at enticement and seduction but, fortified by their conviction that their lives were directly guided by the spirit of God, Noyes and his followers initially paid little heed to village hostility, and proceeded to demonstrate and proclaim their powers of healing.

In June 1847, Noyes 'miraculously' cured Harriet Hall, an associate of the group, who had been an invalid for some years, and had been given up by her doctors as suffering from an incurable, and certainly unusual, combination of dropsy and tuberculosis. Subsequently, the sectarians cited this case as the most convincing proof of Noyes's possession of spiritual powers, but the gratitude of Mr Hall, who had always been ambivalent to the sect, was insufficiently deep to withstand Noyes's admission that sexual intercourse had been part of the treatment, and he lodged a complaint with the State Attorney at Brattleboro.

The rumours of sexual irregularities in the association were confirmed when a member of the group, Clifford Clark, after being told of the institution of complex marriage, became fearful for his wife and consulted a lawyer and the Methodist minister, Hubbard Eastman. As a result of these revelations, and after local hostility had been further inflamed by the death of Mary Knight, a villager whom Mary Cragin had undertaken to cure, Noyes was arrested on 25 October 1847, charged with adultery and fornication, and bailed in the sum of 2,000 dollars by John Miller. Subsequently, fearing that the villagers of Putney might take the law into their own hands, Noyes fled to his relatives at Brattleboro, and thence to lodgings in New York City.

In Putney, Eastman organized the opposition to the sect and, in December, a general meeting of the citizens of Putney condemned the flight of Noyes and demanded the immediate dissolution of the community and cessation of the publication of the periodical, coupled with public renunciation of all offensive principles and remuneration for the injured.

In a letter written from New York on 14 December 1847, Noyes indicated to John Miller, who had been left in charge in Putney, that if the state of affairs became worse, it might be expedient for the group to remove entirely from the village. In January 1848, Noyes received a letter from Jonathan Burt, a Perfectionist of long standing, who was the leader of a semi-communistic group on the Oneida Reserve in New York State, a settlement remote from other habitation. Noyes travelled to Burt's property and swiftly converted him to holiness, bolstering his convictions with 500 dollars in gold and assurances of further aid. A week later, on 4 February 1848, Noyes issued a general call to his followers to join him at Oneida Reserve, and so, in isolation, the sectarians commenced the open establishment of the Kingdom of Heaven.

Summary

In the thirteen years after his initial declaration that he was free from sin, Noyes elaborated a comprehensive theological system, promulgated his doctrines ceaselessly and gradually surrounded himself with a group of followers who, by their almost total subordination to his will, gratified his appetite for power and legitimized his conception of himself as the earthly agent of God. In later years, Noyes interpreted his early career as a deliberate progression towards the communitarianism of the Oneida Community, but in fact, his utopianism only developed as he partly relinquished his ultraist hopes, and as he became dissatisfied with the impact on the world made by his literary evangelism alone.

At the risk of injustice to its complexity, three stages of Noyes's early intellectual development can be distinguished. First, the period of ultraist evangelism from 1834 to 1838; second, the years of transition until about 1844; and after this date, the development of his thought to full-blown utopianism.

Noyes's behaviour and attitude to the world immediately after his theological 'discovery' was qualitatively little different from that of a person imbued with the ordinary revivalistic expectation of an imminent millennium. He appears to have believed that his teachings were destined to climax all the earlier manifestations of religious excitement and of moral concern, and to deal the final blow against sin. In 1835 and 1836, Noyes was preoccupied with the proclamation of his doctrines, and made no attempt to impose even a rudimentary formal organization on his scattered converts.

Noyes's furious denunciation of American institutions was prompted by his despair at the waning enthusiasm of his fellow Perfectionists, and the consequent disappointment of his messianic expectations, as well as by his final rejection by Abigail Merwin. In the years immediately after his marriage, Noyes's interests and understanding of his mission vacillated considerably, but he slowly developed a more gradualistic conception of the way in which the world was to be regenerated, and, with the aid of his few followers, again began the task of disseminating the gospel of holiness. From 1838 to 1844, Noyes concerned himself with establishing his authority among his followers and with elaborating his doctrinal system. In this period, he tempered his denunciations of the world and, in the interests of discipline and of the financial security of the periodical, imposed a rudimentary hierarchical structure on the informally communistic, charismatic fellowship.

No precise point of transformation of Noyes's conception of his mission can be indicated but, after 1844, he became dissatisfied with the results of literary evangelism, and began to conceive himself not simply as the herald of the doctrine of holiness and of a regenerate world, but as empowered to inaugurate a 'visible branch' of the Primitive Church on earth. His faith in his inspiration was deepened by a number of complexly interrelated and mutually reinforcing circumstances: his limited, but gratifying, success in subordinating his immediate followers and other Perfectionists; his discovery of male continence; his conviction of his possession of pentecostal powers; and his elaboration of the moral principles inherent in his doctrines.

After 1844, Noyes explored, and subsequently institutionalized, the social arrangements which he believed appropriate to the regenerate life. Concomitantly, he laboured to cultivate that degree of selfless subordination among his followers which would facilitate this institutionalization, and he evidently considered that the moral foundations of the regenerate life were successfully laid by June 1847.

Once the veil of secrecy surrounding complex marriage was penetrated, Noyes's confidence in divine protection failed him, and, fearing mob violence, he fled from Putney. Characteristically, Noyes later interpreted his flight and abandonment of his followers as God-guided, in that he had followed a 'non-resistant' course, and, as a result, the group had providentially secured a 'retired location' at Oneida Reserve in which to re-establish their association, free from what, at a safe distance, he contemptuously described as a 'small quarrel with an excited village' (*The Spiritual Magazine*, August 1848, p. 200).

A quotation from the group's periodical (*The Spiritual Magazine*, November 1847, p. 182) provides the plainest statement of the utopian faith which led Noyes's followers to join their domineering leader in central

New York, and there to establish the Oneida Community as a demonstration of the selfless perfection of the regenerate life:

> We believe that God has commenced the development of his kingdom in this country; that he has inoculated the world with the spirit of heaven, and prepared a Theocratic nucleus in this the most enlightened and advanced portion of the earth.

Chapter 5

The Oneida Community —
communism of property and affections,
1848–1881

The agricultural and industrial nucleus of the Oneida Community was the forty acres of partially cleared land and the 'Indian sawmill' which Jonathan Burt had purchased in 1845. In the autumn of 1847, Burt and his family had been joined on their holding by a group of Perfectionists, twenty-three men, women and children, under the leadership of Joseph Ackley. Prior to Noyes's arrival at Oneida Reserve, this combined group lacked effective leadership and clearly conceived religious or social goals, and was in desperate financial straits. The latter fact, at least, indubitably influenced the eventual full submission of many of the group to Noyes's authority.

Noyes's call to his followers to rally at Oneida Reserve was issued in February 1848, and by the end of that year, the total membership of the sect was eighty-seven, twenty-nine of these persons being under the age of fifteen. Noyes appears to have been disappointed by the response to his summons but he drew comfort from the fact that the removal of the sect had purged it of a 'herd of treacherous, fair-weather followers'. Despite his disappointment, Noyes's conviction of the importance of literary evangelism remained unshaken, and publication of *The Spiritual Magazine* was resumed in August 1848.

Throughout 1848 and the first months of 1849, Noyes laboured to instil in his followers those qualities of selflessness and submission which he felt were appropriate to life in the resurrection state, and sought to win un-conditional acceptance for his 'social theories' – male continence and complex marriage. The more mundane achievements of the group in this period were impressive: additional land was purchased and cultivated, a variety of minor craft industries was established, a communal dwelling house was erected, a range of administrative committees was established and a pattern of daily activity, which persisted in the community for thirty years, was instituted.

By May of 1849, Noyes appears to have judged, somewhat prematurely, that the Oneida Community was ideologically, socially and economically securely established. Accompanied by Mary Cragin and several other of his intimates, he moved to a house which the community had purchased in Brooklyn, New York, and for several years exercised only a distant control over the affairs of the sect. In this period, Noyes devoted himself to elaborating and publishing his social theories, and held himself in readiness for the time when knowledge of the joys of life in the Oneida Community would lead large numbers of persons to acknowledge his inspiration and to submit to his authority.

At this point it is necessary, in the interests of clarity, to indicate briefly the changes which took place, over time, in Noyes's conception of his mission, and the corresponding stages of the development of the Oneida Community. Broadly, four phases of this development can be distinguished. First, from 1849 to 1854, the Brooklyn period, alluded to above, when Noyes's utopian convictions were strongest and his evangelistic fervour was at its height; in these years, the social arrangements of the Community were successfully institutionalized, although its financial position became increasingly precarious. Second, the decade 1855 to 1865, a period of introversionism and internal purification when, chastened by the failure of his literary evangelism, Noyes returned to Oneida and, after some years, successfully established the Community on a sound financial basis. Third, the decade 1865 to 1875, in which Noyes's attitude to the world became increasingly reformist, and in which the sect enjoyed great prosperity. Finally, the years 1875 to 1880, when a variety of challenges to Noyes's leadership became manifest, and, as a result of internal tension and external hostility, the communistic structure of the sect disintegrated, and first complex marriage, and then, in 1880, economic communism was abandoned. The causes, implications and complexly interrelated structural concomitants of these changes will be analysed after a consideration of the sexual and eugenic arrangements of the sect, and examination of Noyes's conception of the 'spiritual' causes, and appropriate treatment, of disease.

The theory and practice of male continence and complex marriage

The circumstances which prompted Noyes to develop the technique of sexual intercourse which he called male continence, and of the inauguration of complex marriage, have been outlined in the previous chapter. At Putney, the sexual practices of the group were, for a time at least, shrouded in secrecy but, shortly after the removal of the more steadfast sectarians to Oneida, Noyes openly commenced the institutionalization of complex marriage. In 1848, in the pamphlet *Bible Argument*, copies of which were sent to prominent men living in the vicinity of the community and to the Governor of the State of New York, Noyes summarized the scriptural and social arguments in favour of his sexual innovations. The circulation of this pamphlet appears to have been very small, and it was reprinted and some of the arguments in it were expanded in the compendium *Bible Communism* (1853), which provided the fullest statement of the social arrangements of the sect. Some twenty years later, in 1872, the practice of *coitus reservatus* was explained and justified by Noyes in the pamphlet *Male Continence*, which, in the censorious moral climate of the eighteen seventies, was an important factor in stimulating the clerical hostility which led, in 1879, to the group's expedient abandonment of complex marriage.

In his various writings on sexual matters, Noyes was concerned to indicate the deficiencies and evils of monogamous marriage. He asserted that the institution was based on an erroneous conception of the nature of human sexuality, and insisted that the exclusiveness inherent in monogamy ran contrary to man's desire and potentialities. Against those persons who extolled the virtues of exclusive romantic attachments and of monogamy, Noyes (1853, p. 35) insisted that:

> On the contrary, the secret history of the human heart will bear out the assertion that it is capable of loving any number of times and any number of persons, and that the more it loves the more it can love.

Noyes, who appeared to have been devoted to Mary Cragin, who was drowned in the Hudson River in 1851, admitted that an individual might love one person more than all others, but insisted that such a preference should not, morally or psychologically, be a barrier to truly loving, sexual relations with others. He stated boldly that, rather than encouraging the full development of human altruism and selflessness, monogamous marriage tended to warp and pervert the personality since (Noyes, 1853, p. 37):

> It gives to sexual appetite only a scanty and monotonous allowance, and so produces the natural vices of poverty, contraction of taste, and stinginess or jealousy.

More specifically, Noyes claimed that 'the law of marriage "worketh wrath" ', in that in its inflexibility it bound incompatible persons together and 'sundered matched natures', so giving rise to 'secret adultery, actual or of the heart'. Revealingly, in view of his frequently repeated profession that he had had no sexual relationships prior to his own late marriage, Noyes further condemned the prevailing sexual arrangements because they made no morally acceptable provision for young persons at the time when their sexual appetites were strongest.

After marshalling his arguments against monogamous marriage, Noyes summarized those in favour of the employment of the sexual technique of male continence. He asserted that the 'organs of generation' had three functions, the propagative, the amative and the urinary, and, leaving aside the latter function, stated that the sexual act could be theoretically and practically divided into its propagative and amative aspects. Given this distinction, Noyes stated that God had created women primarily for social and not propagative purposes (he based this argument on Genesis 2:18), and added that in all nature, the 'propagative tendency' varied inversely with the evolutionary order of the species.

Noyes held that celibacy was unhealthy, and was an affront to God who had endowed men with their sexual natures. Believing that ejaculation was debilitating, he condemned masturbation and also the practice of *coitus interruptus* and 'various French methods' of contraception. Except when offspring were desired, men should engage in sexual intercourse in such a controlled manner as to avoid 'actual discharge' since the pleasure of ejaculation was entirely personal, and hence entirely selfish. The practice of such male continence would open the way to a full appreciation of the true pleasures of sexual intercourse; those stemming from the spiritual nature of the act, and not from its grosser animalistic aspects (Noyes, 1853, p. 48):

> Sexual intercourse, pure and simple, is the conjunction of the organs of union, and the interchange of magnetic influences, or conversation of spirits, through the medium of that conjunction.

Noyes insisted that discharge of semen by the male during intercourse was not, as selfish and brutalized persons argued, involuntary, but that it was '. . . a matter clearly within the province of the will – subject to enlightened voluntary control' (Noyes, 1853, p. 49). In a more pragmatic vein, Noyes summarized the individual and social benefits of the practice of male continence. The technique would promote the health of the individuals who practised it by freeing men from the evil effects of excessive ejaculation, and by relieving women of unwanted pregnancies. It would increase the pleasure derived from sexual intercourse, the ordinary form of which was 'a momentary affair, terminating in exhaustion and disgust'. Noyes insisted that 'the habit of making sexual intercourse a quiet affair . . . can easily be established . . .', and looked forward to the time when amative intercourse would have its place among the fine arts, for 'there is as much room for cultivation of taste and skill in this department as in any' (Noyes, 1853, p. 22).

At a more general level, Noyes indicated that while he was not opposed to the increase of population as such, his discovery opened the way for scientific propagation; a remark which foreshadowed the later 'stirpicultural experiment' which will be discussed below. Further, he insisted that male continence, as the basis of complex marriage, made possible a type of communal association which would not be fraught with the tensions arising from exclusive attachments and sexual jealousy. Writing in the future tense, but referring implicitly to the Oneida Community and to its 'branch-society' at Brooklyn, Noyes remarked hopefully (1853, p.57):

> A Community-home in which each is married to all, and where love is honored and cultivated, will be as much more attractive than an ordinary home, even in the honey-moon, as the Community out-numbers a pair.

Noyes contrasted such an association with those of the Shakers who he felt had, by their celibacy, banished strife from their communities, but had thereby sacrificed the 'vitality of society'. He added somewhat obscurely that in communities organized on his principles, the strength of the participants would be so increased, and the necessity of work so diminished, that all labour would 'become sport, as it would have been in the original Eden state'. Such expectations, and the sectarians' hopeful dependence on Providence, in conjunction with the expense of supporting the literary élite at Brooklyn, led the Community, by 1854, to the verge of financial disaster.

Throughout his career, Noyes was concerned to distinguish himself and his followers from advocates of uninspired 'free-love', who he insisted were selfish, undisciplined and hypocritical. He delivered stern warnings to all persons who might attempt to reap the benefits of his 'social discoveries' without subscribing to the religious views which underlay them and submitting to his authority as the supreme earthly spokesman of the Primitive Church (Noyes, 1853, p. 57):

> The government in heaven will not employ self-seekers; and whoever meddles with the affairs of the inner sanctuary without being employed by the government, will plunge himself into consuming fire.

In his early writings on sexual matters Noyes said little of the concrete details of the institutionalization of complex marriage, or of the implications of the conception of the 'ascending fellowship' in social, and especially sexual, relations. Once his followers had gathered at Oneida, Noyes faced the task of instructing them in the theory and practice of male continence and complex marriage, and of extirpating all selfish and exclusive tendencies from the group. Throughout 1848, he laboured to destroy every vestige of 'marriage prejudice', and to inculcate the selfless but disciplined morality appropriate for all those who had passed beyond the legal restrictions of the 'law of the apostasy'.

Noyes gradually developed the idea of the desirability of establishing what he termed an 'ascending fellowship' in the life of the sectarians. At Putney, he had taught that the close and exclusive association of believers would magnify their spiritual qualities and powers, and at Oneida, as an outgrowth of this teaching, he stressed that individuals should be encouraged to mix with their spiritual superiors, and so be stimulated to improvement (Barron and Miller, 1875, p. 203):

> We understand by the ascending fellowship, a state in which a person's companionship is with those who are above him in spiritual life, so that the drawing of the fellowship is upward.

This conception was extended into sexual relationships and it was insisted that, as sexual intercourse in its amative aspect was a 'conversation of spirits', the first conversation should be an improving one. Young men and women in the Community were therefore introduced to sexual relationships by older, more spiritually inclined persons of the opposite sex. A majority of the young women appear to have been initiated by Noyes himself, and as

Carden (1969) points out, the median age for initiation was thirteen, a point which, in the years prior to dissolution of the Community, exposed Noyes and at least some of his closest associates to the possibility of charges of statutory rape. Noyes's posthumous eulogist summarized the religious justification of the ascending fellowship in sexual matters (Estlake, 1900, pp. 54–5):

> it was of the greater importance that they should receive these [first] impressions through those members who would be more likely to elevate them with the consciousness of having innocently exercised a pure and natural function on the spiritual plane.

With the exception of their initial experiences, and subject always to the moral constraints imposed by the ascending fellowship, every adult member of the Community was free to request sexual favours from every person of the opposite sex, but from about the period of the Civil War it was strictly insisted that these approaches should be made through an intermediary, usually an elderly woman and, theoretically, each member was free to decline such requests without explanation. Noyes's antipathy to the term 'free-love', and his desire to distinguish his followers from sexual adventurers or libertarians have been mentioned above. He and all dutiful members of the sect were concerned to detect and check any manifestation of over-indulgence or exclusiveness in sexual relations; both forms of behaviour being regarded as threatening to the system of complex marriage.

Once Noyes had educated his followers in his social principles, they appear to have exhibited a tendency to take excessive advantage of their new freedom, and it was not until October 1850 that the editor of the group's periodical could announce that the spirit of 'selfish pleasure-seeking' had been conquered in the Community. Noyes recognized the danger that the sacramental aspects of the sexual act, and its importance as a 'conveyancer of social magnetism', might be forgotten, and, referring to male continence, he roundly condemned (1872, p. 20):

> the temptation to make a separate hobby of it and neglect the religious conditions out of which it originally issued and to which it belongs.

Estlake stated that continence was the watchword of the Community in every aspect of its life, and Noyes sought to counter scandalous rumours of debauches and sexual excesses in the Community by stating (*The Circular*, April 1870, p. 28) that, as a result of the self-control and awakened sensibilities of the members,

> the women of the O.C. [*sic*] are not subject to one-half the sexual exercise that is the average lot of women in the world.

The tendency of individuals to over-indulge in sexual relations could be checked by refusal, but the tendency for some members to develop 'special affections' for others represented a more serious threat to the authority of Noyes and his lieutenants. Persons suspected of being 'sticky', or unduly attached to each other, were explicitly criticized for this failing. They were reminded that 'free circulation' and a consequent widespread exchange of 'magnetic influences' was the ideal of the Community, and were placed under strict surveillance, and encouraged, or instructed, to enter into sexual relationships with other persons.

The implementation of the 'ascending fellowship' appears to have called forth some measure of resistance among the young, who presumably preferred sexual partners of their own age. Noyes frequently stressed that the ascending fellowship was not a vague ideal, but was to be realized in practice in the sect, and on one occasion at least he added a frank comment on the personal and social benefits to be derived from the ascending fellowship (*The Circular*, April 1861, p. 47):

> Our principle has sought to establish circulation through the whole society, with a view to modifying the experience of one class with wisdom, and promoting geniality in the other.

Between 1848 and 1868, procreation in the Community was deliberately limited by the practice of male continence. In these twenty years, some forty children were born, an unspecified number intentionally, in the Community of about two hundred and fifty persons.

The pamphlet, *Male Continence*, published in 1872, was at once a restatement of the sexual theories of the sect, and a report on the effectiveness of male continence as tested by the 'Committee of Providence' – the Oneida Community. Noyes concluded that his 'discovery' was effective in that procreation had been greatly restricted, and the health of the males had been in no way affected by the infrequency of ejaculation. Masturbation had been almost eradicated and male continence had in no way impaired the potency of the male sectarians as, in the previous two years, there had been many 'intentional impregnations' by long-standing practitioners of the technique. Noyes further cited a paper published by his son, Theodore, which showed that the incidence of nervous disease in the Community was lower than that in the external society. Noyes stressed that male continence and complex marriage had not adversely affected the moral health of the sectarians and, as evidence of this, added rather sweepingly that (Noyes, 1872, p. 24):

> The natural desire for children, which has almost died out in general society, has returned to us, with all the vigor that it had in the young and healthy ages.

The stirpicultural experiment

In 1846, Noyes had sarcastically dismissed as 'chimerical schemes' the arguments of advocates of race improvement by means of 'scientific marriages', and he commented only very briefly on the possibility that male continence might facilitate the deliberate improvement of the human race. Throughout his five-year sojourn at Brooklyn, Noyes appears to have believed that widespread publication of his ideas, coupled with the existence of the Oneida Community as a prototype of the regenerate life, would be sufficient, in conjunction with the power of the Holy Spirit, to effect a rapid transformation of American society and eventually of the world. Noyes's changing conception of his mission will be discussed in more detail below; at this point it is sufficient to indicate that he slowly developed a more gradualistic, or to use his own term, 'geological', conception of God's plan for mankind. Concomitantly, after a period of concentration on the regulation of the internal affairs of the sect, Noyes's attitude to the external society changed and he, and at least some of his followers, came to regard themselves as the vanguard of moral and social reform.

Noyes's interest in the possibility of breeding a physically and morally superior group appears to have developed at the time of the American Civil War. In 1865, a leading article in *The Circular* by its co-editor, George Noyes, dwelt on the possibility that 'scientific' control of reproduction within the Community might result in the production of 'geniuses'. George Noyes, who was completely subordinate to his elder brother, cited divine precedent for the project, and claimed that God had exercised 'the herdsman's right' of selection among the progeny of Noah.

From these initial speculations the theoretical basis and justification of 'stirpiculture' was developed in the immediate post-Civil War years. (The term was coined by Noyes to signify selective breeding from a common stock or 'family'.) In this period the sectarians were brought to an appreciation of the sublimity and divine origins of the experiment, which was inaugurated in 1868. Noyes's ideas on this topic were made widely public in the mid eighteen seventies in a pamphlet, *Essay on Scientific Propagation*, in which Noyes provided evidence of his interest in the social sciences, and stated, in markedly Comtean or Spencerian terms that 'it is generally agreed among the highest thinkers that sociology is the science around which all other sciences are finally to be organized' (Noyes, 1875?, p. 3). He added that, as the nucleus of human learning, sociology was inevitably complex, but that its 'nucleolus' was, or would be, the science which presided over reproduction.

Having established the supreme importance of the experiment which was already inaugurated at Oneida, Noyes sought to substantiate his theoretical statements by adducing aspects of the work of Darwin and Galton as additional support for his essentially Lamarckian conception that the acquired characteristics of parents might be transmitted to their offspring. Noyes referred approvingly to Galton's conclusions regarding the hereditary nature of genius, but castigated him for a reluctance to move from scholarship to practical measures and policies. Summarizing Darwin's studies of the selective breeding of domestic animals, he concluded that (Noyes, 1875?, p. 14):

The art of the animal-breeder, so far as mere propagation is concerned, is all contained in two precepts, viz.: Breed from the best, and breed in and in.

Noyes argued that if the same principles were applied to the breeding of a distinct human 'family', they would produce an improvement, not merely in the physical, but also in the moral qualities of the offspring of the group. He asserted that there was no rational reason to doubt that the laws of physiology were the same for man as for the lower animals, and that consequently the difficulties in the way of his proposals were 'not physiological but sentimental'. In his early specifically religious writings, Noyes had attributed the moral superiority which he credited to the Jews, to their consciousness of being the people of the covenant, and to the 'sun and rain of God's discipline', but, in the *Essay on Scientific Propagation*, he attributed their being 'a distinct and superior variety of the human race' to centuries of inbreeding.

Having established the 'scientific' basis of stirpiculture to his own satisfaction, and having maintained that his thought was not merely congruent with, but in advance of, the greatest biologists of the age, Noyes attacked those institutions and social groups which opposed or impeded widespread scientific propagation. He indicated that the general abhorrence of incest, and the specific societal prohibitions against it, were formidable obstacles to the beneficial practice of 'breeding in and in', and he deplored the efforts of 'high-toned moralists' to extend the application of the taboo.

In connection with this discussion Noyes condemned marriage not, as formerly, because it sanctified exclusiveness, but because 'it leaves mating to be determined by a general scramble' and because, while the best men tended to postpone marriage and to restrict the number of their offspring within marriage, the worst men irresponsibly 'disseminated seed' and multiplied their kind. Noyes expressed his animus against the Catholic Church by deploring the practice of priestly celibacy which he felt 'in effect . . . castrates the finest animals in its flocks', and likewise condemned the Shakers in a statement which, bearing in mind that Noyes was no advocate of asceticism, had a hypocritical ring (Noyes 1875?, p. 29):

> They claim to be the noblest and purest people in the world, a sacred generation . . .; and yet, with full power to propagate their kind, they virtually castrate themselves, and expend their labors and wealth on their own comfort and on misbegotten adopted children, leaving the production of future generations to common sinners.

Conversely, Noyes proclaimed that informed by a knowledge of the physiological principles underlying stirpiculture, some generally despised institutions and practices could be seen to have good aspects. Thus he maintained that polygamy tended to promote the reproduction of the best men;

that slavery had to some extent elevated the Negro race, because slaves were often selectively bred, and that even the 'numberless fornications' of Pierrepoint Edwards, the profligate son of the great revivalist, had had a beneficial effect on the genetic composition of the population of New England.

Noyes reiterated his conviction that monogamous marriage must come to an end before God's will could be fully realized on earth, and examining the 'signs of the times', claimed that free-love, the popularity of divorce and the prevalence of abortion, or 'foeticide', all indicated that American society was ripe for institutional change. Employing phraseology similar to that of Marx, Noyes expressed his conviction that he and his followers were leading mankind in accordance with the divine plan (Noyes, 1875?, p. 32):

> If the powers above are summoning us to the great enterprise of peopling the planet with a new race, why should not the old institutions, which are too narrow for such an enterprise, be passing away? The birth of the new always comes with agony and rupture to the old.

As was the case with his other social innovations, by the time Noyes published an abstract and seemingly tentative statement of his theories, the corresponding social practices were already established in the sect – the stirpicultural experiment was commenced in 1868, the first children being born to specially selected couples in 1869. Prior to the commencement of the experiment, Noyes laboured to convince his followers of the validity of his ideas and, in 1868, the young men and women of the Community signed declarations affirming their faith in Noyes, and their willingness to submit themselves totally to his dictates. These declarations merit full reproduction as expressions of the 'selfless dedication' of the sectarians, and of the extent of Noyes's authority over them. Fifty-three young women signed the following articles (cited in Parker, 1935, p. 257):

> 1. That we do not belong to ourselves in any respect, but that we do belong first to God, and second to Mr Noyes as God's true representative.
> 2. That we have no rights or personal feelings in regard to child-bearing which shall in the least degree oppose or embarrass him in his choice of scientific combinations.
> 3. That we will put aside all envy, childishness and self-seeking, and rejoice with those who are chosen candidates; that we will, if necessary, become martyrs to science, and cheerfully resign all desire to become mothers, if for any reason Mr Noyes deem us unfit material for propagation. Above all we offer ourselves 'living sacrifices' to God and true Communism.

Noyes believed that the genetic influence of the father of a child was greater

than that of the mother, and consequently, the selection of the male participants in the experiment was more rigorous than that of the females.
Thirty-eight young men of the Community declared that (cited in Parker,
1935, p. 257):

> The undersigned desire you may feel that we most heartily sympathize
> with your purpose in regard to scientific propagation, and offer
> ourselves to be used in forming any combinations that may seem to
> you desirable. We claim no rights. We ask no privileges. We desire to
> be servants of the truth. With a prayer that the grace of God will help
> us in this resolution, we are your true soldiers.

The arrangements for mating were supervised entirely by Noyes until
1875, by which date a variety of challenges to Noyes's leadership had
arisen, some of which were at least indirectly attributable to the grievances
and tensions generated or exacerbated by the stirpicultural regime. In 1875,
control of the experiment passed to a formal committee of six males and six
females, but reverted to the informal élite of 'central members' in the following year. Sixty-one children were born in the Community in the stirpicultural decade of 1869 to 1879, at least eight of these children being fathered
by Noyes himself. Eleven or twelve of these births were apparently un-
planned. Five of the children born died at or near birth, the remaining
fifty-six, who were collectively referred to as the 'stirps', were brought up in
special conditions until 1879, when complex marriage was abandoned
(Mc'Gee, 1891, pp. 319-25).

Couples selected to form 'scientific combinations' lived together before
and for some indefinite period after the birth of their children. The children
were cared for by their mothers exclusively until the age of nine months, and
at night until they were about eighteen months old, at which time they were
placed in the infants sections of the children's department where they were
cared for by male and female nurses.

Noyes frequently stated that improvement – physical, intellectual and
moral – was the watchword of the Community, and accordingly his attitude
to worldly knowledge and education was liberal. Many newspapers and
periodicals were taken by the Community and were entirely uncensored, and
foreign languages, music, mathematics and other subjects were taught in
open evening classes. The education received by the stirps, and also by the
children born earlier in the Community, was considerably broader than
that provided in the external public schools, and in addition to attending
school the children were required to perform light manual labour for several
hours each day.

The education and general socialization of the children was avowedly
intended to cultivate 'the habit of obedience', and to foster 'softness of heart',
by which was meant receptivity to inspiration, and also the abnegation of the
self and the total surrender of the will to persons possessing superior spiritual

qualities. The stirps were allowed twice-weekly visits to their parents, but both the children and the parents were publicly criticized if they showed signs of becoming unduly attached to each other. In keeping with the general principle that members of the group at every level should 'keep in the circulation', special friendships among the children were discouraged, and if they arose the children involved were, as far as possible, separated.

Healing by faith and criticism

Noyes's ideas concerning the origin of disease stemmed directly from his Manichean theological conception that the universe was a battleground between God, an uncreated good spirit, and the devil, an uncreated evil spirit. Noyes taught that every form of disease, and death itself, were manifestations of the devil's power, and that persons possessing some measure of God's spirit would have a corresponding degree of power to resist and cure disease. As shown in the previous chapter, Noyes believed that the power of the Holy Spirit was 'transmissible' through bodily contact. From this premise he argued that the more intimate and all-embracing the contact, the more complete and effective was the transmission of curative power, and he concluded that in some cases of disease or of mental resistance to inspiration, sexual intercourse might be the only effective method of cure, or of softening the heart to a receptive state.

Conceiving themselves to be the 'theocratic nucleus' of the Kingdom of Heaven on earth, Noyes and his followers regarded themselves as committed to a continuous 'warfare with death', and with its hand-maiden, disease. In the early period at Oneida, and subsequently at Brooklyn, Noyes elaborated his theory of the origins and nature of disease and of the appropriate spiritual methods of its prevention and cure. He did not deny the essential reality of disease, but rather claimed that the possession of sufficient faith in combination with a strenuous exercise of the will, was sufficient to enable an individual to resist disease, and to cure himself and others of disease. Thus, in addition to the 'miracle' which he performed on Mrs Hall, Noyes claimed to have cured Jonathan Burt's brother of insanity, and himself of a tubercular throat infection. His followers reported their cures in the sect's periodical, and in addition frequently attributed these successes, or even their persistence in good health, to the benign influences transmitted through Noyes from the heavenly world.

Resistance to disease was taken by Noyes and his followers as evidence of faith, and of the possession of a 'good spirit', and conversely proneness to disease, or the persistence of illness, was interpreted as evidence of lack of faith and a 'bad spirit'. To deal with recalcitrant physical and mental maladies Noyes developed a curative technique which he grandly entitled 'krinopathy'; an outgrowth of the general method of social control by means of 'mutual criticism', which will be examined below. In an article on krinopathy or 'criticism-cure', Noyes provided an unassailable justification of the employment of this technique (*The Circular*, August 1854, p. 430):

> No one is too sick for criticism if there is any thing wrong in his spirit. He may be saved from death by it – if not, he will be better prepared to die for having received it, and will thank you from the other side.

The characters of persons deemed fit subjects for krinopathy were publicly discussed and examined in an attempt to extirpate those negative qualities of 'unfaithfulness of mind' which were believed to be at once demonstrated by, and ultimately responsible for, their physical state. Verbatim reports of curative criticisms were published frequently in *The Circular*. Thus in 1874, a member reportedly suffering from a prostrating spinal affliction which a doctor had pronounced incurable, was criticized by a committee of several persons. Summarizing the criticism, Noyes stated (cited in Nordhoff, 1875, p. 297):

> I do not care what the doctors say about L's back. It is very likely incurable as far as they know, and yet it may be very easily curable to any body who knows about the doctrine of possession of the devil.

At this late date, to add empirical weight to this vague assertion, he cited the cure of Harriet Hall as incontrovertible proof of the validity of his teachings.

In another reported case of krinopathy, a woman whose arm had become paralysed after it had passed through the rollers of a wringing machine, was first criticized by a committee appointed by Noyes, and this criticism proving ineffective, was criticized by Noyes himself, and was apparently cured – 'a private criticism soon after penetrated her spirit, and separated her from the brooding influence of evil that she had come under in a heart affair' (cited in Nordhoff, 1875, p. 273).

Evil spirits and 'devil's providences'

The quotation immediately above provides an illustration of a secondary strand in Noyes's thought concerning disease and physical misfortune. Not only did he believe in the existence of the devil as an uncreated evil being, but he also believed that the devil was aided by a legion of evil spirits.

In the discussion which preceded the momentous 'declaration' of June 1847, Noyes had informed his followers that the Spirit of God needed only 'confession to give it room', that is, to enable it to extend its operations on earth. At a more mundane level, the sectarians were urged to make public acknowledgment of the spiritual and social blessings that they enjoyed in the Community. Similarly, the periodical of the sect contained numerous accounts of 'special providences' which had beneficially influenced individual action, or the development of the sect.

Conversely, Noyes appears to have believed that excessive discussion or contemplation of evil events would similarly 'give room' for the further operation of evil spirits. At an individual level, members of the Community were frequently criticized for being preoccupied with thoughts of disease and misfortune. More generally, in the periodical Noyes occasionally criticized the non-religious newspapers of the day, which he felt dwelt excessively on shameful and horrific topics, and so perverted men's imaginations and prevented them from recognizing the blessings they enjoyed and the operation of benign spirits in the world.

Noyes did not attribute evil influences only to places, and to 'unhealthy' or morbid thoughts, but also to persons. The clearest evidence of this conception that evil intentions and thoughts could give rise to evil effects, is provided by Noyes's extended account of the 'Mills affair', published in *The Circular*, between November 1864 and March 1865.

William Mills had seceded from the group after his sexual approaches had been totally rejected by the female members. He was subsequently re-admitted on probation, and receiving no warmer reception appears to have become half-crazed. Somewhat ironically, his mania took the form of proclaiming himself commissioned by God to destroy the Community, and he threatened several persons with heavenly wrath if they refused his demands or obstructed him in any way. Mills was eventually expelled from the sect, and reporting these events Noyes claimed that Mills's 'oppressive power' had worked evil in the Community. More specifically, he stated that those persons whom Mills had threatened had suffered a number of minor accidents, which Noyes interpreted as 'Devil's providences'. Noyes reiterated his belief in evil spirits, and the malignant influence of evil thoughts, and concluded that 'holding these beliefs, we are free to say that Mills's case is one of the best proved cases of malignant sorcery we have ever seen' (*The Circular*, January 1865, p. 346).

The 'warfare with death' – an attenuated campaign

The intensity of the struggle which Noyes and his followers waged against disease and death was at a pitch in the Brooklyn period, 1849 to 1854, when the utopian convictions of the sect were strongest. In these years, Noyes was convinced that the earth would shortly be transformed into the Kingdom of Heaven through the example of the Oneida Community and by his 'power of utterance' in the periodical. Every 'cure' effected, and every 'testimony' or 'confession' of faith in the healing power of the Holy Spirit was seen as bringing nearer the time when that Spirit, channelled through the Community, would pour out over the earth and abolish sin. Testimonies and reports of cures were regularly printed in the sect's periodical, and in 1852, when Noyes sanguinely reviewed the achievements of the Oneida Community, he reported that in three years he and his followers had made a considerable advance towards their goal of complete victory over death (*The Circular*, May 1852, p. 110).

In the two years after the publication of this statement, several prominent members of the Community died, but Noyes interpreted these seeming setbacks as presaging the imminence of the second general resurrection, and the associated abolition of death. He stated that believers should consider the deaths at Oneida to be the casualties which were inevitable in that most furious stage of any battle – the final engagement before the rout of the enemy.

The zenith of Noyes's ultraist evangelical ambitions and achievements was reached in 1854, throughout which year *The Circular* was issued thrice-weekly. At the end of this year, the Community at Brooklyn was closed (ostensibly in order to escape from the malignant 'spiritual influences' of the city) and Noyes returned to Oneida. In the decade that followed this 'concentration of life', Noyes developed a more gradualistic conception of his mission and a reformist attitude to the world. Earlier he had roundly condemned American government and institutions, but in the latter part of his career he came to conceive of the Community as the moral and social vanguard of the United States, whose national destiny was to exert a beneficent and progressive civilizing influence on the less enlightened portion of the world.

Immediately after his return to Oneida, Noyes set about the task of purifying the economic, moral and spiritual condition of the sectarians in preparation for a renewed outpouring of the Holy Spirit. Earlier, Noyes had rejected all legalistic restrictions on behaviour and consumption, but as part of this programme of purification, he instituted moral campaigns against the use of tobacco, tea, coffee and meat. These restrictions were justified on medical, social and spiritual grounds. The use of tobacco was condemned as obnoxious to refined sensibilities, and essentially selfish. Tea and coffee were declared to impose 'spiritual bondage' on their votaries, and vegetarianism was adopted in order to free the Community from the gross spiritual influences which emanated from meat.

The increasing gradualism of Noyes's interpretation of the divine plan for redemption of the world was reflected in his writings on the abolition of disease and death. Throughout the eighteen sixties and eighteen seventies, his statements on these subjects became vaguer in content and less optimistic in tone. Accounts of the administration of curative criticisms and confessions of faith in the healing power of the Holy Spirit continued to appear in the pages of *The Circular*, but they were somewhat perfunctory, and reliance on faith healing was increasingly supplemented by reliance on practical medicine. No cures to rival the miracles performed on Harriet Hall and George Burt were claimed, but the accounts of these early cures were frequently republished.

In 1865, Noyes announced in an article that, as the leaders of the human march to redemption, the sectarians were committed to becoming 'Anastasists' or 'Resurrectionists'. By this he meant that, at an unspecified date, their spiritual struggles would free them from the power of death; but despite such doctrinal restatement masked by terminological innovation, by 1870 it must have been plain to the members of the group that they were making little progress in their battle with disease. This 'warfare' culminated somewhat bathetically after 1875, in the sectarians' enthusiastic proclamation of the invigorating, restorative and curative properties of Turkish baths, especially when combined with krinopathy.

From the early eighteen seventies, Noyes himself was plagued by growing deafness, and by a return of the throat condition which in 1847, he had claimed to have cured by faith and will power. His voice dwindled to a whisper, and occasionally entirely failed him, and his conversation was almost totally confined to the central members of the group, themselves ageing men. Noyes's physical deterioration inevitably diminished his authority. He had never explicitly laid claim to immortality, but he had asserted that the second general resurrection and the concomitant abolition of death, would occur within the lifetime of the generation living when a branch of the Primitive Church was established on earth. Further, he had taught that receptivity to disease was a sign of the possession of 'an unclean spirit'.

The declining vigour of their prophet, the man they acknowledged as furthest advanced in the regenerate state, must have shaken the faith of many of the older members, and caused them to have doubts concerning the validity of Noyes's religious claims and their own future security. Noyes's dependence on a few elderly lieutenants was resented by many of the younger sectarians, some of whom, including Noyes's eldest son, Theodore, had been led by their education and general experience of the external world, to doubt the validity of 'Bible religion', and even of the 'inspiration' and 'manifest miracles' which formed the basis of Noyes's charismatic authority.

Noyes's changing conception of his mission

In their declaration of June 1847, Noyes and his followers provided a clear statement of the two partially conflicting commitments involved in religious utopianism: separation from the world and evangelism. Believing that the Kingdom of God was realized in their own association, the sectarians took upon themselves the related tasks of establishing the 'fashions and institutions of heaven upon earth', and of 'extending God's everlasting domain over men'. They committed themselves to developing that degree of perfection in their association which would demonstrate the superiority of the regenerate life, and they believed that their selfless devotion to God's will would be rewarded by, or would 'make room for', an out-pouring of the Holy Spirit sufficient to enable them to convert all those who were capable of regeneration. (It was taken for granted that all members of the sect who died before the final conquest of death would enjoy eternal bliss.)

By 1849, Noyes appears to have considered the Community to be securely established as a standing demonstration of the heavenly form of society. In May of that year, he moved to Brooklyn and for the next five years devoted himself to literary evangelism. In this period he paid only infrequent visits to Oneida, and entrusted the routine management of the Community to a lieutenant, Erastus Hamilton. Not only did Noyes remove himself physically from the Community, but to some extent he sought to disclaim responsibility for its affairs, and concerned himself with 'harvesting' the world for God or, more accurately, with preparing the harvest of the world through the medium of the periodical. The author of the *Second Annual Report* of the Oneida Community was at pains to repudiate suggestions that the Oneida Community was held together solely by the force of Noyes's personality, and provided a clear indication of Noyes's lofty conception of his mission at this time (anon., 1850, p. 22):

> J. H. Noyes . . . has been absent from Oneida for the most part of the last year, residing in Brooklyn, N.Y., and engaged in a sphere of occupation above the superintendence of any local Community.

In his years at Brooklyn, Noyes, who proclaimed that 'the press is the king of trades', was inspired by a vision of the time when he, as God's representative and editor-in-chief on earth, would preside over and co-ordinate the affairs of a multitude of perfectionist communities. To this end, 'sustained and nourished' by the devoted sectarians at Oneida who suffered considerable poverty and physical hardship in this period, Noyes and the literary élite concentrated their efforts on extending the circulation of the periodical and the frequency of its publication. The press was removed to Brooklyn in 1851 after a fire had destroyed the Oneida print-shop, and *The Circular* was issued on a weekly basis until 1853, twice-weekly for most of that year, and thrice-weekly throughout 1854.

It must be emphasized that, after the 'gathering period' at Oneida, admission to the Community was greatly restricted, and a considerable number of applicants were simply instructed to hold themselves in readiness for the coming expansion of the Spirit and consequent transformation of the world. Noyes's evangelism was of the most general nature; he sought to awaken the American nation to a consciousness of the virtues of regeneration, and to the imminence of the second resurrection. At Brooklyn, his immediate aim was the establishment of a free daily paper 'devoted to the sovereignty of Jesus Christ'; a paper which he confidently expected would supplant all others. Noyes's persistence in ultraist modes of thought can be illustrated by his statement that the establishment of such a newspaper was the *sine qua non* of the conversion of the world – 'we need not expect to see the tide of evil rolling back, till this victory is won' (*The Circular*, April 1853, p. 163).

Noyes's return to Oneida in December 1854 was prompted by evangelical disappointment and financial considerations. Announcing the closure of the Brooklyn Community, Noyes condemned the iniquity of the American people who had ignored his message of redemption, and were unmoved by the attractions of a life of sanctified, selfless subordination. He prophesied national strife and disorder, and indicated that he and his followers thought it desirable to withdraw themselves from the coming disruption of American society.

In the previous chapters it has been suggested that the members of a utopian sect tend to explain the non-achievement of their goals by reference to prior over-concentration on one component of their dual ideological commitment, and that consequently, the pattern of development of such a sect is likely to be marked by alternating phases of concentration on evangelism and on internal purification. In the case of the Oneida Community, Noyes primarily explained his failure to 'roll back' the tide of sin in terms of the extreme corruption of the world, but he appears also to have attributed this failure to the impurity and imperfections of his followers. On his return to Oneida, he instituted a regime of 'improvement' of every aspect of the lives of the sectarians, and justified this action as a necessary purification of the Community; a prerequisite for the further expansion of its influence. Thus, in 1857, referring to the future establishment of a daily newspaper, Noyes stated succinctly that '. . . when our subjective preparation is complete, God will open the way for its accomplishment' (*The Circular*, January 1857, p. 206).

In the early years of the decade 1855 to 1865, Noyes sought to establish the Community on a sound economic basis, and in this 'industrial phase', condemned as exploitative the 'hireling system' of the world, and elaborated general proposals for reforms which he insisted would abolish labour unrest and industrial strife.

Such a concern with the specific social problems generated by the industrial depression of the late eighteen fifties is indicative of the more general changes in Noyes's idea of his mission, and of the role of the Oneida Community. In this decade, his interpretation of God's plan for the world became increasingly gradualistic, and he came to regard himself and his followers as the vanguard of worldly reform, as well as the potential progenitors of a new, morally superior race of men. Indeed by 1870, Noyes had developed what may be termed a relativistic conception of his life-work, and discussed the Oneida Community not as God's final and unalterable blueprint for mankind, but as a single species of 'religious socialism'.

Noyes's tendency to 'edit' his own biography has been indicated earlier. In 1860, he looked back on the years which he had spent at Brooklyn, and remarked that in this period he had commenced the study of geology, and had been led to realize that God dealt in millennia, and not in single years. Noyes stated explicitly that this realization had led him to be in less 'hurry for a daily paper' and, implicitly, for the conversion of the world.

Further evidence of Noyes's increasingly reformist attitude to the world was provided when he commented on the Community's 'providential' avoidance of the Civil War drafts in Madison County. Referring to the departure of conscripts from the neighbourhood, Noyes remarked (*The Circular*, August 1863, p. 95):

> ... while they go to the war, we will still continue to work in the not less noble task of making human society a better place for them on their return.

After 1865, Noyes's ideological gradualism and reformism became still more pronounced. In this period he was initially preoccupied with the inauguration and superintendence of the stirpicultural regime, and with his study of 'American socialisms' and, after 1870, with combating external hostility and internal challenges to his authority. In 1866, he announced that the sectarians were preparing for a 'change from the silent policy of the past' in regard to their sexual arrangements, but Noyes's ambitious plans for extensive lecture tours and a great expansion of the publishing activities of the group did not come to fruition.

Increasingly, Noyes expressed his approval of the general development of the American nation, and did not stress, as earlier, the uncompromising nature of the 'searching-power' of his testimony against sin and selfishness. In his writings in the group's periodical, Noyes indicated his agreement with the evolutionary conviction that the United States had a God-given destiny to civilize and modernize the rest of the world. At a less exalted level he sought to show that, 'to the believer's eye', a wide range of inventions and social innovations could be seen to be in conformity with the divine plan for the redemption of the world. Thus, he claimed that the laying of the transatlantic cable would play an important part in unifying and pacifying mankind, and, more tenuously still, stated that the development and expansion of hotels and watering places was indicative of a widespread nascent desire for co-operation and communal living.

In the latter years of his career, Noyes sought to establish himself not as a prophet, commissioned by God to denounce sin and reveal the ultimate form of society to mankind, but rather as a 'moral advocate' of social reforms of every level of generality. A quotation from another of Noyes's articles indicates the degree of his identification and *rapprochement* with other religious movements and reformist groups. Expressing his faith that sin would eventually be destroyed by a 'true work of redemption', and incidentally justifying the prosperous stagnation of the Oneida Community, Noyes bracketed himself and his followers with all other men of good will, and stated rather lamely that – 'we can only wait with others, and hope that the same power which began the work will go on and complete it' (*The Circular*, March 1872, p. 100).

These changes in Noyes's conception of his mission, and of the role and importance of the Oneida Community, were given clear expression in his *History of American Socialisms*, which was assembled from manuscripts which Noyes had acquired in 1864, and published in 1870. In his ten-page summary of his six-hundred-page work, Noyes attempted to establish the causes of the success or failure of these 'social experiments'. In a style reminiscent of his earlier diatribes in *The Berean*, Noyes stressed the failure of the secular Owenites, and of the 'semi-religious' followers of Fourier, to establish lasting, harmonious communities. He insisted that such 'deductive socialists' were misguided, in that they based their new forms of society on untested conjectures. Noyes asserted that (Noyes, 1870, p. 668):

> God's appointed way for man to seek the truth in all departments, and above all in Social Science, which is really the science of righteousness, is to combine and alternate thinking with experiment and practice, and constantly submit all theories, whether obtained by scientific investigation or by intuition and inspiration to the consuming ordeal of practical verification.

Noyes stated that the case of the Oneida Community and of the other enduring 'socialisms' demonstrated that the only sure basis for communitarianism was a religion 'of the earnest sort, which comes by recognized afflatus', such religion being necessarily combined with discerning selectivity in recruitment (Noyes, 1870, p. 656):

> Earnest men of one religious faith are more likely to be respectful to organized authority and to one another, than men of no religion or men of many religions held in indifference and mutual counteraction.

Given that only earnest religion could modify human depravity in such a way as to make 'continuous Association' possible, Noyes concluded from the success of the 'sporadic experiments made by various religious sects' (including the Oneida Community), that all hope of 'Association' on a world-wide scale should not be abandoned. In a manner completely at variance with his earlier utopian insistence that the Oneida Community was the unique nucleus of the Kingdom of Heaven on earth, he stated that while 'Exceptional Associations' might be formed from time to time by means of careful selection and special good fortune, only the infusion of the major denominations by the Spirit of God could effect the moral transformation of the world (Noyes, 1870, p. 657):

> Our hope is that churches of all denominations will by and by be quickened by the Pentecostal Spirit, and begin to grow and change, and finally, by a process as natural as the transformation of the chrysalis, burst forth into Communism.

The limited, but indubitably gratifying, external success of the *History of*

American Socialisms appears to have rekindled and redirected Noyes's literary ambitions and, after 1870, he came to conceive of himself as especially qualified to be the spokesman and leader, or perhaps better, the doyen, of the communitarian movement in the United States. This change in the nature and focus of Noyes's ambitions was undoubtedly also prompted by the variety of challenges to his leadership which, after 1870, developed within the Community. The extent of Noyes's disappointment at the failure of his ultraist evangelism and at the unfaithfulness and insubordination of some of his followers, can be gauged from *The Circular* for January 1876, in which he stated that the experience of the group had made them 'conservative', and that he had 'no wish to hurry the world into Oneida Communism'.

In March 1876, *The Circular* was replaced by a new weekly paper, *The American Socialist*, which, edited by Noyes, was intended to provide a 'public record of facts relating to the progress of socialism everywhere'. In this periodical Noyes offered a forum of debate to socialists of every variety, but the subsequent debates were somewhat one-sided, and the eloquent 'Appeal for Union' addressed to all American communitarians appears to have been unheeded by the Shakers, Rappites and other similar 'inductive' experimenters in social science.

By 1877, external hostility to the sexual arrangements of the Community, and internal challenges to Noyes's authority had intensified, and, in May of this year, Noyes conferred the Presidency of the Community on his eldest son, Theodore. Noyes's announcement of his resignation concealed the conflicts in the Community, but illustrated the relativistic way in which he had come to view the Oneida Community as but one division in the army of reform. Noyes stated that his leadership of the Community was incompatible with his grander editorial duties, '. . . because The American Socialist aspires to be the organ of Socialism in all its degrees, while the O.C. [*sic*] is the exponent of only one form of Communism' (*The American Socialist*, May 1877, p. 164).

Two years later, confronted by the possibility that the opponents of the sect might secure special legislation against complex marriage, and facing the total breakdown of his authority, Noyes fled to Canada, and initially sought sanctuary with some sympathizers near Strathroy, Ontario. On 20 August 1879, he wrote to the sectarians advising them to abandon complex marriage in deference to public sentiment, and stated, 'for my part, I think we have great reason to be thankful for the toleration which has so long been accorded to our audacious experiment' (*The American Socialist*, August 1879, p. 276).

Complex marriage was duly abandoned on receipt of this letter, and many members of the group contracted monogamous marriages shortly thereafter. Noyes appears to have expected the economic communism of the group to persist despite the cessation of complex marriage, but, in September 1880, a tentative agreement to reorganize the economic and domestic arrangements of the group was signed by all but one of the adult members. Shortly afterwards, a detailed plan for the distribution of the assets of the sect was adopted, and on 1 January 1881, economic communism was formally at an end.

Throughout these changes Noyes lived in Canada. In addition to his considerable share of the divided communal property, he was granted a pension by the Community, and after 1882, exercised an important influence in all the major decisions of the Corporation. *The American Socialist* had been discontinued at the end of 1879, but in 1885, Noyes's literary ambitions appear to have briefly revived, and he discussed the possibility of establishing another periodical. However, weakened by influenza, he went into a decline and died in April of 1886, before this ambition could be realized.

It remained for Noyes's apologist, Estlake, to rationalize the apparently total disintegration of Noyes's life-work. This he did by adopting a gradual-istic, evolutionary conception of God's plan, closely akin to that of Noyes in his last years, but employing natural rather than sexual analogies. Estlake asserted that in all nature, 'integration must be preceded by disintegration' and stated that (Estlake, 1900, pp. 134-5):

> The Oneida Community was also an object lesson in direct connection with the plan of Christianity, demonstrating the possibility of realising the state of civilisation that Christ foreshadowed, and it was another instance of coming events casting their shadows before.

Estlake looked confidently ahead to a time when a free mingling of the blood of the superior Anglo-Saxon and Jewish races would produce a race in which many individuals would approximate in intelligence to Noyes himself, and, not content with this prediction he forecast, '. . . a religious awakening that will usher in such an era of revivalism as has never before been experienced'. Citing the 'signs of the times', which indicated the imminence of this revival, Estlake stated optimistically that, in the field of international relations (1900, p. 106):

> Already the tendency of the best intelligence is toward arbitration rather than campaigns. The soldier's occupation is vanishing.

The organization of charismatic communitarianism

The charismatic nature of Noyes's authority over his followers has been partially discussed in the previous chapter. He announced himself to be the representative of the Primitive Church, and to be entrusted with the twin tasks of proclaiming the gospel of holiness, and of establishing the Heavenly Kingdom on earth. In his own words, he considered himself to be 'a child of inspiration' and, as such, claimed to possess some measure of the Pentecostal power of healing, and to be able to discriminate between the promptings of good and evil spirits. His followers legitimized Noyes's claims by their submission to his authority, and, in the first two decades at Oneida at least, paid frequent 'spontaneous' tributes to his spiritual and intellectual supremacy. Noyes's brother, George, writing in 1850 on behalf of the whole body of sectarians at Oneida, stated that, '. . . we cannot but recognize him as the man of this age, the central point of junction between this and the heavenly world' (*The Spiritual Magazine*, January 1850, p. 376–7).

Once his followers had regrouped at Oneida, Noyes imposed a formal organizational structure on the group. He established various industrial and domestic 'departments' and appointed foremen to these, he instituted weekly general meetings and a range of committees to co-ordinate the policies of the departments, established 'Business Boards' to plan the long-term policy of the group, and elaborated principles to regulate the admission of members to the sect.

Persons wishing to join the sect were required to understand and subscribe to its doctrines, to realize that they were making a commitment for life, to have paid their debts or at least disclosed them, and to be free of obligations to their kindred. On joining the Community their whole property was transferred to the Association, and a record of the transaction was kept. If a member seceded he was refunded an amount equivalent to the property he had dedicated, but no allowance for interest or labour was made, and the publications of the group stated emphatically that the practice of returning property rested 'on the ground, not of obligation, but of expediency and liberality'.

The departmental and committee structure of the group expanded with its numbers and economic enterprises until, at the time of Nordhoff's visit in 1874, there were twenty-two standing committees, the concerns of which varied from general finance to hair-cutting, and forty-eight departments. The latter ranged in importance from 'hardware', which included the trap manufactury, the economic mainstay of the group, to a department whose sole function was the repair and regulation of the clocks of the Community. Routine administrative business was conducted at the Sunday morning meeting attended by the heads of all the departments, and decisions made at this meeting were communicated in the evening to the sectarians for their comments, and usually, their unanimous approval.

In 1848, Noyes and Jonathan Burt had drawn up a loose and informal document as the contractual basis for the group. This rarely cited document, the 'Principles of the Oneida Association', remained unchanged until 1867, when the whole property of the sect was transferred to four 'owners', one of whom was Noyes himself. This transference was made as a result of threats of legal action stemming from a seceder, Charles Guiteau, who won the temporary support of some members of the administration of the New York Y.M.C.A. Noyes did not yield to Guiteau's demands, and, as the latter's instability became pronounced (he shot President Garfield in July

1881, and was subsequently hanged), his supporters deserted him. However, it seems likely that Guiteau's calumnies found a ready audience in New York, and that he sowed some of the seeds of the later clerical persecution of the sect. With the exception of this expedient change in the contractual basis of the group, the formal organization of 'Bible communism' remained largely unaltered until its abandonment in 1881. The causes and details of this abandonment will be fully examined below, after consideration of other aspects of the development of the sect until the early eighteen seventies.

It must be emphasized that the development of a formal organizational structure did not imply any diminution of Noyes's authority. The 'bureaucratic' structure was imposed by Noyes on the sect, and was understood by his followers to be a direct fruit of his inspiration, a fruit which, incidentally, relieved Noyes of everyday administrative concerns and left him free to concentrate on the higher task of literary evangelism. Noyes's removal to Brooklyn, and the infrequency of his visits to Oneida in the period 1849 to 1854, did not diminish his authority over the sectarians. In the early years of poverty and physical hardship at Oneida, Noyes remained largely 'uncontaminated' by mundane matters until, in 1854, he returned from 'fronting the enemy' at Brooklyn to inaugurate a regime of spiritual and behavioural purification, and to rescue the sectarians from the uncertain financial state to which his evangelical ambitions had brought them.

In the Brooklyn era Noyes's claims to possess extraordinary spiritual powers were rarely tested, and were neither rendered familiar by promiscuous display, nor disconfirmed by equivocal 'successes' or simply by repeated failures. Surrounded by his intimates, and visited periodically by the members of his 'staff' – the central members of the group – Noyes lived in relative magnificence at Brooklyn, and appears to have been content that rumour, and the propensity of the followers of a charismatic leader to justify their devotion by magnifying the leader's qualities, should together enhance his reputation.

Until after the end of the Civil War, when Noyes moved for a time to the sect's commercial 'depot' in New York City, his authority over his followers was almost absolute. In the first two decades of the existence of the Oneida Community, the attitude of many of the members of the sect probably resembled that of Noyes's son, Pierrepont, who, as a child in the eighteen seventies, scarcely differentiated his father from Christ, and regarded the central members as being like the Apostles (Noyes, 1937, p. 70).

Social control

As shown in the previous chapter, after an early flirtation with antinomianism Noyes laid great emphasis on the fact that the attainment of regeneration did not preclude further spiritual improvement, and stressed that the regenerate life was necessarily one of unity and subordination. In *The Berean*, he indicated that the leading members of the Primitive Church had overlooked and corrected the conduct of 'lesser vessels', and he added that God could be expected to punish presumption or insubordination by the providential administration of suffering. More immediately, referring to the eventual establishment of a terrestrial branch of the Primitive Church, he indicated that persons living in the heavenly state would be subordinate to one guiding spirit, and he left his followers in no doubt that he was to be the vessel of that spirit.

The object of education and discipline alike, at Putney and at Oneida, was the total abolition of selfishness – the tap-root of sin. By banding together in community the sectarians would 'condense', and so magnify, their good qualities, and establish their Community as a fit channel for ever greater out-pourings of the Holy Spirit. Noyes frequently asserted that the duty of his followers was to become as little children, not in the quality of their minds, but in their wills, which should be subordinated and humble. Every manifestation of the 'canker of egotism' was condemned and, in 1850, Noyes stated bluntly that, 'individuals are to the Association as lumps of ice in water, good for nothing only as they are melted into the water' (*The Free Church Circular*, May 1850, p. 118). Only by the destruction of his ego could the individual hope to be of service to God, and to attain true spiritual knowledge.

Noyes frequently remarked that he placed no reliance on codified systems of regulations as a means of inducing self-denial and the fusion of the individual into the greater 'public-spirit'. The pamphlet *Bible Communism* (1853), which was almost certainly entirely written by Noyes, stated that the regulation and discipline of the sectarians rested on 'religious influence', 'education' and 'free criticism'. The latter, more specific disciplinary technique, will be considered after a brief discussion of the implications of 'religious influence' and 'education', which in this context can be treated as synonymous terms.

In *The Berean*, Noyes had dismissed the observation of the Sabbath, together with the Decalogue and the sacraments of baptism and marriage, as legalisms, and insisted that his followers should regard every day of their lives as intrinsically holy. On the same grounds he eschewed set religious services, the nearest approximation to which were the daily evening meetings which Noyes bracketed with criticism as the sole instruments of governance in the Community.

Every member was encouraged to attend these meetings, and was liable to be reprimanded as selfish and 'possessing a private spirit' if he did not. The meetings generally lasted for at least an hour, and usually included discussions of perfectionist theology and social teachings, 'home-talks' delivered by Noyes himself, communal singing, stylized expressions of faith and submission and earnests of good intentions and good conduct. At the Sunday evening meeting attended by Nordhoff, orchestral music was played, hymns were sung, extracts from newspapers read, and a discussion was held on the healing power of prayer. At the close of this discussion, a large number of the members present made short, ejaculatory 'confessions' of 'the power of healing', 'a tender conscience', 'the power of Christ in my heart', and of other spiritual attributes and items of faith (Nordhoff, 1875, pp. 298–301). Such confessions, and longer accounts of 'miracles' performed by members of the group, and of special providences bestowed on the members, were frequently reprinted in the periodical.

Noyes's insistence that his followers should learn to see or read all events with 'the eye of faith' has been mentioned above, and in the periodical he frequently demonstrated his proficiency in this skill. Thus, a moral lesson against the development of special affections was drawn from the death of an infant, and a report of the arrest in New York of a man who threw acid on the dresses of women entering theatres, was made to serve a dual didactic purpose. It was interpreted as an illustration of the wickedness of great cities, and also as a 'criticism from the Lord' who disapproved of all 'costly array' (*The Circular*, November 1854, p. 615).

Such unremitting moralizing, in combination with reiteration of the principles of the sect, and assertions of the joys of the regenerate life, served to educate the sectarians and, presumably, to convince them of their superiority to the world, and of the happiness of their lot. However, Noyes and his lieutenants did not rely solely on affirmation and instruction to stamp out every manifestation of selfishness. Adults and children alike were encouraged to report any incidence of 'exclusiveness' or indiscipline to the central members, and individuals who transgressed were remonstrated with by one or more of the central members, and were to some degree shunned by their fellows until they had publicly 'confessed a tender conscience', and provided evidence of their remorse and renewed fusion with the 'public spirit'.

Mutual criticism

Noyes described the system of 'mutual criticism' as being the fulcrum of the Community. He claimed that the technique channelled hostility into socially useful directions, and disarmed gossipers, whom he described as 'the soldiers of the Devil'. The technique represented a development of the exercise he had engaged in with the Andover Brethren, and, although instituted at Putney, was elaborated at Oneida. Early in 1848 Noyes selected four judges who, after being individually criticized by Noyes himself, made enquiries regarding the conduct and spiritual condition of every member and then as a group criticized each individual in turn. Subsequently the practice evolved, and individuals volunteered for, or were requested to undergo, criticism, their examination being conducted by a committee of from five to twenty members, and occasionally by the whole Community. Criticisms were regularly held on Sunday afternoons, and were frequently reported verbatim in *The Circular*.

The critics appear to have concentrated on three major faults: want of repose or restlessness, levity and individualism. However, it should not be thought that the criticisms levied were couched in such abstract terms. Even the most minute aspects of the subject's conduct and attitudes were itemized and commented on by the 'practised tongues' of the critics. Thus individualism, the soul-destroying 'canker of egotism', was held to be manifested by a desire for privacy, by contempt for others, intellectual arrogance, laziness, spiritual pride, and also by such seeming peccadilloes as excessive sensitiveness, and fastidiousness in regard to food. Criticism was not entirely negative, the individual's good qualities were remarked upon, and he was frequently urged to be thankful for the beneficent influence of communal life which had engendered, or at least fostered, his virtues. The criticism was usually concluded by a balanced assessment of the subject's spiritual condition and prospects for moral advancement. The assessment was usually provided by Noyes, who appears to have offered himself for criticism on occasion, but failed to 'draw fire'.

The example of a criticism cited by Nordhoff is especially interesting as illustrating the tensions generated by the 'temporary monogamy' involved in the stirpicultural experiment. The subject, a young man, had volunteered for criticism, and had confessed a selfish attachment to the women who was to bear his child. He had, according to Noyes, struggled against this temptation, and on Noyes's advice had isolated himself entirely from the woman and had 'let another man take a place at her side'. Despite such self–denial, he was criticized for being over–fastidious, proud, insincere and insufficiently religious. Not altogether surprisingly, '. . . as the accusations multiplied, his face grew paler, and drops of perspiration began to stand on his forehead' (Nordhoff, 1875, pp. 290–3).

Prior to Noyes's move to Brooklyn, applicants for admission to the Community were accepted relatively indiscriminately; their acquaintance with perfectionist doctrines and willingness to travel to Oneida were taken as sufficient proof of their faith and sincerity. Inevitably the institution of criticism and the physical hardships endured by the sectarians in the early eighteenfi fties resulted in a number of secessions. From 1854, applicants for admission were only accepted after an informal probationary period of correspondence or visits and after having demonstrated their spirituality, and in some cases provided more tangible proofs of their devotion. Until the outbreak of the Civil War, the sufferings 'providentially administered' by God on the Community were primarily financial, but after 1860 there was growing dissatisfaction among the younger members, many of whom had been brought into the Community as children. As indicated, in 1860 Noyes had occasion to rebuke the younger members for their lack of appreciation of the joys of the ascending fellowship, and in the following decade such strictures and less specific expressions of misgiving became more frequent.

In 1870, by which year the conflicts and jealousies generated by the stirpicultural experiment were apparent, Noyes openly expressed anxiety concerning the future of the Community, and attributed its malaise to the corrupting effects of prosperity. After this date, the disaffection of the younger members rapidly increased, and the deterioration of Noyes's health and the relativization of his conception of the Community also shook the faith of many of the older members, and gave encouragement to those individuals who doubted his inspiration and resented his pre-eminence.

Social composition

In 1852, when considerable hostility to the sect was expressed in New York State, Noyes stated that he was not interested in proselytization. He described his writings as educational, and sought, through the medium of the periodical, to generate widespread intellectual and moral support for his religious and social theories as a necessary preparation for the imminent transformation of the world by the Holy Spirit. When sufficient men had demonstrated their eager desire for the 'final work', it would commence, and every manifestation of sin would be driven from the world.

After Noyes returned to Oneida in 1854, he insisted that the immediate task of the group was economic stabilization rather than numerical expansion. In the next decade, only a small number of persons were admitted to full membership in the sect. To the 'scattered believers', those subscribers to *The Circular* who were 'exposed to the deadly, oppressive influences of surrounding worldliness', and were denied access to the spiritual haven of the Community, Noyes had little to offer beyond vague evocations of 'the good time coming', and suggestions that they should demonstrate their faith by providing moral and financial support for the sectarians at Oneida.

As early as 1855, Noyes felt impelled to reply at length to a correspondent who had stated that a small and exclusive Community would make no significant impact on the world. Noyes insisted that rigorous selection of members was necessary if insincere applicants were to be eliminated, and stated that the immediate task of the group was that of establishing itself on an independent economic basis. In the same issue of the periodical he justified the group's reluctance to engage in charitable activities by reference to the will of Christ who, '. . . wishes to have us husband our means for wholesale operations, and not that we should be impoverished by the claims of needy individuals' (*The Circular*, June 1855, p. 91).

By the outbreak of the Civil War, the booming trap manufactury had removed the threat of financial disaster. Thereafter, as Noyes compromised his 'industrial principles' and employed large numbers of hired labourers, the prosperity of the sect steadily increased. On average about five new members were admitted to the Community each year after 1855, and, as the sect's attitude to the world became more markedly reformist, the sectarians came to regard themselves as an enlightened élite, far in advance of the mass of mankind who were slowly struggling towards regeneration and improved forms of social organization. Increasingly, the exclusiveness of the group was attacked by external readers of *The Circular*, and Noyes repeatedly published lengthy refutations of accusations that the sectarians were selfish and withdrawn, and indifferent to the problems of the common mass of humanity. In November of 1866, Noyes apologized for the slow growth of the Community, but insisted that its great achievement was that it had 'won the power to be', and stated that he had come to realize that the magnitude of the task of transforming the world 'required veterans instead of conscripts'.

A year later, after Guiteau had threatened the sect with legal action, Noyes announced that for defensive reasons the Community would decline all applications for membership under consideration, and all future applications, until further notice. Presumably, the task of establishing the degree of subordination necessary for the inauguration of the stirpicultural regime had taxed Noyes's energies to the utmost, and he appears to have recognized that his authority might be endangered by any considerable expansion of the group.

Shortly after the publication in 1870 of his *History of American Socialisms*, Noyes indicated that no new communities, or branches of old communities, could hope to be successful until the right human 'material' for their construction was abundant in the world. With reference to the situation at that date, 1870, he stated gloomily (*The Circular*, October 1870, p. 244):

> Owenites, infidels, Spiritualists, irresponsible 'free-lovers', and the riffraff of defunct Communities, stand ready to take possession of every social experiment.

After 1870, Noyes's reluctance to admit new members appears to have alienated many of his external sympathizers, and added fuel to the fires of those clerical opponents of the group who depicted the sectarians as living lives of luxurious promiscuity under a hypocritical cloak of religiosity and of professed interest in social reform. External hostility increased rapidly in the early eighteen seventies, and in 1874 Noyes admitted James Towner and the eleven members of his 'Cleveland family' to membership. Towner had corresponded with Noyes since 1867, when, as a qualified attorney, he had advised Noyes that he had little to fear from Guiteau's threats of legal action. As will be shown below, Towner and his relatively worldly followers became a centre of disaffection in the sect, and Towner himself aspired to overthrow Noyes, and to assume the mantle of his authority.

At the beginning of 1849, the total membership of the Community was eighty-seven. Twenty-nine persons were under the age of fifteen and the sexes were equally represented among the adults. By 1850, the membership totalled 172, but a year later had fallen to 150, and it seems likely that the intensification of the use of criticism in the sect, and the physical hardships and poverty suffered by the sectarians in this period, led a considerable number to secede. By 1860, the membership had risen to a total of 250, by 1874, to 270, and by 1879, after more than fifty stirps had been born, it had reached a peak total of 300.

The vast majority of the members were independent farmers or skilled artisans. Noyes cited members who had formerly been lawyers, teachers, editors and ministers, but also occasionally lamented the fact that men of substance and reputation remained aloof from the group. He does not seem to have dissented from Nordhoff's judgment that the members were largely drawn from among 'the better class of farmers', and he cited without comment an extract from a New York newspaper which described the sectarians, in 1867, as having an air of 'bookish rusticity'.

The male to female ratio was almost equally balanced throughout the first two decades at Oneida, but in 1874 there were about twenty more females than males in the group; a fact probably attributable to females' greater longevity.

Noyes sought to counter the scurrilous speculations of visitors and commentators by roundly denying that the sectarians were especially concerned to recruit young women. He stated that, on the contrary, he and his followers felt a considerable reluctance to accept unmarried women because of the 'jealousy' of the outside world. The majority of recruits entered the Community with their spouses, and the motives of unattached males who applied for membership were subject to close scrutiny.

In 1879, of the total population of 299 persons, 57 were under the age of ten, 26 between ten and twenty, 25 in their twenties, 48 in their thirties, 46 in their forties, 40 in their fifties and 57 over the age of sixty. The total of perhaps 35 young adults thus formed a small minority between the stirps, the supposedly morally and physically superior fruits of controlled breeding, and the mass of middle-aged or elderly members, many of whom had spent the greater part of their lives subordinated to Noyes's authority, and whose attitude to the world was largely compounded of distrust and contempt.

Economy

The expansion and fluctuations of the economy of the Oneida Community have been detailed elsewhere (see Parker, 1935, pp. 200 ff.); consequently it is necessary only to consider the general pattern of the economic development of the group, and the relationship between this pattern and the broader structural and ideological development of the sect.

In the course of the year 1848, Noyes established the rudiments of the network of labour departments and administrative committees which, in a greatly expanded form, persisted until the retreat from economic communism in 1881. Convinced that horticulture should be the basis of the Community, Noyes purchased land contiguous to Burt's original holding until, by 1853, the Community owned 235 partially cleared acres. The skills of the artisan members were employed in a wide range of minor craft industries: the manufacture of brooms, rustic seats, sewing silk, shoes, traps and, in addition, flour and lumber milling. Despite this variety of production, and the sectarians' frequently reiterated trust in Providence to provide for them in the period while they awaited the transformation of the world, the capital of the group dwindled alarmingly, until by the year 1857 only $67,242 remained of the $107,700 brought into the group by adherents.

The economic difficulties of the group were compounded by the death of the former Putney storekeeper, John Miller, who had managed the business affairs of the sect. In 1854, Noyes returned from Brooklyn to assume control of the Oneida Community, and to inaugurate a regime of purification as 'subjective preparation' for a fresh outpouring of the spirit and also, more mundanely, as an economy measure.

In the years after his return, Noyes sought to establish the group on a sound economic foundation but, in the uncertain economic conditions of the early eighteen fifties, he was initially unsuccessful. In these years Noyes lauded the virtues of industry and manual labour and, in keeping with his increasingly more gradualistic conception of the divine plan, he rationalized his search for a cure for the economic ills besetting the group as the third part of God's plan for the progressive redemption of the world through the Community. He stated that his religious and social teachings had reconciled man with God, and the sexes with each other, and that the third part of the plan was the reconciliation of capital and labour by the abolition of the 'hireling system', and of everything which rendered labour unattractive. In true ultraist fashion Noyes announced his scheme to abolish economic exploitation; employers should stop hiring workmen, but should rather make them full partners in their enterprises and 'take them into their families'. This ambitious panacea for industrial strife attracted little attention in the degenerate world.

The economic salvation of the Oneida Community was the trap manufacturing business which had been carried on in a small way since 1849, after Sewell Newhouse, a backwoodsman from the vicinity of Oneida Reserve, had joined the Community. Prior to his conversion, Newhouse had sporadically manufactured traps which, because of his secret method of tempering the springs, commanded a ready market. He was an independent individual, and initially refused to reveal his secret even to Noyes himself. The latter worked in the group's foundry in the first half of 1855, and either discovered Newhouse's secret process, or persuaded him to reveal it, and thereafter the trap manufactury was established on a regular, and greatly expanded, basis. Sales of traps boomed in 1856, and, though the group's net earnings plummeted to a nadir of under $2,000 in the wake of the industrial depression of 1857-8, after this recession the trap business flourished, and was the basis of the group's prosperity in the post-Civil War period.

The expansion of the trap manufactury was such as to lead Noyes to conquer his earlier, vehemently expressed, aversion to the hireling system of the world. In December of 1863, the demand for traps was so great that the group's school was temporarily closed and the children drafted for work, and by the end of 1864, forty hired hands were employed in the trap-shop. Subsequently, external labourers were employed in most other 'departments' of the Community. At the time of Nordhoff's visit in the early eighteen seventies, the number of external labourers almost equalled the total population of the two Communities. At Oneida, 201 men and women were regularly employed; 75 of the women in the silk factory, and 67 men in the trap-shop and foundry. At Wallingford, Connecticut (the only one of several small branch communities, established in the early eighteen fifties, to survive the period of financial retrenchment after Noyes returned from Brooklyn in 1854), thirty-five hired women worked in the silk factory. In addition a minimum of twenty farm workers were employed at the two societies, and external labourers worked in the Community kitchens, laundry rooms, furnace rooms and shoe and tailor's shops.

Nordhoff succinctly remarked of the prosperous sectarians that 'mere drudgery they nowadays put upon their hired people', but Noyes appears to have been uneasy about the sect's compromise with worldly ways, and justified the employment of labourers as a temporary measure, the need for which would cease as the world became enlightened and moved spontaneously to communism. More pragmatically, he also stated that the Community did a useful service by providing employment in good conditions and at good wages.

In 1870, Noyes expressed fears that the sectarians would become corrupted as their prosperity increased, and his fears appear to have been justified. Many of the older sectarians were very content with their comfortable lives, and lost, if not their faith, at least their 'crusading zeal'. In the case of the younger members, contact with the world, and in some instances higher or university education, led them to be 'infected' by agnosticism, or at least by scepticism, in religious matters. Externally, the Community's prosperity infuriated its opponents, who were enraged by the spectacle of vice unpunished and of 'licentiousness' combined with good living. Further, as already indicated, the group's exclusiveness, and Noyes's refusal to participate in charitable activities or practical measures for social reform alienated many of its sympathizers, whose views were epitomized by a correspondent who stated with sarcastic wistfulness (*The American Socialist*, January 1879, p. 33):

Could I have known of the Oneida Community before its soul departed, I might have been one of the selfish aristocrats who, from the secure heights of her Communistic walls, look down and enjoy the fratricidal struggle in the arena beneath.

Relations with the world

The predominant attitude of Noyes and his followers to the world outside the Community was one of contempt, aversion and moral superiority. The external society was corrupt; it was 'occupied territory' held by Satan, and subject almost totally to sin, disease and death. By contrast, the Community was regarded as God's stronghold in the world; a stronghold from which, when the time was ripe and Satan's grip on the world was loosening, the sectarians, God's soldiers and propagandists, would rally forth to its conquest. Pierrepont Noyes, speaking of his boyhood as one of the stirps stated (1958, p. 3):

> We Community children lived in a little world bounded on all sides by walls of isolation. We believed that outside those walls were philistine hordes who persisted in religious errors and social formulas under which they sinned and suffered. When I was a child the world 'outside' was a world of taboo.

The children were forbidden to speak to hired men or visitors, and adults who dwelt too much on worldly things were liable to be criticized for a lack of appreciation of the blessings of communal life. It must be emphasized that the sectarians' attitude to the world was not solely, but only predominantly, one of disdain and aversion, and that throughout the life of the Oneida Community Noyes and the other literati sometimes expressed their approval of persons, or social movements, who they believed were acting in accordance with God's plan for the world.

Although Noyes's attitudes became increasingly reformist, hostility to the external society continued to be expressed occasionally in the periodical, and by those simpler sectarians who could not comprehend the subtlety of God's later evolutionary plan for the regeneration of the world through the 'civilizing power' of the American nation. Hostility and fear of the world were given symbolic expression in the few hymns and ritual observances of the group. Thus, the most important 'Community Hymn', which was probably written during the introversionist 'industrial phase' of the late eighteen fifties, expressed the sectarians' conception of themselves as the unified, unrelenting enemies of the evil, exploitative world (*The Circular*, June 1862, p. 77):

> We will build us a dome
> On our beautiful plantation,
> And we'll all have one home,
> And one family relation;
> We'll battle with the wiles
> Of the dark world of Mammon,
> And return with its spoils
> To the home of our dear ones.

Still more explicit illustration of the belief that the Community was the dwelling place of the Spirit of God, and the world a place of corruption, is provided by the fact that persons departing from the Community for long periods customarily requested a criticism in order to draw 'sustaining power' from the whole communal 'family'. Conversely, returning travellers were given a purificatory spiritual 'bath' of criticism and (Estlake, 1900, pp. 60–1):

> After a rush of visitors, those who had been most exposed to contact with them usually offered themselves for criticism, that their spirits might be freed from contamination by worldly influences.

Before proceeding to the details of the sect's relationships with the external society, the broad pattern of the development of these relationships must be indicated. Noyes's conception of the sect's position *vis-à-vis* the world in the utopian years at Oneida and Brooklyn can be summarized by a single quotation (*The Perfectionist*, November 1843, p. 73):

> We are resident foreigners; citizens not of the United States, but of the kingdom of Christ; and as such we claim the protection of the government of the United States, while we disclaim allegiance to it, and participation in its evil deeds.

As Noyes became preoccupied with literary evangelism, his earlier vigorous denunciations of American institutions tended to be replaced by articles eulogizing the United States as the nation destined to 'civilize' the world, and so prepare barbarian nations for the reception of perfectionist religious and social teachings. After the Civil War, Noyes again became preoccupied with thoughts of large-scale and intensive evangelism, but his plans did not materialize, and his openly reformist interests and frequently professed sympathies with all progressive works, were channelled into the comparative study of American communal groups and the stirpicultural experiment.

By 1876, increasing indiscipline in the Community and his unremitting desire for widespread influence, had led Noyes to 'move beyond' the Oneida Community, and to attempt to establish himself as the person best qualified to guide and co-ordinate 'socialistic experiments', according to the inductive principles of the 'science of righteousness' – social science.

As indicated earlier, Noyes insisted that he was primarily concerned with intellectual evangelism rather than with active proselytization, and indubitably such statements were influenced by expedient considerations. Hostility to the group had arisen at Putney when it became known that they were not only practising complex marriage, but actively seeking converts to the system, and the early hostility in New York State appears to have been prompted, or at least rationalized, by fears that the Community might be a corrupting influence.

Between 1848 and 1853, Noyes openly publicized his social theories but, after his return from Brooklyn, caution prevailed, and persons enquiring about 'delicate' aspects of the sect's teachings were referred to earlier publications or, if sufficiently pressing and apparently sincere, were invited to visit or correspond with the Community. By 1867, prosperity, and the mistaken assumption that American society had become less prudish, had emboldened Noyes, and for some five years male continence and complex marriage were frankly discussed, and worldly marriage was excoriated in the periodical. Correspondence relating to these matters was terminated by the passage of the 'Comstock Laws' of 1873, which rendered illegal the transmission of information relating to birth control and other 'obscene' topics through the United States' mails. However, by this date, many persons had become enraged by the knowledge that in New York State, the cradle of the 'American Empire', a sect was practising and publicizing sexual arrangements even more offensive to orthodox morality than those of the Mormons.

Noyes's attitudes to other sects and to denominational religion became more moderate as his reformism developed, but on occasion something of the acidity of his earlier diatribes infused the generally approving, if patronizing, discussions in the later volumes of *The Circular*. He exhibited considerable interest in the Shakers, praised their moral qualities and discipline, and indicated (1875?, p. 29) that the decline of their membership would be halted, and mankind best served, if they would;

> . . . expend the vast fund of self-denial and cross-bearing purity which they have accumulated in celibacy on a conscientious and persevering effort to institute among themselves the noble art of breeding from the best.

Noyes continued to denounce secular 'Associationists' as misguided, and indeed, as perversely ignorant in their refusal to recognize the importance of 'earnest religion' as the basis for successful communal life, and to acknowledge his authority as doyen of 'social experiments'. The pages of *The American Socialist* gave considerable attention to such reformist movements as vegetarianism, feminism and anti-vivisectionism, and every aspect of the progress of such movements was taken as indicative of the slow, but cumulative, enlightenment of mankind. In addition, numerous articles dwelt on topics relating to bodily health, and the curative properties of exercise, special diets, and especially, as mentioned above, Turkish baths, were extolled by the ageing contributors to the periodical.

No significant conflicts arose as a result of the sect's economic activities; their products and business methods were highly regarded by all who dealt with them, and the employees of the Community enjoyed good wages and working conditions, and considerate, if extremely paternalistic, treatment. The sectarians did not vote, and paid the taxes required of them. Their attitude to war was equivocal; Noyes did not deny that some wars were justifiable, but was concerned to emphasize that his followers were reserved by God for more elevating and elevated struggles than simple physical combat.

Noyes's abolitionist sympathies have been indicated in the previous chapter. Although he condemned the intransigence of the slave-owners, prior to the outbreak of the Civil War he advocated that the South should be allowed to secede peacefully from the Union and, in 1859, he interpreted the failure of John Brown's schemes as, '. . . a pretty good indication that Providence does not favor armed interference on part [sic] of the North to free slaves' (*The Circular*, November 1859, p. 170).

However, once war was declared, Noyes proclaimed his sympathies with the Union, but also indicated that he and his followers 'certainly think that our best function is not fighting'. Owing to 'Providential protection', or to extreme good luck in the draft ballots, only two members of the Community were liable to conscription, and their draft-commutations were speedily paid. In May 1865, in an article on the Community's attitude to the Civil War, Noyes indicated that the group had paid 10,000 dollars in war taxes, in addition to state and county taxes quadrupled by bounty-levies, and added that the sectarians did not fight because they had not received orders to do so from the 'supreme Government of God'.

Noyes's statements that the Union Army was commissioned by God to scourge the evils of slavery and of southern aristocratic degeneracy, illustrates his belief that it was the destiny of the United States to civilize the world and to prepare its barbaric populations for 'Christ and Communism'. Thus, in 1853, at the height of his evangelical enthusiasm, Noyes discussed the state of the 'swarming inhabitants' of China, and stated that, aided by the freedom and energy of the American nation, 'our Social Theory we believe is destined in conjunction with the Bible, to work the civilisation of those nations' (*The Circular*, April 1853, p. 158).

Noyes favoured the annexation of Canada by the United States, and hailed American military triumphs against the 'inferior' Spanish peoples as being 'an illustration of the old Bible-doctrine of election'. In 1858, he predicted the march of empire into South America, and the conversion of its brutalized, degenerate population to true Christianity and communistic living. By such an expansion in addition to the already posited annexation of Canada, the American nation would unify the two continents in conformity with God's will. He asked (*The Circular*, March 1858, p. 34):

> . . . does not the finger of manifest destiny point to a time when the whole of this continent will be the home of an integral and united people.

After the Civil War, Noyes dwelt less on the impending conversion of whole nations to the gospel of holiness, and more on interpreting, and demonstrating his approval of, many aspects of modern civilization. Scientific discoveries, inventions, social reforms of various kinds and 'enlightened' changes in attitudes were alike seen by Noyes as steps forward in the march of human progress, a march led by the United States; the nation whose democratic constitution furthered this progress by permitting 'a thousand experiments' in 'socialism' to flourish.

Persecution and the disintegration of 'Bible communism'

The persecution which the sectarians suffered at Putney arose as a result of the breakdown of the secrecy surrounding their sexual arrangements, and because of their enthusiastic attempts to convert the young women of the neighbourhood. At Oneida, Noyes resolved on a policy of openness in regard to his social theories, but, as the sexual practices of the sect became widely known, considerable hostility developed in the vicinity of Oneida Reserve, and in 1850 complaints regarding the sectarians' 'immorality' were lodged with the local magistrates. The Grand Juries of Madison and Oneida Counties investigated these complaints, and apparently found no legal basis on which to proceed against the sectarians, but the members of the Oneida Jury informed Noyes and his followers that they would be well advised to leave the State. Some New York City newspapers echoed this criticism, but hostility died down after several important landowners in the area had signed a petition affirming the good conduct and reputation of the members of the Community.

Noyes's reaction to this hostility was compounded of panic and exultant evangelistic enthusiasm. From his eminence at Brooklyn he sought to disclaim responsibility for the Community, and, when the public obstinately persisted in associating him with his humble followers, he announced that because of the 'jealousy' of the surrounding population, he and his followers had decided to 'forgo' complex marriage. He stated (*The Circular*, March 1852, p. 66) that:

> the Oneida Association, and all Associations connected with it, have receded from the practical assertion of their views, and formally resumed the marriage morality of the world, submitting themselves to all the ordinances and restrictions of society and law on this subject.

In making this decision, Noyes seems to have been influenced in part by his tendency to retreat when faced by apparently stern opposition, and also by the conviction that the Oneida Community had demonstrated its principles sufficiently to render them irresistible when widely communicated to the world. In the article cited above, he stated that, by their abandonment of complex marriage, his followers had 'loosened their hands' for the attainment of the 'central object of a Free Press', and for the 'Abolition of death'. He added (*The Circular*, March 1852, p. 66) somewhat vindictively:

> Our present transition is like that of the insect passing from its chrysalis state revivified by experience, and shedding its envelopement. The forms that we leave behind are mere cast-off exuviae which the New York Observer may tear to pieces at its leisure. We shall be found elsewhere.

The present transition was not of long duration. In August of the same year, Noyes published his 'Theocratic Platform', a statement of the religious and social principles of the group, which included, among its other planks, the 'Abandonment of the Entire Fashion of the World and Marriage', and the 'Cultivation of Free Love', meaning, in the sect's terminology, disciplined and responsible communism of affections.

After 1854, Noyes was reticent about the details of his social theories, and in the next two decades the sect suffered little persecution, except from the leading questions of prurient visitors, and from the routine 'revelations' of scurrilous newspapers. However, in 1867 Noyes announced plans for a great expansion of the group's 'educational' activities, and for five years discussed sexual matters with a frankness which roused great hostility, especially among the clergy of New York State.

Clerical persecution – 'the Mears crusade'

An exception to the earlier statement that, as the years passed, Noyes's attitudes to other sects became more tolerant, must be made in the case of the Mormons. In 1858, Noyes had described the Mormons as a 'deluded and fanatical sect', but had advocated governmental tolerance towards them. In 1870, he stated that, for their obstinate persistence in polygamy, the Mormons deserved to be proceeded against by legal means. In 1862, an Anti-Polygamy Act had been passed by Congress, and since that date the United States government had been seeking to implement the Act among the Mormons by force and persuasion. Noyes's hardening of heart against the Mormons is attributable to the fact that, by 1870, some of the opponents to the Community bracketed its members with the Mormons as libertines and standing threats to public order and decency. Further, in 1870, the indignation generated by Guiteau's accusations was heightened by the publication of a book by J. B. Ellis, *Free Love and its Votaries*, which was primarily directed against Noyes and his followers.

The example of government action against the Mormons, and Noyes's open publication of his sexual theories, stimulated dormant hostility to the Community in New York State, originally among those Methodist clergymen who had been prominent in the anti-polygamy campaign. A paper denouncing the Oneida Community was read at a meeting of the Methodist clergy of Central New York State in August 1873, and by this date Professor John Mears of Hamilton College had emerged as the leader of the Community's opponents. In October 1873, the Synod of the Presbytery of Central New York appointed a seven-man committee, chaired by Mears, to investigate the Community, and in October 1874 the committee reported back on the teachings, sexual arrangements and generally good reputation of the Community. Not to be outdone as champions of public morality, the Baptists of Central New York State had also held a meeting, and had appointed a committee to co-operate in suppressing the Community.

An awareness of the good reputation and the apparent legal immunity enjoyed by the sectarians under the existing laws of New York appears to have damped the ardour of all but Professor Mears, the most obsessive of the 'crusaders', who, for several years lectured and petitioned against the Community. In January 1879, doubtless after having read the 'signs of the times' in the equivocation and dissent apparent even in *The American Socialist*, Mears called for a conference of all persons interested in putting an end to the 'impure emanations' from the Community. The conference was duly held at the University of Syracuse on 14 February 1879. On entering the hall, the delegates were handed copies of an article by Noyes which rejected all analogies drawn between the Community and the Mormons, and stated that the members of the Community had never forced their views on their neighbours or held the laws of the United States in contempt.

This document had no effect either on Mears, who opened the conference by calling for the extermination of the Community, or on the majority of the delegates, who condemned complex marriage as an 'outgrowth of vile passion', and the sect as a 'pernicious institution' which was based on 'a system of organized fanaticism and lust'.

The assembled clergy concluded that action must be taken against the Community for the sake of the morals of the State, and appointed a committee to consider possible measures. Reports of this conference engendered a considerable reaction in favour of the Community, and in March 1879 Mears was persuaded to moderate his aims from the 'annihilation' of the Community, to the abolition of its 'scandalous social custom'. On 29 June 1879, after a number of well-publicized meetings held *in camera*, Mears stated to the *New York World* that he and his associates meant to make a great moral effort to persuade the sectarians to abandon complex marriage, and if that failed, would seek special legislation from the State. However, by this date Noyes had fled to Canada, leaving his followers in a state of demoralized apprehension.

The abandonment of sexual and economic communism

Noyes's replies to the first attacks on the Community by the Methodist opponents of the Mormons were spirited. He dismissed the clerics involved as ignorant and intolerant, and stated in October 1871, that he was not disturbed by the opinions or machinations of the members of, '. . . an English sect, almost as fanatical and quite as bigoted as the Mormons themselves . . .' (*The Circular*, September 1872, p. 308).

However, in the course of the next few years, tensions and conflicts which had earlier been muted or suppressed by the insistence on unanimity in the group, were articulated and, while external opposition was encouraged by signs of dissension in the sect, such opposition increased the insecurity and doubts of the sectarians. After 1870, Noyes's authority over his followers declined as a result of several mutually reinforcing factors: his own failing health, the disaffection of the younger members and the mounting disillusionment and apprehension of the older sectarians including, most importantly, several of the central members.

As indicated above, after 1870 Noyes's health steadily deteriorated. He grew deaf, and could rarely speak above a whisper. His authority had rested on his followers' belief that he was commissioned by God to undertake a special mission, and that he was endowed with extraordinary powers, but by 1870 it must have been apparent to even his most devoted followers that his mission was unaccomplished, and that his powers were insufficient to preserve him from infirmity and encroaching old age. For years Noyes had 'lived' on the reputation derived from his past 'miracles', but, as has been shown, in the later volumes of *The Circular* the accounts of faith cures were perfunctory, and considerable attention was given to worldly medicine. Even the élite who contributed regularly to the periodical had come to put their primary trust in practical medicine, rather than in the power of Christ and krinopathy.

From the scattered discussions and strictures in *The Circular* for the years 1865 to 1870, it can be inferred that the increased emphasis on discipline prior to the inauguration of stirpiculture was especially resented by the younger adults, many of whom had been born in the sect and took its prosperity for granted. They formed a small and relatively cohesive group between the stirps and the middle-aged majority of the sectarians, and were not only especially exposed to the possibility of humiliating rejection as unsuitable material for stirpiculture, but also, if selected to form 'scientific combinations', were at risk in that they might, and frequently did, develop selfish affections for their partners.

In addition, the higher education received by many of the younger members had led some of them, including most importantly Noyes's eldest son, Theodore, to doubt the inspiration on which Noyes's authority rested, and even to doubt the validity of religion itself. There was no censorship of books and newspapers in the Community, and, while Noyes displayed an amazing capacity to reconcile scientific knowledge with his own conception of the divine plan, many of the scientifically educated younger men appear to have been unimpressed by his sophistry. Theodore Noyes was converted to 'positivistic' atheism by his reading and medical studies and by the Darwinian conflict which raged throughout the eighteen seventies, and he and other younger members appear to have regarded many aspects of Noyes's teachings as outmoded and irrelevant.

The failure of Noyes's health generated doubts among many of the older members, and led them to be uneasy regarding the validity of his claims to inspiration, and more particularly with regard to their own future security. Decades of relative ease and prosperity had undoubtedly led many of the sectarians to abandon their earlier zeal for the transformation of the world, but in addition, the faith of the more fervent members was shaken by Noyes's relativistic conception of the Community as 'only one form of socialism'.

The majority of the older members believed that the nature of heavenly society had been revealed to Noyes, and that their task, for the performance of which they would receive the gratitude of the world and eternal bliss, was to establish that form of society on earth. Many of the older sectarians were probably intellectually and psychologically incapable of the subtle reinterpretations of the divine will in which Noyes indulged. To these members the passing years brought only bewilderment and incomprehension. Harriet Worden spoke for many when she stated plaintively after the distintegration of the communistic structure of the sect (cited in P. Noyes, 1937, pp. 18–19):

> It was never, in our minds, an experiment; we believed we were
> living under a system which the whole world would sooner or later
> adopt.

The demoralization of the sectarians increased as the duplicity of some of Noyes's 'lieutenants' became apparent. William Hinds, Noyes's assistant on *The American Socialist*, nurtured and expressed grudges against him, and allied himself with the 'Towner family' who had been admitted in 1874, and who acted as informal *confidantes* to disgruntled members of the group. Such a role would almost inevitably have been forced on any apparently neutral person or persons who entered the group at this stage in its development, but Towner actively sought adherents with the ultimate object of usurping Noyes's authority.

Noyes responded to this range of challenges to his leadership by resentful condemnation of the Communities at Oneida and Wallingford as 'far enough from being paradisaic' models for the transformation of the world, and by concentrating more on his self-imposed role as leader of the American communitarian movement. He thus heightened the unease of the older sectarians and increased the indiscipline of the young, who chafed under their submission to the authority structure of a social system which even its founder had ceased to regard as the unique, divine blueprint for the world. By May of 1877, Noyes had succeeded in convincing himself that the importance of his editorship of *The American Socialist* outweighed, and was incompatible with, his leadership of the Community. He therefore conferred the Presidency on his son, Theodore, a man of thirty-six whose short incumbency greatly intensified the conflicts within the group.

In his personality and intellectual background Theodore Noyes was totally unsuited for the task of leadership of the sect, especially at such a troubled period in its history. He was naturally diffident, and was reluctant to assume command of the group. On so doing he sought to exercise his authority impersonally and bureaucratically, presumably in part as an attempt to circumvent his father's 'lieutenants', some of whom bitterly resented his elevation to the Presidency. Following his father's precedent, and in order to 'keep himself apart from the generality', he moved, with his consort, to New York and (P. Noyes, 1937, p. 161):

> It was not long before the surprised Communists found themselves regimented to such an extent that they were called upon to render written reports of each day's work or play in order that this ruling couple might know what was going on in the Community without personal contact or residence at Oneida.

Noyes and his followers had frequently expressed their horror of 'forms', by which they meant codified system of regulations, which to them smacked of 'legalism'. Consequently, the resistance to Theodore Noyes's half-hearted attempt to rule the Community at a distance was such that, after less than a year, *de facto* control of the Community was resumed by Noyes and the central members.

The elevation of Theodore Noyes to the Presidency, and his subsequent abdication, provided clear evidence of the unrest in the Community and stimulated the opponents of the group to fresh action. As already stated, in January 1879 Mears had called for a conference to debate means of exterminating the Community, and although Mears subsequently modified his statements and demanded only the abandonment of complex marriage, the threat of possible future legal action was sufficient to bring the conflicts in the group to a climax.

Pierrepont Noyes's account best illustrates the atmosphere of apprehension, indiscipline and recrudescent individualism which prevailed in the Community in the first half of 1879. Towner and Hinds and their followers appear to have threatened Noyes with the possibility of their providing the external enemies of the group with evidence which would enabled them to charge Noyes with statutory rape. (Although as Carden, 1969, points out, many of Noyes's opponents would also have been potentially subject to similar charges.) Such information does not appear to have been given to Mears, who spoke only of obtaining 'special legislation' against the Community, but, faced with internal opposition, factionalism, jealousies and threats of legislative action directed primarily against him as founder and leader of the Community, Noyes panicked, and allowed himself to be persuaded that for his own and the general good, he should leave Oneida.

Noyes fled to Canada on 29 June 1879, and Hinds, the assistant editor, took charge of *The American Socialist* which continued to be published until the end of the year. Noyes's departure threw his internal opponents into disarray, and the sectarians floundered without effective guidance until, on 20 August 1879, Noyes wrote counselling the abandonment of complex marriage. In his letter, Noyes indicated that the sectarians should be thankful for the past toleration accorded to their social arrangements, and proposed that, as a concession to public opinion, the Community should abandon complex marriage and adopt 'Paul's Platform' of tolerating marriage but preferring celibacy. Noyes emphasized that even after making such a concession to the world, the sect would still have its communal property, household, meals and arrangements for the rearing and education of children, and would continue to hold daily evening meetings.

The letter was read to the assembled sectarians on 26 August 1879, and they agreed, with one dissenting vote, to 'retreat from their social principles'. Complex marriage ended two days later. Many marriages took place in 1879, and the remaining communal arrangements rapidly collapsed before the 'individualistic impulses' which were generated by this outburst of the despised 'instinct of monogamy'. By June 1880, the 'administrative council' of the group, headed in Noyes's continued absence by Erastus Hamilton, had decided that communism was unworkable in a group composed of single individuals and monogamous families. After consultation with Noyes, an 'Agreement to Divide and Re-organize' was signed by all the adult members on 1 September 1880. Two weeks later a 'Plan of Division' was adopted (only Sewell Newhouse, who despite years of selfless subordination appears to have retained a measure of independence, opposed it) and the assets of the Community were redistributed by 1 January 1881, when economic communism formally ended, and the Oneida Community was reconstituted as a joint stock corporation.

The 'Plan of Division' provided that the Corporation was to maintain a free school, offer company jobs to members of the Community in preference to outsiders, and furnish non-profit-making accommodation in the main dwelling house to all who required it. More important, the assets of the Community were represented by 24,000 shares in the Corporation, each share having a par value of twenty-five dollars. Each adult member received sixty dollars in cash, shares equalling half of the value of the property he had dedicated to the Community, and four and one quarter shares of stock for each year spent in the Community since the age of sixteen. Each child was allotted one hundred dollars annually until the age of sixteen, and on attaining this age was given a cash grant of two hundred dollars to help with his education. Each person was allowed to retain a small amount of 'personal' property, and to buy the remainder if desired. In addition to his allotment, Noyes was awarded a pension of 150 dollars a month for life.

A board of nine directors had been appointed in November 1880, but bitter faction fights continued in the Corporation until the annual election of 1882, when the 'Townerite party' was decisively defeated and, subsequently, Towner and some thirty of his followers departed for California. From 1882, the majority of the directors were 'Noyesites', in that, until his death in 1886, they consulted Noyes about all major policy decisions.

Summary

After his expedient flight from Putney, and 'providential' arrival at Oneida, Noyes, who believed that God had entrusted him with the unique blueprint of heavenly society, commenced his task of establishing this society on earth, and of announcing its existence and merits to the world. In the period 1849 to 1854, he temporarily resolved the dilemma of the conflicting commitments involved in his utopianism by reserving the 'higher sphere' of literary evangelism for himself and a few associates. At Oneida the humbler sectarians laboured to construct a concrete demonstration of the heavenly life, while at Brooklyn, Noyes sought to galvanize the world by the proclamation of his religious and social principles. In these years the sectarians expected the imminent transformation of the world, and their attitude towards existing institutions, and to persons who refused to recognize the moral and social superiority of the lives led by the malnourished sectarians at Oneida, was one of contempt.

After five years of exemplary communitarianism and exhortatory intellectual evangelism, knowledge of the deteriorating financial position of the Community forced Noyes to concern himself with the routine matters of its administration. He seems to have realized that even the thrice-weekly publication of *The Circular* had made little impact on the 'tide of sin', and explained the failure of his evangelism by reference to the extreme corruption of the world, and also to the insufficent moral development of the sectarians, whose impurity was, in a sense, blocking the channel through which the Spirit of God was to pour out over the earth.

For five years Noyes concentrated on the task of establishing the sect on such a lucrative economic footing as would eventually enable it to support renewed, intensive, literary evangelism. In this pre-Civil War period the seeds of his reformist interest were sown. The impact of external economic conditions led him to consider the causes of industrial conflict, and to suggest ultraist, and essentially tautological, proposals for its resolution, but, from the last years of the war, large numbers of labourers were employed by the sect, and Noyes's earlier denunciations of the evils of the hireling system were expediently ignored.

After 1860, Noyes's conception of the nature of God's plan for the redemption of the world became ever more gradualistic, and his attitude to the world more reformist and conciliatory. He came to believe that the United States was the tool of God, destined to accomplish the civilization of all mankind. Concomitantly, in place of his earlier utopian conviction that the social arrangements and moral principles of the Community would rapidly spread throughout the earth, he came to believe that he and his followers were an especially enlightened and advanced group, whose morality and institutions 'foreshadowed' the state which the external society would achieve after a long process of cumulative improvement. The stirpicultural experiment indicated his loss of faith in the possibility of any rapid transformation of human society. The regenerate order might eventually be established as a result of the 'upward striving' of ordinary men, but its establishment would be hastened by the generation of a new breed of morally superior men to lead the human march to redemption.

Such exalted conceptions apart, it appears that, by the late eighteen sixties, the zeal of many of the sectarians to do battle with the 'wiles of the dark world of Mammon' had been diminished by prosperity and advancing age. For many of the members of the group life in the 'resurrection state' had ceased to be a challenge to constant spiritual improvement, and had become, despite their professed horror of 'forms', a matter of sedate and comfortable routine. After 1865, some of the contributions to *The Circular* began to betray a romantic and antiquarian interest in the early history of the group at Putney and Oneida, and documents and accounts relating to these stirring pioneer days were frequently republished.

The prosperity of the sect was not productive solely of complacency, although complacency, spiced with a sense of the moral superiority of 'the Communal Home', was evident in many of the articles in the periodical in the eighteen sixties. As indicated, Noyes himself was concerned that prosperity might have a corrupting effect on the sectarians. He strove to convince the readers of *The Circular*, and himself, that the sect was not settling into stagnant, exclusive inaction, but was really conforming to God's will in witnessing to the possibility of true Christian communism, while it awaited a fresh infusion of the 'divine afflatus' to the world.

Conflicts and dissension indubitably existed in the group throughout the eighteen fifties and early eighteen sixties, but many of the members who suffered doubts concerning the nature of Noyes's inspiration, or the future of the group, must have suppressed their anxieties or attributed them to 'evil spirits' preying on their own 'morbid imaginations'. Malcontents and potentially disruptive individuals were exposed to the withering blast of public opinion in the form of criticism, and after the Brooklyn period the number of persons annually seceding from the group approximately equalled those entering it.

The strictures and admonitions which appeared with increasing frequency in *The Circular* after the Civil War, were primarily aimed at the adolescents and young adults of the group, many of whom had been born in the sect, or brought into it as children. Indiscipline among this group posed far more serious problems for Noyes and his lieutenants than did recalcitrance among new members, which could be blamed on the corrupting influence of the world. The younger members of the group had, in some cases from infancy, received an education intended to inculcate 'softness of heart'. They had had the benefits of criticism from an early age, and of the ascending fellowship in their adolescence. They should, if Noyes's theories were correct, have been paragons of selflessness and subordination. Instead, many of the

younger members were 'sticky' in their affections, and resented their subordination to the dictates of the older members, who, as a group, were
presumed to be further advanced in spirituality, and hence endowed with
something of the reproving powers of the Apostles.

Those young sectarians who experienced the strains and tensions of
adolescence in an extreme form directed their rebelliousness against the
informal, but oppressive and pervasive, authority structure of the sect, and
intellectual rebellion was manifested in atheism or agnosticism, or less
coherently, but perhaps more destructively, in scepticism and cynicism with
regard to the joys of communal life. Further, the higher education received
by some of the young members led them to doubt whether the findings of
modern science could be readily subsumed under those of 'Bible-religion',
and they came to realize that social change might, for better or worse, be
brought about more quickly than through attendance upon the Spirit of
God. They learned that the world regarded their leader as, if not a licentious
and hypocritical fanatic, at best as dogmatic and deluded, and most damaging
of all, in relation to the much bruited march of human progress, totally
insignificant.

The indiscipline of the young, the unease of the older sectarians, and the
jealousy and ambitions of some of Noyes's lieutenants, increased and became
more evident, as Noyes's health deteriorated and as he sought refuge in
interests 'above', or removed from, the Community. The recrudescence of
significant external hostility was the catalyst which, in conjunction with
Noyes's ill-advised bestowal of the Presidency on his agnostic son, precipi-
tated the distintegration of the entire communistic structure of the sect.

Throughout all but the last years of his life, Noyes's control over the lives
of the sectarians and the structure and affairs of the Oneida Community
was almost complete. The Community was the embodiment of Noyes's
idiosyncratic religious and social conceptions, which have necessarily been
discussed extensively in the above two chapters. The complexity of these
conceptions, and every aspect of the history of the Putney and Oneida
Communities, reflected the complexity of the personality of their charismatic originator and founder. When discussing Noyes's intellectual development and actions, this very complexity renders it extraordinarily difficult,
but essential, to steer between the Scylla of cynicism and the Charybdis of
naïvety. In Noyes's personality, intellectual boldness and originality, sensuality and impetuosity, existed uneasily with physical cowardice, extreme
arrogance and a moral nature which, although unorthodox, was essentially
'legalistic'. In addition Noyes possessed shrewdness of such an intuitive and
practical type that it might better be termed 'horse-sense'.

Noyes was primarily a religious visionary, but a visionary possessed of
considerable scientific knowledge and 'secular' wisdom and ability. While
he claimed allegiance by virtue of his divine commission, he cemented the
loyalty of his followers (who were mainly self-educated farmers and artisans

– essentially practical men) by his forceful personality, intellectual capacity, and ability to translate his abstract religious conceptions into concrete, workable and satisfying modes of behaviour and social forms.

In 1900, Estlake stated that he had written his book on the Oneida Community, not to promote a new association, but to demonstrate the nature of the social changes which enlightened politicians might seek to bring about in the course of a few generations. Estlake glossed over the defects of Noyes's character and stated that Noyes was a man ahead of his time; the most important of God's messengers since Christ. With a facility which his mentor would have admired, Estlake exculpated Noyes from blame for the collapse of the Community, and transferred the burden of guilt to the corrupt and unappreciative inhabitants of the external society. Referring to Noyes, Estlake (1900, p. 5) stated:

> If he was too sanguine, it was because he credited Christendom with some earnestness in seeking the happiness it craved, and with a higher cerebral development than his critics put in evidence.

Chapter 6

A contemporary utopian sect –
the Society of Brothers (or Bruderhof)

The pacifist communitarian sect, known formally as the 'Society of Brothers', and more colloquially as the 'Bruderhof', today consists of three communities in the eastern United States, which together have a total population of between eight and nine hundred persons. In the half century of its existence, the sect has at various times established now defunct communities in Germany, Liechtenstein, England, Paraguay and Uruguay. The original community was founded in Germany in 1920 by Eberhard Arnold, who led the group until his death in 1935, and whose religious teachings and heirs continue to dominate the Society of Brothers.

Arnold was born in 1883 in Königsberg, East Prussia, in an academic, Lutheran family. According to Arnold's wife Emmy, as a child he displayed a warm sympathy towards tramps and poor people, and soon came into conflict with his parents, who were staunchly bourgeois in their social attitudes (Emmy Arnold, 1964, p. 6). At the age of sixteen, influenced by a clerical uncle of Christian Socialist persuasion, and after some contact with the Salvation Army, Arnold 'experienced Christ' and dedicated himself to the service of God and to social reform.

For several years after his conversion, Arnold associated with members of the Salvation Army. He spoke at their meetings, and participated in visits to the 'darkest taverns' of Breslau and to the 'submerged tenth' of the city's population. Despite such participation, Arnold did not join the Salvation Army, because he felt that the group's approach to social and moral problems was insufficiently radical.

On leaving grammar school, Arnold succumbed to his parents' insistence that he should study theology with a view to entering the Lutheran Church, and while at university he spoke for various inter-denominational groups associated with the radical wings of the Baptist and Lutheran Churches. In March 1907, at one such discussion, he met Emmy von Hollander, a probationer nurse from a background similar to his own. The couple were united by their somewhat vague, but exalted, religious enthusiasm, by their sympathy with the poor and by disapproval of their parents' style of life, and they became engaged within a month of their first meeting.

By 1908, Arnold appears to have decided against entering the State Church (primarily because he disagreed with infant baptism) and for this reason was disqualified from sitting for his first theological examination. In the following year, he received his doctorate from the University of Erlangen for a thesis on 'Early Christian and Antichristian Elements in the Development of Friedrich Nietzsche', and in December 1909 he married Emmy von Hollander. The couple were undeterred by the fact that Arnold had no secure source of income, but saw their marriage as a decisive step away from middle-class restraints. They wanted to put their lives into God's hands, 'entirely on the basis of faith' (Emmy Arnold, 1964, p. 15).

For the next three years, Arnold and his wife were supported by fees and collections from lectures, by various evangelical groups which formed the 'Fellowship Movement', and, to some extent, by their parents. In 1913, Arnold was discovered to have tuberculosis and, with his wife and two children and his sister, moved to the mountains of the South Tyrol. In this period of enforced retreat Arnold read widely, wrote articles for various inter-denominational periodicals and studied some of the sixteenth-century writings of the Anabaptists.

On the outbreak of the world war, Arnold was called to his reserve unit, but was discharged after short service with a transport corps. He rejoined his family in Halle, and in 1915 accepted a post as literary director of the publishing house of the German Christian Student Union. Arnold retained this post until after the end of the war, and in this capacity edited the monthly magazine of the Christian Student Union. In addition, he supervised the publication and distribution of a wide range of nationalistic reading matter for wounded servicemen and prisoners of war.

This work involved visits to military hospitals and to the families of servicemen, and in the course of these visits Arnold became more deeply aware of the variation in the treatment received by different ranks, and of the differing impact of the war on their families. Such experiences appear to have heightened his conviction of the corruption of the German upper classes and bourgeoisie, and after the Armistice, his interpretation of his duty as a Christian became increasingly radical. At Whitsun of 1919, Arnold attended the Marburg Conference of the Christian Student Union. He spoke passionately on the implications of the Sermon on the Mount, insisting on its 'unconditional absoluteness', and on the inadequacy of denominational translations of its principles. Some months later, at another conference, Arnold stressed that bearing arms was incompatible with Christianity, and stated that the duty of the Christian was to be a corrective of the state, and not its minion.

In the immediate post-war period, Arnold's dissatisfaction with the values and pretensions of bourgeois society grew steadily deeper, but for more than a year he was unable to decide on a concrete alternative to the middle-class style of life. He and his wife and associates shared the romantic notions of rural life, and the nostalgia for the vanished 'folk-community' which imbued the non-political youth movements of the period, and they variously contemplated the establishment of folk-schools, co-operatives and land-settlements.

By the winter of 1919, study of the Acts of the Apostles had convinced the Arnolds that any truly Christian community must be based on economic communism. In the spring of 1920, by which date Arnold had largely alienated the more orthodox directors of the Christian Student Union, he and his followers began to look for a site to establish such a community. The zenith of the nascent group's romantic, but unfocused, enthusiasm for the 'organic' life was reached at the 1920 Whitsun Youth Conference of the Student Union, which was held at Schlüchtern in Hesse. Some two hundred persons attended, many armed with guitars and violins, the girls wearing bright 'peasant' dresses. An atmosphere of spontaneity and naturalness prevailed (Emmy Arnold, 1964, p. 37):

> We would sit around on the ground forming a large circle, the girls with garlands of daisies in their hair, the boys in their shorts and peasant blouses. Outward formality and convention were cast off. We simply felt as men among men.

After this conference and visits to a Lutheran communistic settlement, the Arnolds travelled to the nearby village of Sannerz and inspected a large house, with orchards and a small area of agricultural land attached. Some months later, Arnold severed his connections with the Christian Student Union publishing house, and accepted an offer from his Christian Democrat associates to start a publishing house for them once the necessary funds had been raised. Encouraged by this proposal, and by receipt of a gift of 30,000 marks to establish a 'primitive church-community', Arnold and his family returned to Sannerz, and took a ten-year lease on the house which they had previously inspected. To seal their renunciation of middle-class habits of prudence and forethought, and to supplement their capital, they sold their insurance policies, and once again resolved to put their future entirely into God's hands. Five other adults joined the Arnolds shortly after they had concluded the rental transaction, and these seven adults, plus their children, formed the nucleus of the Sannerz Community.

The original members of the Sannerz Community, and all those persons who were subsequently admitted to the 'inner-circle' of fully committed members, believed themselves to be divinely commissioned to establish a community which would form the nucleus of the 'coming order' of God's Kingdom on earth. Arnold believed that such a community should support itself primarily by agriculture, and additionally by craft industries and publishing, the latter activity also serving to propagate knowledge of the sectarians' ideals and of their translation of these ideals into a 'living witness'. In addition, the 'Church-community' should demonstrate its concern for the plight of the world by maintaining a home for orphans, and by offering at least temporary refuge to persons who were oppressed by the 'evil forces' which were rampant in the external society.

The land at Sannerz was brought into cultivation in the autumn of 1920, but despite, or because of, their romantic idealization of the joys of the rural life, the middle-class sectarians were poor farmers. No attempt appears to have been made to initiate craft industries on any large scale in the first year at Sannerz; instead the central members were kept fully occupied with meetings and discussion groups, and with attempting to exorcize the 'evil spirits' and 'bad attitudes' manifested by many of the numerous visitors to the community. The group's financial position was precarious, but garden and orchard crops, occasional gifts from visitors, contributions from the members' families and a small income from the publishing house, enabled the sectarians to eke out the kind of frugal 'independent' existence which they thought appropriate to their calling.

Throughout summer 1921 visitors thronged the Community, and some participated in work camps to renovate the farm buildings and to clear fields. Arnold looked back to this period as one in which the rooms of the Community were filled with the power of the Holy Spirit, and at least some of the guests came to share the central members' conviction that their group was a beach-head of the Kingdom of Heaven in the world (anon., 1964, p. 5):

> ... whoever really had the vision that saw into the depths and could look into men's hearts inevitably realized that here there was a spiritual mission of the gospel and the church of Jesus Christ, a mission station right in the middle of a Germany, a central Europe that was pagan and yet under the visitation of God.

Throughout Germany, by the spring of 1922 the enthusiasm of most of the other post-war religiously inspired 'life-reform' groups and evangelical fellowships had collapsed, and many of their members had reunited with the denominations, resolving to leaven them from within. At the 1922 Whitsun Conference of the Christian Student Union, many of the delegates condemned the unworldly utopianism of Arnold and his followers. In addition, throughout 1921 and 1922 the group at Sannerz received many visits from members of the political youth associations, who variously accused the sectarians of being irresponsible, idealistic, parasitic and, most wounding of all, of being essentially and inescapably bourgeois.

In July 1922 (by which date some fifty persons resided at Sannerz) Arnold and his family accepted an invitation to spend a month's holiday in Holland. While they were there, the rapid inflation of the mark led many of the persons who had invested in the Sannerz publishing house to call in their money, and the Arnolds received frantic letters from their followers in Germany. However, Arnold 'received the inner certainty' that he should not allow his calm to be interrupted, and remained in Holland for the planned period.

On the Arnolds' return to Sannerz, they found that the publishing house had been put into liquidation, and, at a hastily convened meeting, were accused of gross irresponsibility, economic ineptitude, secretiveness and misrepresentation.

At the close of the meeting some forty persons decided to leave the group, and departed as soon as they could find accommodation and employment. By October 1922, only Arnold and his wife and five loyal followers, together with their children, were left at Sannerz. This mass defection was interpreted by the Arnolds as a demonstration of the power of worldly evil – of 'Mammonism'. Arnold stated that the seceders became enemies of the true way of life because they rejected unity in submission to the spirit of God, and (Emmy Arnold, 1964, p. 81):

> . . . because they wanted to go back again into ordinary middle-class
> life, to normal private life and their own pocket book. At the time, the
> movement was led into bondage again through the middle class
> influences of capitalism and its business and professional life.

After this nadir of the group's fortunes, its numbers slowly increased. The sectarians were not entirely destitute as some money was forwarded to them by sympathizers in Holland, and in 1923 publishing was resumed under the imprint of the 'Eberhard Arnold' publishing house.

By 1926, as a result of the accession of a few converts, the continued adoption and temporary fostering of children and natural increase, the total population of the Community had risen to about forty-five persons and more extensive accommodation was needed. Eventually, the sectarians discovered the 'Sparhof', near Fulda, in the Rhön mountains, a dilapidated farm on poor, high ground. Ten thousand marks down payment was required, but as the group lacked such a sum, it was decided in 'the Brotherhood', the inner, secret assembly of the full members, to proceed with the purchase on the basis of faith, and accordingly the contract was signed. The sum required was 'providentially' received from a sympathizer a few days later, and by early 1927, the group had removed completely to the Sparhof, which was subsequently renamed the 'Rhönbruderhof'. (The name 'Bruderhof' and the term 'hof' for an individual community were adopted by Arnold after he encountered them in his studies of Anabaptist writings.)

Religious teachings

Eberhard Arnold did not attempt to develop a completely distinctive theology. He regarded himself as inspired by God to proclaim the continuing practical relevance of certain passages of scripture (especially the Sermon on the Mount and sections from the Acts of the Apostles), and to establish and promulgate a form of society based solely on Christ's ethical teachings.

However, despite the sectarians' insistence that their common life was inspired directly by the Spirit of God, Arnold's religious teachings can be seen to embody (in an extreme and simplified form) many of the characteristics of the 'dialectical' theology which was elaborated in Germany after the First World War. More broadly still, Arnold's teachings and ideals, and consequently the whole style and tenor of life in the Bruderhof communities to this day, were influenced by his participation in, or belated identification with, the German 'Youth Movement'.

The exponents of 'dialectical' or 'neo-orthodox' theology wrote in reaction to the 'liberal' theology which was predominant in nineteenth- and early twentieth-century Germany. At the risk of superficiality, it can be stated that the liberal theologians decreased the orthodox emphasis on the supernatural and eschatological aspects of Christianity; said little of the nature of God, and much of 'Jesus the man'; encouraged an evolutionary and relativistic approach to the study of religion, and sought to reconcile religion with scientific knowledge. Their thought developed in concomitant and apologetic relation to the individualistic, capitalist, middle-class society of nineteenth-century Europe. Nowhere was this rationalistic, 'de-mystifying' approach to theology and to the study of religious phenomena more highly developed than in Germany in the second half of the nineteenth century.

In the chaos and confusion of post-First World War Germany, dialectical theology represented a reaction to the compromises and essential 'man-centredness' of liberal theology, and can be understood as part of the widespread intellectual rejection of the values of bourgeois Germany. Dialectical theology dismissed all anthropomorphic conceptions of God and asserted his 'otherness'; stressed the corporate nature of Christianity; insisted on Christianity's essential immunity to invalidation by science; reasserted the actuality of the future coming of Christ; emphasized that Christian duty necessarily involved suffering, and insisted that the paramount duty of the Christian was to attend and act upon the word of God, as revealed through the actions and teachings of 'Jesus the Christ'.

As already indicated, Arnold shared fully in the distaste of many of his contemporaries, and especially of younger Germans, for the values and style of life of the middle classes of Wilhelmian Germany, and more specifically he condemned denominational condonation of individualism in all its aspects. Like the dialectical theologians (with whom his followers bracketed him) Arnold stressed the 'objectivity' of the Christian message, emphasized that the way revealed by Christ necessarily involved suffering and complete subordination to the will of God, and asserted, in an extremely radical form, the essential community of lives of Christian witness. It is not suggested that Arnold established the community at Sannerz as an enshrinement of ethical principles derived purely from the study of dialectical theology, but rather that his thought was subject to some of the same influences as that of the dialectical theologians, and that the post-war theological revolution was one context of the development of his religious teachings and ideals.

While the development of dialectical theology can be understood as the reaction of religious intellectuals to the self-confidently militaristic, nationalistic and bombastic society of late nineteenth- and early twentieth-century Germany, the development of the 'free' youth movements appears as a juvenile reaction against the values and life style of the urban middle classes.

The free youth movements, those originally loosely organized by young people themselves (as distinct from the 'youth tutelage' movements of the denominations and political parties), originated in the mid eighteen eighties. The founder of the pristine movement, the Wandervögel (Roamers), was a schoolboy, Karl Fischer, who rejected the evocatively termed 'culture of the sofa' of his middle-class parents. Fischer organized the more idealistic, or more disgruntled, of his associates into bands of Roamers, groups of adolescents who scorned urban life and revelled in the freedom which they found in hiking, and in pitting themselves, for weekends at least, against nature.

The movement expanded rapidly, until by 1911 the Roamers totalled perhaps 60,000, but they were splintered into numerous groups which differed in the degree of their rejection of bodily comforts, in their sexual inclinations, and in the extent of their rebellion against adult society. These variations aside, the members of the various groups of Roamers were alike in their distaste for their overwhelmingly middle-class origins; in their nostalgia for a vanished 'folk-community'; in their consequent aspirations to 'solidarity' with the peasantry and positive estimation of 'spontaneity' and 'naturalness'; and in explaining their general aimlessness in terms of a quasi-mystical desire to 'get to the bottom of things'.

By 1913, the Free Youth Movement had grown sufficiently to attract the attentions of the youth tutelage associations, many of which pirated the less threatening aspects of the free movements' culture – their picturesquely 'natural' clothing, their hikes and campfire sing-songs, and adult-free meeting places. In October 1913, in an attempt to reassert their distinctiveness, the free movements organized a conference of all sympathetic groups at Hohe Meissner. At this conference the vast majority of delegates merged their groups into a loosely structured federation of 'Free German Youth', and subscribed to a vague confession which stated that the members were determined to shape their lives independently and would take 'united action' to protect their freedom to do so.

This seemingly innocuous statement was deemed threatening by the adult world, and Gustav Wyneken, who had emerged as leader of the Free German Youth, was vilified as a homosexual by members of the Bavarian Catholic Centre Party. Consequently, in May 1914, a more conciliatory confession was adopted, which paid tribute to the store of values transmitted by the adult world. Some months later many of the Hohe Meissner delegates established their devotion to Germany by being killed in the first battles of the world war, reportedly going into action singing songs from *Pluck-Fiddle Jack*, the folk-song hymnal of the Roamers (see Becker, 1946).

Arnold and his wife do not appear to have participated at all extensively in the pre-war free youth movements, but after the war they acknowledged the original Hohe Meissner confession, and regarded themselves as members of the radical wing of the Free German Youth. As will be shown, spontaneity, naturalness, simplicity and humility are all greatly valued in the Bruderhof, and the manner in which these virtues are demonstrated today exhibits the lingering influence of the culture of the German Youth Movement. Despite their age (Arnold was thirty-six in 1919, and his wife thirty-five), throughout 1919 the Arnolds shared the feelings of dissatisfaction and exaltation which characterized the adolescent members of the Youth Movement. However, by mid-1920, Arnold's conception of his mission had crystallized, and the mass defection from Sannerz in 1922 did not serve to change his ideas, but only to deepen his conviction of the corruption of bourgeois society. Arnold's specific religious teachings can best be considered in terms of his understanding of the nature of evil; his interpretation of the characteristics of the Primitive and Early Churches; the idea of 'organic community', and his conception of his mission.

Arnold believed that the world was the principality of evil, the domain of Anti-God whom most men worshipped in preference to God. Anti-God, or Mammon, stood 'in contradiction to the future and to eternity', in that, while the distinction between good and evil would persist in all eternity, Anti-God was destined to be replaced in the world by God, the fount of all goodness. Arnold, who believed that the world was 'quite literally peopled . . . by death-bringing spiritual beings' (anon., 1964, p. 121), stated that the spirit of Anti-God and his demonic minions was manifested in all forms of violence, in lust, deceit, greed and in private property – the quintessence of greed (anon., 1964, p. 19):

> The poisonous root of private property is disintegration, death and corruption. Private property arises through self-isolation, through the self-seeking of the covetous will. Private property brings a curse with it; there is a lack of relationship of individuals one to another and of the individual with God. . . . Humanity lies in agony, on the verge of death, and the most obvious sign of its mortal sickness is private property.

Arnold especially condemned capitalist society, which he felt glorified individualism and acquisitiveness, and destroyed the capacity for men to enter into selfless relationships, and so estranged mankind from God.

There is a marked similarity between Arnold's condemnation of the evils of capitalism, and his implicit evocation of a past era when all human relationships were characterized by fellowship and effect, and the youthful writings of Karl Marx, but Arnold consistently opposed political, and especially violent, remedies for the evils of bourgeois society. Such solutions he felt were also destructive of community and of personal relationships. Arnold admitted that Marx, and Marxists, had some appreciation of the great truth of man's loss of 'organic community'. He praised the 'revolt of the spirit' which underlay Marxism, and the vision of a future community of men which inspired Marxists, but he condemned their denial of the power of the Spirit of God, and their elevation of material considerations to supreme importance.

Having rejected the claims of revolutionaries and secular utopians to be able to inaugurate an era of qualitatively different human relationships, Arnold asserted that the overthrow of Mammon, and the consequent establishment of world-wide fellowship, would only come about through the action of Jesus Christ, who would eventually overthrow and drive from the world the 'powerful and dark spirit' of Mammon (Arnold, 1939a, p. 78). Arnold denied that he and his followers were 'utopians' in that they were looking to a future which would never come, but stated that the eradication of evil was imminent, and that by this act the world would be eternally transformed and redeemed (Arnold, 1939a, p. 27):

> This earth will become like one land, one garden, where one
> righteousness and justice and one joy, one truth and one purity of
> mutual relationships, hold sway; so that only then shall joy really begin
> on this planet. This planet, the Earth, must be conquered for a new
> kingdom, for a new order, for a new unity, for a new joy.

Arnold considered himself to be an instrument of God, commissioned to do His will on earth in obedience to the promptings of the Holy Spirit. As such an instrument, he was the most recent of a line of persons and groups who had received some measure of the Spirit since the time of apostasy of the Early Church. Arnold and his followers acknowledged their brotherhood with the prophetic Montanists; with the 'genuine monasticism' of the early centuries of Christianity, the itinerant community of Francis of Assisi, the Bohemian and Moravian Brethren, the early Quakers, and especially with the 'ethically pure' original Anabaptists of the sixteenth century (Arnold, 1967, pp. 6–7). All these groups were to be revered for their sacrifices for Christ, but none were so important as ethical and organizational exemplars as the Primitive and Early Churches. Arnold devoted much time to the study of the Early Church, and concluded that its essential characteristics, those in accordance with the 'leadings' of the Holy Spirit, were openness, communism, purity, pacifism and unity.

Arnold stressed that the Early Christians (whom he broadly termed 'apostles') had been charitable. Their larders and stores were at the disposal of all wayfarers, who were welcomed lovingly and warmly. He emphasized that the apostles had recognized their obligation to work, and that they were characterized by their 'equality in poverty and in the grace which answered it' (Arnold, 1939b, p. 44). All who sought to witness to a truly Christian life should similarly be charitable, diligent and communistic, and should demonstrate their humility and equality in simplicity of dress, manners, artifacts and every other aspect of their lives.

The Early Christians, or at least those whom Arnold judged to have given a 'true witness', attached great importance to purity, and maintained complete continence prior to, and faithfulness after, marriage. Arnold extolled the joys of family life, and described the monogamous family as the necessary foundation for 'the building of all human fellowship and association' (Arnold, 1939b, p. 54). While Arnold considered monogamy to be the only form of sexual relationship compatible with Christianity, he did not regard a marriage as a partnership of equals. From his study of the Early Christians Arnold concluded that the duty of women was to be 'loving, loyal and quiet'. The wife would influence her husband, but could in no way lay claim to exercise the 'chief authority' in the relationship (Arnold, 1965a, p. 32).

Arnold taught that complete pacifism and non-resistance was the duty of all Christians, and that they should in no way actively uphold 'the order of Law'. They should not act as judges or officials, or vote, or hold political office. However, he recognized the necessity for the state as a temporary institution which had vital functions to perform in the period before the establishment of God's coming order over the earth.

The above paragraphs implicitly indicate Arnold's vision of the future of mankind, which was, in God's time, to become united in an 'organic community'. For Arnold the tragedy of the modern world was that man had become increasingly individualistic, and set his petty desires above those of God. Arnold described individualism and egoism as states of putrefaction of the fellowship which was the true destiny of mankind. Individualism, manifested in the 'covetous will', represented the 'advanced decomposition of the context of life' (Arnold, 1938, p. 20). In consequence, the lives led by most men in contemporary societies were totally divorced from the lives which all men consciously or unconsciously desired. Community, implying the total subordination of the individual will to that of God, was the underlying goal of all the best efforts of mankind – 'the secret of life is expansion, movement, community and reciprocity. Life is the conquest of isolation through community' (Arnold, 1938, p. 9).

In the future, when God's will was done on earth, there would be no more 'isolated questions', no factionalism, no social stratification, no privilege or exploitation, and most fundamentally, no life-destroying individualism. All mankind would eventually be bound together in ego-less harmony, united by Agape, the love stemming from the spirit of God.

Arnold's religious teachings were explicitly this-worldly; he castigated those persons who concentrated their efforts on the attainment of other-worldly salvation, and condemned the 'grandiose misunderstanding' of Christ's mission which led the denominations to restrict themselves to the solitary redemption of the individual. Arnold urged his followers to delight in life and in all natural things, and said little of the future existence of the individual soul, but insisted that his followers should concentrate their efforts on realizing God's plan for the transformation of the earth.

The task of all members of the Bruderhof was to establish and expand the Church-community, as a demonstration of the coming Kingdom. Arnold cautioned his followers to guard against arrogance, and to remember their absolute dependence on God's spirit, as the only mortar which held together the fabric of their societies. While the individuals composing the Church-community were unimportant *qua* individuals, the continued existence of God's 'mission station' on earth was only possible through the regeneration and spiritual rebirth of the members of the group. The rebirth of individuals was to be manifested in their total renunciation and subor-dination of their querulous, covetous, impure, individualistic personalities. The task of the sectarians was to render their lives as far as possible perfect witnesses to Christ, and so to transform themselves into 'cells' or 'building-blocks' suitable for utilization in God's Kingdom.

Arnold did not only commit the Bruderhof to witnessing to the possibility of leading lives of true Christian fellowship on earth, but also to 'conquering the earth', and 'to winning back the garden' from Anti-Christ. Translating Arnold's metaphors, he taught that the mission of the sectarians was to establish unity, purity and selflessness in their communities, and to evangelize. Their task was not simply to maintain the beach-head of God's Kingdom, but to be, in a sense, offensive. They were to wage war against Mammon, and carry the war into Mammon's stronghold - the world. The Church-community was to be a 'fighting church', engaged in a constant struggle with the evil powers which raged without, and which sought constantly to penetrate the sect's defences and bring it to apostasy.

Believing himself to be divinely commissioned to extend the coming order of God, Arnold condemned introversionist groups which 'hid their light', and stated explicitly that the members of the Bruderhof should actively seek converts and should extend brotherly aid to distressed persons in the world. In a letter written a few days before his death in November 1935, Arnold in a sense recommissioned the Bruderhof as a utopian sect. He de-plored the limited nature of the group's evangelism and counselled his fol-lowers to take an active interest in all partially enlightened social movements, without 'being infected by them', and to demonstrate their understanding of the root causes of distress and social unrest.

The religious teachings of Eberhard Arnold remain the canon of the Bruderhof. No aspect of his teachings has been repudiated by the sect. No subsequent leader has done more than reiterate and reaffirm his teachings. The publications of the groups in England and the United States have very largely consisted of translations of Arnold's works, and of the source-books of Christian witness which he and his associates compiled in the last decade of his life. The members of the Society of Brothers thus remain utopian in their ideological commitment to the maintenance of internal purity, and to evangelism and an active response to 'movements of the times' in the external society. To use the terminology at present current in the Bruderhof, they are committed both to 'creative withdrawal' and to 'out-reach'.

Despite this persisting formal dual commitment, for about fifteen years after 1941 the majority of the sectarians were settled in Paraguay, in a region so remote, and a culture so divergent from their own, as to preclude more than a minimum of evangelistic activity and success. Since 1962, after a prolonged period of 'purification', in the course of which the total population of the group was halved, and as a result of which, all the communities outside the United States were eventually abandoned, the posture of the sect *vis-à-vis* the world has become increasingly introversionist. In recent years few persons have been admitted to the sect, the total population of which has increased only slightly in the last decade, despite a very high birth-rate.

The above paragraph has unavoidably telescoped and distorted the development of the sect in the thirty-four years since Arnold's death. Before examining the formal structure of Bruderhof communitarianism, and the sect's relationships with the world, it is necessary, in view of the repeated migrations and geographical dispersal of the group, to present a summary of its history from the time of the establishment of the Rhönbruderhof.

Historical overview – 1927–1970

The move to the Rhönbruderhof in no way mitigated the group's economic difficulties, and in the five years after 1927 the sectarians suffered great poverty, and much of their property was confiscated by bailiffs in lieu of settlement of various minor debts which had been contracted 'in faith'. Their land was poor and exposed and yielded only very meagre crops, and the health of many of the members was adversely affected by an inadequate diet and strenuous labour. Despite poverty, the group continued to foster children, and, in accordance with their 'open-door' policy, offered hospitality of a kind to all who visited them.

Throughout the late nineteen twenties Arnold and his associates published a series of 'source-books' of Christian witness, and in the course of research for this work, studied some of the early writings and accounts of the Hutterian Brethren. The members of the Bruderhof were struck by the similarity of their own doctrines to those of the Hutterites, and were excited to discover that the descendants of these pacifist Anabaptists were living in relatively prosperous communities in Canada and the United States. In 1928, fired by a complex mixture of evangelical and financial motives, the sectarians wrote to the Hutterites expressing their conviction that the Hutterians were true witnesses to the Holy Spirit, and their desire to unite with the Hutterian Church. (On the Hutterites see Peters, 1965, Bennett, 1967, *et al.*)

The members of the Bruderhof were disappointed by the Hutterites' unenthusiastic response to their letter, but after a protracted correspondence Arnold was invited to visit them. Early in 1930 he travelled to North America, and for more than a year journeyed between the communities, seeking to gauge the spiritual qualities of the Hutterites, to convince them of his sincerity and to raise funds for the Society of Brothers. On 9 December 1930 Arnold was received into the Hutterian Church, and ten days later, was confirmed as 'Minister of the Word' or 'Bishop' of the Hutterian Church in Germany (see the appendices to Arnold, 1940b.)

Arnold appears to have been disappointed by the Hutterians' response to his appeals for money, but after his return from America the group's financial worries were eclipsed by the increasingly threatening political situation in Germany. After Hitler's elevation to the chancellorship of the Reich in 1933, educational and religious establishments and communities were subjected to compulsory 'Nazification'. In the plebiscite held in November 1933 the members of the Bruderhof declared, by gumming statements of their views on to their ballot slips, that they could only support and acknowledge a government appointed by God. Four days after the ballot (which appears to have been the only occasion on which the sectarians have voted) the Rhönbruderhof was searched by police and stormtroopers, and many papers were confiscated. A month later the group's school was closed on the pretext that the patriotic instruction provided was insufficient, and shortly afterwards, the sectarians sent their children to sanctuary in Switzerland.

In February 1934, Arnold and his wife travelled to Liechtenstein, and rented a summer hotel near Triesenberg, which they rechristened the 'Almbruderhof'. This community provided a refuge for the children of the group and, temporarily, for those young men who were liable for military service.

In the summer of 1935, Arnold travelled to England to explore the possibility of establishing a community there, and to raise funds among his pacifist correspondents. Throughout his stay in England he suffered severe pain from a leg he had fractured in 1933 and which had remained unhealed. In November 1935, Arnold entered a hospital in Darmstadt to undergo an operation to re-set his leg. Complications developed, necessitating amputation, but Arnold did not recover from this operation and he died on 22 November 1935.

Arnold's death exacerbated the tensions and conflicts which had arisen in the group at least in part as a result of its incorporation with the Hutterites, but the majority of the sectarians were united by their desire to escape from the threat of Nazi totalitarianism. By 1936, it was apparent that Liechtenstein would not long provide sanctuary for pacifist Germans, and in October of that year, the group purchased a two-hundred acre farm in England, at Ashton Keynes in Wiltshire. The Rhönbruderhof was closed by the Gestapo in April 1937, under a law prohibiting 'communistic disturbances'. The

Almbruderhof was closed in March 1938, by the end of which year some thirty to forty adult English converts had been made, and the 'Cotswold' Bruderhof at Ashton Keynes had a total population of 210 persons, ninety of whom were children. A year later, the 'Oaksey' Bruderhof was established on a farm in the vicinity of Ashton Keynes.

As refugees from Nazi persecution the sectarians received a warm welcome and considerable financial aid from a variety of pacifist groups and, convinced that their escape was providential, they embarked enthusiastically on recreating Arnold's vision of the Church-community. However, after England's entry into the war, many of the neighbours of the sectarians became bitterly antagonistic towards them. (For more detail of this period see Whitworth, 1971.) Faced by local hostility and demands for the internment of the German majority of the membership, the Bruderhof negotiated with the British Government, and received permission to emigrate to Paraguay, the only country which would accept them and which offered freedom from conscription, freedom of conscience and abundant cheap land. In the first weeks of 1941, approximately 350 sectarians sailed for Paraguay, leaving behind three English converts to supervise the disposal of the group's properties.

The last party of sectarians arrived in Paraguay in May 1941, and, shortly after this date, the group reassembled in east Paraguay on the 21,000-acre 'Primavera Estancia' which the group had agreed to purchase for some £4,500. The sectarians suffered severely from a variety of tropical diseases, and from a strange and inadequate diet, but with help from Mennonite neighbours, soon established two hofs on their property: 'Isla Marguerita' and 'Loma Hoby'. Subsequently, a third hof, 'Ibate', was established at Primavera, and a hospital was built at Loma Hoby which extended its services freely to the local Indians. By 1951, the total population of the Paraguayan hofs had risen to more than 600, almost entirely as a result of natural increase. In 1952, a small hof, 'El Arado', was established near Montevideo, in Uruguay.

It had been intended that the members who were left in England should travel to Paraguay as soon as the sale of the Ashton Keynes properties was completed, but the negotiations were prolonged, and by Christmas 1941, this residual group had been joined by sixteen other adults and children. The British Government was unwilling to grant them permission to travel to Paraguay, and accordingly, after correspondence with the Paraguayan hofs, in 1942 a farm was purchased near Bridgnorth in Staffordshire, and the 'Wheathill' Bruderhof was founded. By 1950, as a result of evangelism, natural increase and the return of a number of members from Paraguay, the population of Wheathill had risen to a total of almost 200 persons. In 1958, the 'Bulstrode' community was established near Gerrards Cross, Buckinghamshire, on the fringe of London.

During the first decade of the existence of the Paraguayan hofs, and of the 'revived' Bruderhof in England, the members were primarily concerned with establishing the communities on a viable economic basis, and had little money or energy to spare for evangelism. However, in the early nineteen fifties, the sectarians finally severed their connections with the Hutterians, and, freed from the legalism and introversionism which this connection implied, turned again to consider the ways in which they might reflect their 'light' more widely in the world.

The extent of the sectarians' evangelistic activities, and of their reconciliation with the world, was greater in England than in Paraguay, where the mass of the membership were located. From 1948, the leaders of the Paraguayan hofs corresponded with sympathizers in North America, and in 1952 missionaries were sent to the United States, and aroused the interest of several small communitarian groups, whose members were predominantly from Quaker backgrounds. In 1954, a property was purchased at Rifton, eighty-five miles north of New York City, and the 'Woodcrest' community was established. Subsequently, two other hofs were founded in the northeastern states: 'Oak Lake' near Farmington, Pennsylvania, and 'Evergreen' near Norfolk, Connecticut.

In November and December 1956, an Interbruderhof Conference was held in Paraguay. The main topic discussed and agreed upon was the proposed gradual transfer of personnel and resources from Paraguay to the United States – the country which seemed to promise the greatest success for evangelism. Subsequently, much contention arose in the Paraguayan and English hofs, and a rift developed between those members who wanted the sect to ally itself with reformist religious and political groups, and those who insisted that the Bruderhof should be 'the Church set on a hill', aloof from the world, and content to accept those few recruits whom God sent to it.

Heinrich Arnold, the leader of the American hofs, and second eldest son of Eberhard Arnold, acted as one of the arbiters in these disputes, and resolutely maintained that the cultivation of internal purity was the essential, or at least the immediate, task of the sect. Between 1958 and 1962, many of those persons who sought greater community contact with the world, were individually expelled into it. Since this period of purification and purge, all the hofs outside the United States have been closed. Heinrich Arnold's power has continued to increase, and since the mid nineteen sixties he has been acknowledged as 'Vorsteher' or 'Bishop' of the group. At the present time the sectarians do not appear to be taking any active, externally directed measures to realize Eberhard Arnold's vision of a world transformed by 'the fire of the Spirit' into a 'network of organic living cells'.

The formal organization of Bruderhof communitarianism

The members of the Bruderhof insist that their lives are not bound by fixed regulations, or by established, rigid, modes of behaviour. They state that 'the life' is, like an organism, constantly evolving, but in reality the daily and annual cycles of life in the communities, and the formal structure of Bruderhof communitarianism, have persisted without significant alteration for upwards of thirty years. Many rituals and customs, and the whole 'ceremonialism of informality' which pervades the life of the sectarians, date from the earliest years of the Community at Sannerz.

As a consequence of their nominal incorporation with the Hutterian Church, the sectarians took over aspects of 'the orders' of the Hutterite communities – their hierarchical structure and terminology of office, and the disciplinary system of graded 'exclusions'. However, the Bruderhof's conformity to the model of Hutterite life was only partial and approximate, and as a result of geographical separation and Hutterite inertia, the Society of Brothers was almost entirely independent of Hutterite control. By the end of the Second World War, the sectarians' identification with the Hutterites was more nominal than real.

Arnold's appointment as Hutterite 'Bishop' for Germany simply reaffirmed his paramount position in the Bruderhof. Throughout his life he laid claim to authority by virtue of his divine commission, and consequent understanding of God's will for mankind, and his charismatic claims appear to have been strengthened by his education and intellectual superiority to his followers. All important decisions were made unanimously by the Brotherhood, the assembly of full members, but Arnold's voice was dominant in that body. Any member who persisted in dissent after the 'leading of the Spirit' had become apparent to the majority of the Brotherhood, was liable (as today) to be denounced for harbouring a 'bad spirit' which prevented the emergence of that unanimity which betokened the Spirit's presence in the united, 'ego-less', Brotherhood.

The power and will of the Holy Spirit which is believed to descend to the United Brotherhood, needs to be translated and given expression, and the primary agent of this task is the Servant of the Word, or Word-Leader, the spiritual and temporal leader of the group. Arnold summarized the duties of the incumbent of his position, and emphasized that the group was not, or should not be, subject to control by human will or authority (1965, pp. 236–7):

> The word-leader cannot speak or act out of himself. He says or does
> that which moves in the others and wants to be expressed in word or in
> deed. Never should there prevail a human leading. . . . We believe in
> the revelation of truth in the living community.

The task of the Servant of the Word or Vorsteher of the sect is to keep himself informed of the spiritual condition of the group, and, necessarily, of the individuals composing it. Such knowledge of the spiritual 'standing' of the individual 'cells' of the body of the group is necessary if the Servant is to be able to distinguish between opinions stemming from the Spirit of

God, and those prompted by evil spirits. Further, the Servant should be able to comprehend and communicate the significance of all the seemingly mundane vicissitudes of the sect, each of which is believed to stem from the action of God or of the powers of evil, and which must necessarily have an 'inner meaning' and significance.

The Servant of a single hof is likewise responsible for the spiritual condition of the members of his community, and for articulating, or, more desirably, bringing to unanimous articulation, the one clear prompting of the Spirit which seeks expression in the assembled Brotherhood, and which is suppressed by individualism, which is manifested in factionalism, persistent dissent and the 'unbending will'.

Shortly before Arnold's death, he nominated his son-in-law, Hans Zumpe, to be his successor as leader of the group, but Zumpe appears to have been unable to establish complete control over the sect, and was never hailed as Vorsteher. For more than a decade after 1935, Zumpe was the most influential individual in the group, but throughout this period the sectarians were primarily concerned with the establishment of their hofs in Paraguay and England, and with subsistence. By the nineteen fifties, there had developed marked inter- and intra-hof ideological and attitudinal divergences, which were only resolved by the purge of 1958 to 1962 after which Heinrich Arnold was recognized as Vorsteher of the sect.

Since Heinrich Arnold's emergence as leader, the period from the death of Eberhard Arnold in 1935 to the end of the purge in 1962 (in the course of which Zumpe was expelled) has come to be regarded as an era of apostasy. These years, in which the sect lacked coherent leadership and unity of purpose, and which, in England at least, were characterized by laxity in regard to admissions, and eager alignment with reformist movements, are now described as the period in which 'the Brotherhood ceased to exist'. By this phrase the sectarians mean that the group was not guided by a single clear leading from the Holy Spirit, but was led into disunity by the forces of worldly evil.

Although theoretically all members of the Bruderhof are necessarily and essentially equal in their 'poverty' and in their submission to the Spirit of God, each community is complexly stratified; the different groups varying in terms of their access to information, their participation in worship and influence in decision-making, and hence in their prestige and power. Four groups can be distinguished in descending order of religious and administrative importance. The Servant and his associates, who together form what may be termed the 'executive' of the hof; the full members of the group not included in the above category; novices; guests and children. The stratification of the communities, and the attempt to rank any particular individual, is greatly complicated by the generally subordinate status of women, by the ambiguous position of unmarried adults, by the question of the spiritual 'standing' or condition of individuals, and by the sectarians' marked positive estimation of youthfulness. However, the above fourfold division of the population of the hofs is adequate for the purposes of exposition.

Except in very exceptional circumstances effective power lies with the 'executive' of the hof. All appointments to the executive are made only after prolonged discussion and with the unanimous agreement of the full members of the community. In the case of the appointment of a Servant, or Assistant Servant, the discussions are also attended by the leaders of other hofs. Appointments to the executive are made for life, but are conditional upon good conduct. The executive of a hof consists of the Servant, the Assistant Servant (if there is one), the Steward, the Housemother, the Witness Brothers and subordinate housemothers.

The Assistant Servant stands as potential successor to the Servant and generally understudies his duties, and may take the Servant's position if the latter is absent from the hof. The Steward is responsible for the finances of the hof and superintends its economic activities in daily consultation with the leaders of the male work departments. The Housemother, who is almost invariably the wife of the Servant, supervises the female work departments, which are headed by housemothers, who again almost invariably, are the wives of the Witness Brothers. The latter, usually five or six in number, act as general assistants to the Servant in his pastoral duties of counselling, arbitrating in disputes, and supervising the conduct and spiritual standing of the members.

The executive of the hof are responsible to its remaining full members, and the decisions and recommendations of the executive, as well as matters of general policy and administration, are discussed in the Brotherhood meetings which are held for several hours on two evenings of each week. All full members of the hof who are in good standing attend these meetings, as on most occasions do novices, and every member, male or female, may speak, and indeed all are urged that it is their duty to 'open' any doubts or disagreements they may have to the Brotherhood. In addition to being the deliberative and consenting assembly of the hof, the Brotherhood constitutes its legal body, all property being formally owned by it.

The novices of a hof are those persons who have been accepted as probationers for eventual full membership of the sect, and who have furnished proof of their sincerity by transferring all their money and property to the Brotherhood as the legal representative of the Church-community. Normally, a person who becomes interested in the Bruderhof will make several short visits to the communities, and subsequently may request permission to stay for an indefinite period as a guest, contributing his labour without payment, but receiving his keep and lodging in return. If a guest is deemed unsuitable he will be asked to leave the hof, but if he seems serious he will, after some weeks or months, be invited to participate in the 'Gemeindestunde', the 'inner' religious meeting of the sect. Eventually, such a serious guest may request to be allowed to enter the novitiate, and if his request is granted by the Brotherhood, he will take the novice's vows, and his entry to the novitiate will be celebrated by the whole hof in a 'Love Meal'.

The novice vows to put himself and all his property at the disposal of the Church-community, to surrender himself totally to the Spirit of God, to accept reproof, and, when necessary, to reprove others. After taking his vows the novice is regarded as being 'engaged' to the sect, and must demonstrate his suitability for full membership. Specifically, he must come to a realization of the fact that as an individual he is corrupt and incapable of redeeming himself. Further, he must by his humility and selflessness, give evidence of this realization, and of his total reliance on the Church-community for rebirth, and entry into the 'true life' to which all mankind unconsciously aspires.

If the novice passes successfully through the engagement period which may last for up to two years, and through the intensive baptism classes which conclude it, he is accepted into full membership of the sect. In the baptism ceremony he is reminded that the contract he is entering into is undertaken with the true Church of Christ, which has the power to 'bind' and 'loose' the individual in earth and in heaven, and that he has consigned all his property to the group without any right to future reimbursement. At baptism, the former novice becomes a full member of the sect, and privy to all the information which the executive of the group feels is expedient to pass down to the Brotherhood meetings.

As indicated, serious guests will eventually be invited to attend Gemeindestunde, which is held regularly on Sunday evenings and occasionally also in mid-week. This privilege of attendance is frequently revoked with little explanation other than that the individual 'is not standing right' in spiritual matters. Casual guests are not permitted to attend Gemeindestunde, although they are invited to the more relaxed 'Family' and 'Household' meetings which are held on Sunday mornings. Throughout the Bruderhof's existence, with the exception of periods of severe internal crisis, guests have been provided with food and accommodation in return for labour. Casual visitors are given tours of the hof by the Guest Warden or one of his deputies. Persons staying at the hofs overnight, or for somewhat longer periods, are allowed little privacy but are provided with relays of guides who readily answer questions concerning the more obvious 'outward-forms' of the lives of the sectarians.

Social control

The members of the Bruderhof insist that their lives are governed solely by the Spirit of God as manifested to the united Brotherhood. Certainly, they have never been governed by detailed, formally codified regulations, but, from the early years at Sannerz to the present, there have existed certain relatively explicit behavioural principles, and a normative system so pervasive as to influence even the minutiae of the sectarians' lives, and to induce a high degree of conformity of action, and, presumably, of thought. Put differently, while correct behaviour is not, with a few important exceptions, specified and itemized, incorrect behaviour is instantly recognized by the sectarians, and is interpreted as a symptom of an 'unhealthy' mental attitude, and of the individual's not standing right in relation to God and the Church-community.

The aim of social control in the Bruderhof is to enable the sectarians to lead lives which witness to the love of Christ, and so to demonstrate the joys of life in God's Kingdom. The task of each individual is therefore to purge from himself, and from his fellows, all the corruption and vices of the world. Only by 'dying to the world' can the individual render himself fit to be used in building God's Church-community, which is believed to be the only environment in which such a dismantling and reconstitution of the self is possible. By such an act of sacrifice, or, put in a manner which better expresses the sectarians' conception, of emancipation, the individual 'finds resurrection' in this life, and implicitly, if he remains faithful to Christ, in the next. The duty of the individual is to submerge himself in ego-less submission to the Spirit of God, and in this context Bruderhof writers frequently compare individuals to grains of corn which must be crushed if their goodness is to be released.

The ideal towards which every imperfect individual must constantly struggle is total selflessness, and consequent complete openness and faithfulness to the promptings of the Spirit. The persons respected by the Bruderhof are those who, in their every action and deed, body forth their submission to the Spirit.

The virtues prized by the Bruderhof are humility, chastity, co-operativeness and simplicity. Humility should be demonstrated by a negative estimation of one's powers and capabilities, and by submissiveness to the reproofs of others. Chastity should be total before marriage, and implies complete post-marital fidelity and constant purity of word and thought. Co-operativeness is a corollary of humility – no individual should think himself above the company of others, but should seek to merge his spirit with theirs in joyful fellowship. Co-operation in work and recreation is intrinsically valued, as it is the antithesis of isolation, which is regarded as the nursery of 'life-destroying' selfishness. Simplicity is consciously demonstrated in every aspect of Bruderhof life, and finds psychological expression in what may be termed the 'child-like character' – the individual embodiment of the sect's ideals.

The sectarians' conception of the moral nature of children is a romantic one. Children arrive in the world, and for a time remain, as unspotted souls, if not actually trailing clouds of glory. They are essentially selfless, gentle, pure and free from taint of sin. Moral qualities and types of behaviour which are thought to express the innocence of childhood are valued in adults as evidence of their simplicity of spirit. Thus harmless mischief is seen as demonstrating praiseworthy exuberance and love of fun, and surprises (gifts, unexpected outings, secretly prepared dramatic entertainments and the like) are institutionalized in Bruderhof life. The childlike man is cheerful, friendly, unassuming and ingenuous, filled with a joyful appreciation of communal life, and of God's goodness and gifts. Naturalness and informality of behaviour are extolled, and indeed, insisted upon. Most important, members of the group should be childlike in their realization of their absolute dependence on the Church-community, which is spoken of as the 'mother' of the sectarians.

The members of the Bruderhof regard themselves as engaged in a constant battle with the forces of evil. Each sectarian is thus a soldier in God's army, fighting to maintain, and theoretically to extend, God's earthly Kingdom, and is also himself a battleground – a minor theatre of the struggle between the Holy Spirit and demonic forces. Each individual is not only responsible for his own spiritual condition, but also for that of his fellows.

The Bruderhof believe the world to be the 'principality of Anti-God', and consequently seek to insulate themselves from its corrupting influence. The adult member has little contact with the world, and such contacts as he does have are closely regulated. Throughout the group's existence the ordinary members have been required to ask permission from a member of the executive if they wish to leave the grounds of the hof for any reason, and virtually all journeys 'outside', whether for business or pleasure, are made in groups. Indeed, for the Bruderhof, isolation and true pleasure are virtually incompatible. In summer, religious meetings are often held outdoors, and the delights of nature are vociferously appreciated, but an individual who repeatedly communed with nature by himself would be taxed with having a 'bad attitude'. Friendships with persons in the outside world rarely develop, but if they do, are strongly discouraged, and the adolescents who, in the United States, attend the high-schools in the vicinity of the hofs, travel in groups, and have little or no contact with their schoolfellows outside classes.

Until fairly recently members' incoming and outgoing mail was censored, and while today the sectarians may correspond with external kin and friends made before their conversion, it is likely that any member who engaged in a particularly voluminous correspondence would be 'spoken with' by one of the Witness Brothers. Readings at mealtimes tend to deal with topics which demonstrate the selfishness and lack of fellowship of the world, and letters from absent members, especially from younger persons receiving higher education, are read publicly. Understandably, these letters often reflect their writers' longings for the secure and predictable world of the hof.

One cardinal regulation, which dates from the early years in Germany, ranks as a 'law' of the Bruderhof, and its observance is believed to be essential for the maintenance of harmonious communitarianism. This 'First Law in Sannerz' totally prohibits gossip, and binds all members who hear gossip immediately to challenge the gossiper to repeat his statements to their subject's face.

This law forms the basis of the regulatory system of 'admonishment'. All members are required to reprove misconduct and every manifestation of wrong attitudes. Such reproof must be immediate and face to face. Admonishment is not a vague ideal or a rare occurrence, but is believed vital to the well-being of the sect. Novices are schooled in the administration and reception of admonishment, which must be delivered with all due sternness but in humility. An individual who took pride in his ability to detect sin and to administer telling reproofs would himself be open to admonishment. Admonishment should be received humbly and gratefully, and usually the person reproved will immediately confess his error, and resolve to mend his ways. Should brotherly remonstrance give rise to recrimination, the dispute is taken to a Witness Brother or, in serious cases, is submitted to the assembled Brotherhood. In either case, the person or persons deemed sinful must confess their sins and humbly ask forgiveness, or be excluded from worship and face greater sanctions.

It must be emphasized that, while the 'brotherly act of correction' is directed against spiritual failings, such failings are frequently inferred from the concrete minutiae of the individual's behaviour. Thus, repeated absence from communal meals, insufficient verbal expression of humility, reluctance to participate in group recreational activities, excessive concern about personal appearance, moodiness, reticence, or even inadequately demonstrated delight in nature or 'simple things', are all liable to interpretation as evidence of absence of the 'childlike spirit', and to give cause for admonishment.

The development of special affections and attachments (beyond the exclusive sexual attachment of marriage) is forbidden. Each member should strive to love every other member of the hof equally, and even public demonstration of special affection for one's children is frowned upon. Cliqueishness is abhorred, and budding cliques or exclusive friendships may be ended by transferring some of the persons involved to another community. In most cases however, admonishment, combined if necessary with remonstrance by a member of the executive, and public condemnation in the Brotherhood meeting, is sufficient to elicit abject confession and repentance.

While every member shares in the responsibility for the spiritual condition of his fellows, the maintenance of spiritual harmony is the especial concern of the executive of each community. There is no confessional secrecy in the Bruderhof, and all important information received by the Witness Brothers and Housemothers is relayed to the Servant. Similarly, no conversation can be regarded as private or 'off the record', indeed the very desire for such privacy is sinful and would merit remonstrance. When incorrect behaviour is obvious, admonishment will usually follow immediately, but in cases where a member merely suspects incorrect behaviour, or where the basis of his inference is very insubstantial or ambiguous, a member may unburden himself of his suspicions by confessing his own 'bad feelings' to a Witness Brother. By so doing, he can avoid committing the sin of gossiping, while convincingly demonstrating the nicety of his conscience, and furnishing the executive members with information which may serve them as a basis for investigation or further enquiries.

The power of the Servant of the hof and, by extension, of his executive, derives primarily from his task of 'leading-out' the Holy Spirit which 'moves in' the Brotherhood. Unity in submission to the Spirit, which in practice tends to mean unity in submission to the Servant as 'spokesman' of the Spirit, is the goal of the lives of the sectarians, who believe that the attainment of such unity will be rewarded by greater out-pourings of divine power. For an individual or group to challenge the executive is to jeopardize the fragile unity which binds the sectarians to God. In most cases such challengers will be repudiated by the Brethren and will be regarded as the dupes of evil spirits – witting or unwitting agents of the 'powers of darkness'.

The power of the executive of the hof is heightened, first by the insistence that every member must individually and immediately voice his disagreements and doubts (which implies that if some members voice disagreement as a group, they are self-confessedly guilty of factionalism, and the mere fact of their collusion demonstrates their bad intentions and places them in the wrong); second, by the requirement that each member must constantly scrutinize the conduct of his fellows; third, by the upward flow of information; and finally, by the executives' ability to withhold information from their 'constituents' – the Brotherhood.

Intensive and unremitting surveillance of the conduct of the members of the hof is facilitated by the small size of the communities, by the regimentation of the members' lives, and by their constant interaction at work, communal meals, religious and administrative meetings and in the group recreational activities which occupy the greater part of their remaining waking hours.

After their incorporation into the Hutterian Church, the Bruderhof adopted a semblance of the Hutterite disciplinary sanctions, the system of graded 'exclusions' from participation in the worship, administration and communal life of the sect. Every member of the group is likely to receive occasional admonishment, but an individual who repeatedly transgresses the informal normative system will attract the attention of the executive, and will be more formally remonstrated with. If the individual is recalcitrant, or if he has difficulty in resolving his doubts or mending his ways, he will be temporarily excluded from religious meetings and will be re-admitted only after making a full confession of his sin.

More serious offences are punished by – in ascending order of severity – 'small exclusion', 'great exclusion', and expulsion from the sect. A member placed in small exclusion is debarred from participation in religious or administrative meetings, and, while continuing to work and to live with his family, is prohibited from more than essential conversation with any of the other inhabitants of his social world – the hof. The individual in great exclusion is separated from his family and lives in isolation. His meals are brought to his quarters, and he is visited daily by the Servant of the hof who strives to bring him to an appreciation of his total dependence on the Church-community for redemption, and ego-less self-realization. Expulsion, which is preceded by public anathematization in the Brotherhood meeting, is also graded. A member may be expelled for a definite period, or indefinitely, and may or may not be allowed to engage in correspondence with the hof. No offence is beyond forgiveness, and indeed the Bruderhof state that no member has ever been expelled, but this statement rests on a semantic peculiarity. The sectarians believe that no sinner is so depraved as to be beyond the redeeming power of God's grace (should that grace be extended to him), consequently no person is utterly and irrevocably expelled.

The struggle against sin must be waged without cessation by every hof, and by every individual. No member of the sect is beyond the reach of temptation, indeed the most virtuous of men may fall prey to the subtle sin of spiritual pride. The individual's this-worldly rebirth is effected by baptism into the sect, but this redemption is not secure. Membership of the group is thus the condition of spiritual improvement, but not its guarantee, and the powers of evil are always waiting to snare the lax or the unwary. Probably every member of the sect has at one time been condemned for bad attitudes and behaviour, and has been forgiven after making confession and, literally, craving the forgiveness of the Brotherhood.

Even members of the executive of the hof are liable to be admonished, and are fairly frequently demoted. The demotion of a Witness Brother, Steward or Housemother is most likely to occur as a result of action by the Servant and of other members of the executive. Demotion of a Servant, a rare event, is likely to be instigated by the executive of other hofs, or by the Vorsteher of the group if there is one, and produces a general crisis in the affected hof, whose members are guilty of having condoned the actions and accepted the 'wrong leading' of their spiritual mentor.

From 1922 until his death in 1935, Eberhard Arnold was the undisputed leader of the Bruderhof. In this period, all the major decisions appear to have been made by Arnold and to have been subsequently ratified by the Brotherhood, entry to which of course depended on Arnold's fiat. In the twenty years after Arnold's death, the absence of any strong paramount leader and the geographical bifurcation of the group facilitated the development of inter- and intra-hof ideological conflicts, and of more mundane jealousies and rivalries, which culminated in the successive hof crises and purges of 1958 to 1962.

All the conflicts which came to a head in the late nineteen fifties appear to have stemmed from the group's dual commitment to withdrawal from the world and to evangelism. Some members argued that the group's withdrawal from the world was a perversion of Arnold's teachings, while others insisted that if the group was to succeed in 'maintaining its light', it should shun the contamination of worldly interests and associates. In each hof this essential ideological divergence generated a host of subordinate questions of practical policy, each of which could only be resolved by tacit or actual resolution of the central dilemma. Such questions included: the appropriate attitude of the group to higher education; the degree to which the sect should associate itself with other pacifist and communitarian groups; the possibility of abandoning the ideal of an agriculturally based community; the importance and effectiveness of literary evangelism; and whether or not the sectarians should participate in national elections.

The events of the years 1958 to 1962 are shrouded in secrecy, and the sectarians speak of this period with the greatest reluctance, but it appears that, by the former date, the conflicts in the Paraguayan and English hofs had developed to such an extent that, successively, the executives of the individual communities were forced to admit their incapacity to establish unity, and sought advice from the leaders of the other groups. At this time only the communities in the United States were expanding and were relatively harmonious. Heinrich Arnold, the dominant Servant in the United States, thus appeared to have a 'clear leading', and, with other leaders, was called upon to help resolve the conflicts in England and Paraguay.

Secure in his own following, esteemed because of his demonstrated capacity to expand the American communities while maintaining their unity, and indubitably attributed with something of the charisma of his father, Heinrich Arnold sought to purify the group. He and his associates accomplished successive purges of all those persons who had 'brought in a disturbance' by advocating closer alignment with the world. Presumably, for many of these persons secession appeared a logical alternative to remaining in a sect which they believed to have lost its relevance and vital spirit, but many members were also expelled by the introversionist majority who clung to the sect as the storm-tossed, but divinely commissioned, 'ark' which alone could preserve them from the evils of the world.

Since Heinrich Arnold's acknowledgment as Bishop, the group's introversionism has become steadily more marked. The world is today condemned as a place of selfishness, greed, violence and, perhaps especially, sexual corruption, but the sectarians seem to be attempting to ignore Eberhard Arnold's insistence that his followers should 'conquer the earth' by evangelism. Instead, the present leadership of the group, blessed with followers who have 'suffered through' the trials of the period of purge, is preoccupied with internal purification. The American sectarians stress the difficulties and 'dangers' of leading lives of Christian witness in the contemporary world, but appear concerned only with separating themselves from the world, and with intensifying the joys of their ego-less, sheltered, *gemütlich* lives of submission to the Spirit of God as manifested to the leaders of 'the all-nuturing mother', the Church-community.

Worship

The members of the Society of Brothers deny the efficacy of sacraments to bring about any significant or lasting change in the conduct and character of the individual. Even the water baptism which marks the individual's entry into the Brotherhood is not 'necessary' or indispensable, but is merely a symbol. Rebirth comes about only through the individual's total dedication to Christ, and through the continued sacrifice of his individualism in communal life.

The sectarians insist that their lives are their worship, and consciously seek, symbolically and actually, to minimize the distinction between the sacred and the profane. For this reason the religious meetings of the sect are held in the hof dining halls, which are also used for administrative meetings and for recreational activities. As is the case with reference to every other aspect of their lives, the sectarians insist that their worship is not governed by set forms; but the various religious meetings, the sect's distinctive style of silent prayer, and all the rituals and seasonal observances of the group appear to have changed little since they were 'given' to the believers at Sannerz.

The core of the religious life of the Bruderhof is the Gemeindestunde meeting, which is held on Sunday evenings, and frequently also on an evening in mid-week. Gemeindestunde is open to all those invited guests, novices and full members who confess themselves to be free from doubts and all animosity towards their brethren, and who are recognized by the hof executive to be in such a state of 'clarity'. Past sins and evil states of mind are confessed in the first part of the meeting, which lasts for perhaps an hour and a half, and this 'clearing' is followed by a lengthy reading by the Servant of a text which is likely to emphasize the worthlessness of the individual, and the joys of unity. After this reading the group is called to prayer, and the members, presumed purged of their individuality and merged into the body of Christ's Church, pray silently, kneeling in a circle with palms upturned to symbolize their readiness to receive the Holy Spirit, and their humble gratitude for God's grace.

Two 'less inward' religious assemblies are held on Sunday mornings – the Family and Household meetings. Family meeting is held after breakfast, and is attended by almost the entire population of the hof, including guests and very young children. Songs are sung, guests are welcomed, birthdays and forthcoming activities are announced, and the short meeting, less than an hour in length, is often concluded by a tableau or short dramatic performance by the older children. Household meeting follows shortly after Family meeting, and is attended by all but the younger children. The tone of this meeting is more serious and reflective. Hymns are sung, selections from the sect's writings are read, and this somewhat more lengthy meeting, about an hour and a half in duration, is closed by a short period of standing silent prayer.

The members of the Society of Brothers believe that every object and every event has an 'inner meaning', discernible by those who walk in the light of God's spirit. This quasi-mystical immanentism, in conjunction with the dualistic conception of an eternal struggle between good and evil, leads the sectarians to interpret virtually all their vicissitudes as the direct results of the action of Providence, or of Anti-God. Just as every item of a person's behaviour is explained as an expression or symptom of his spiritual condition, so there are no random or fortuitous happenings in the lives of the sectarians. A member will not say that he came to the group 'by chance', but that, unconscious though he may have been of it at the time, he was 'sent' to the sect. Ideas do not 'occur' to individuals, but are 'given' to them, and success in any venture is not attributed to 'good luck', or to individual skill and enterprise, but to God's liberality and blessing.

The sectarians' concern to render every aspect and action of their lives a witness to Christ and an act of worship, in conjunction with their positive estimation of communality and simplicity, gives rise to what has earlier been termed the 'ceremonialism of informality'. Formality in its two senses of adherence to established rules, and of impersonality in relationships, is abhorrent to the sectarians, who insist that it is 'life-destroying' in its denial of fellowship, and that it is, in a sense, a refuge for individualism. As indicated in the above discussion of social control, informality, implying spontaneity of expression and personal man-to-man relationships, is highly valued by the sectarians, who insist that the outward forms of their lives and social organization are unimportant and transitory.

Paradoxical as it may seem, in the Bruderhof, informality is *de rigueur*. The sectarians insist that all the choices made by the members of the group are free ones – individuals are free to dress as they will, to attend meetings and communal meals if they will, to work if they will – but if they behave in a manner markedly different from that prescribed by informal convention and custom, they are deemed to have lost their 'free will', and to have fallen victim to an evil spirit which is manifested in 'bad attitudes'. The 'free' individuals who manage to resist such snares 'body forth' their childlike virtues in very similar ways. Self-deprecation and humility are given utterance in what, to the observer, appear stylized forms of speech, and the responses of the sectarians to events and objects are, linguistically and substantively, highly predictable. For example, natural objects, children and unexpected entertainments will, respectively, evoke voluble expressions of awe and vague exaltation, delight in innocence and naturalness, ingenuous surprise and humble gratitude.

Every meal, communal or familial, is, or should be, a sacral event and, as indicated above, all group activities are valued, not instrumentally but sacramentally, as acts of communion, in the sense of sympathetic intercourse infused with the Holy Spirit. The daily communal lunches and dinners are each preceded by a hymn and by a short silent grace, and are eaten in silence, and closed by another hymn. Every important event in the hof – the admission of novices, engagements and marriages, funerals, visits by members from other hofs, baptisms – is celebrated by a solemn communal 'love-meal'. In some years, during the Easter period, the sect's continued unity in submission to the Spirit is celebrated in the most solemn rite of all, the 'Lord's Supper', which is the climax of weeks of spiritual preparation.

The national and secular holidays of the world are scarcely acknowledged by the Bruderhof, but Advent and Christmas, Easter and Whitsun, are all regarded as special seasons, and are each celebrated with appropriate observances, as well as generally with love-meals, songs, dramatic presentations and a general intensification of the emphasis on unity of thought and action. Two 'ritual' concessions to individualism and to vestigial desires for privacy are worthy of note. Birthdays are celebrated with songs, small gifts and by the granting of a special wish, which usually takes the form of a request for a foodstuff or item of clothing, and newly married couples are sent on a short honeymoon away from the hof.

Economy

Among the organizational and ethical principles of the true witness provided by the apostles of the Early Church, Eberhard Arnold included their economic communism, and their recognition of their obligation to work. As indicated, Arnold appears to have had a romantic view of the lives, characters and work of the peasantry, and he envisaged that agriculture would be the mainstay of the Church-community. He also insisted that all work was of equal value provided that it was performed as an act of worship, and that no individual was entitled to esteem himself above his fellows because God had bestowed special talents on him, but should employ those talents for the benefit of all.

The principles outlined in a statement made in 1939 (anon., 1940?, p. 10) with reference to the products of the small turnery of the Cotswold Bruderhof, are still acknowledged today, although the contemporary sectarians are supported almost entirely by the profits of a complex industrial enterprise manufacturing educational toys.

The object is to produce beautiful work on very simple lines,
expressing in this, as in all aspects of the life, the absolute simplicity
which grows out of the life.

In outline the organization of Bruderhof communism has persisted with few significant changes since before 1930. All the property of a hof is vested in its full members as a body, and in the United States today each hof is incorporated under state law as a religious and manufacturing association. In the past each hof had its own economic hierarchy and kept its own accounts (although there was much transference of persons and funds) but today the economic affairs of the three hofs are more closely interrelated. The products of Evergreen and Oak Lake are taken to Woodcrest for finishing and dispatch, and the Business Manager of Woodcrest necessarily maintains close contact with the Business Managers of the two smaller hofs. In financial affairs, as in all others, the members are encouraged to think of themselves as members of the overall Church-community, rather than as inhabitants of a particular hof, and all members must be willing to change their place of residence if this is desired by the Brotherhood.

Internally, responsibility for the finances and for the productive and labour departments of each hof rests with its Steward, who supervises communal purchasing and the distribution of foodstuffs, clothing and every variety of personal and household necessities to individuals and families. The Steward is also responsible for supervising the management of the male and female work departments, and meets regularly with the work distributors and departmental foremen. Among the present work departments, in addition to the toy manufactury, are maintenance, publishing, the school, office, stores and several purely domestic departments each supervised by a housemother: kitchen, laundry, dressmaking and the like. With the exception of persons employed in a few specialized departments, the labour force is fluid, and the work distributors readily draft persons from one department to another. Virtually all work is performed in groups, and the most menial tasks are allotted in rotation to every adult member of the hof.

Throughout the sect's existence in Germany its main economic activity was subsistence agriculture. Craft industries were only minimally developed, and it seems likely that the profit, if any, which the group derived from its publishing house was small. The sectarians suffered intermittent privation, and the group appears to have survived only by drawing on the capital brought in by converts, and with the aid of gifts from guests and well-wishers, and remittances from the families of members. In addition, after 1930, the sect received quite substantial donations from some of the Hutterite communities.

After the move to England, the generosity of Quaker sympathizers and capital derived from converts enabled the group to establish a small turnery at Ashton Keynes, and to publish a quarterly magazine. By comparison with the land at the Rhönbruderhof, the farms at Ashton Keynes were fertile, and until local hostility developed, the sectarians sold their surplus of bread, milk and eggs on regular rounds in Swindon and the villages adjacent to the two hofs.

The sectarians' available capital was greatly depleted by their migration to Paraguay, and by the down payment required to secure the Primavera estate, but with the aid of funds, equipment and labour donated by their non-communistic Mennonite neighbours, and after much hardship, land was cleared and brought into cultivation, and a brickworks, tannery and carpenter's shop established. Subsequently fruit juice was bottled and sold, and a shop was purchased in Asuncion to sell craft work and literature, but the profits of these diverse activities were probably entirely offset by the cost of maintaining the free hospital at Loma Hoby. The Paraguayan hofs were never completely self-supporting, and this fact appears to have been among the arguments adduced at the Interbruderhof Conference which, in 1956, resolved upon a future transference of personnel and resources to North America.

By 1956, Woodcrest, the hof in New York State, had a total population of approximately 150, and in the following year, the Oak Lake Bruderhof was established as a result of a Bruderhof-induced schism in the Forest Hill, North Dakota, Hutterite colony. From their inception, these two American hofs were industrially based. Among the original members of Woodcrest were several converts from the pacifist, co-operative 'Macedonia' community which had for some years been established in Georgia. Since 1947, the Macedonians had manufacturered toys and educational play equipment under the trademark of 'Community Playthings'. Between 1954 and 1957 the manufacture was carried on jointly by the two sects, but in the latter year, the majority of the few remaining members of Macedonia joined the Society of Brothers, and Community Playthings passed entirely into Bruderhof control.

Today, at each of the three hofs, unified sawmills and manufacturies produce toys from bulk timber, and Woodcrest serves as the collection point and dispatch centre for the products of the two smaller hofs. The majority of the male labour force, and most guests, are employed in the manufacturing shops, in which the style of supervision is relaxed and instructions are given in the form of suggestions rather than commands.

From 1961, the English hof at Bulstrode also engaged in the manufacture of toys under the Community Playthings label, but the scale of this enterprise was small, and the Bulstrode hof derived the major part of its income from tubular steel products. The Wheathill hof, whose members were primarily engaged in agriculture, was closed in 1960. In 1966, when Bulstrode was closed, the British rights to the trademark and designs were sold to a Scottish firm of toy manufacturers.

The financial success of Community Playthings has been such that, for the first time in their history, the sectarians have been freed from constant concern with subsistence, and indeed, if the sectarians expanded Community Playthings to the utmost, they would probably become affluent. As indicated above, the manufactury at each hof is supervised by a Business Manager, and, presumably, relief from nagging economic worries and from the task of supervising several small productive departments has freed the other hof executives to concentrate more intensively on internal purity and order. Heinrich Arnold, the Vorsteher of the sect, is resident at Woodcrest, but commutes regularly between the three hofs, and, except when important policy decisions have to be made, is almost exclusively concerned with sacral affairs.

The relative prosperity enjoyed by the American sectarians was such that, by the early nineteen sixties, when the annual sale of toys totalled more than a million dollars, the sectarians faced a literal 'embarrassment of riches'. The group is assessed for federal taxes by dividing its total income by the number of persons who would presumably be gainfully employed in normal society.

By 1964 its income had risen to a point which made it seem likely that the sect would soon be liable to pay income tax, and so would 'directly' support American militarism. The sectarians were deeply worried by this impending compromise of their pacifist principles, and in 1965, it was decided that Community Playthings should cease to deal with agents or retailers, and that the group's products should be sold only to persons applying directly to the hofs, where small showrooms and shops are maintained. As a result, the group's profits fell considerably, and the sect was relieved of a possible taint to its ideological purity, and freed from one aspect of the insidious corrupting influence of Mammonism.

As the above survey of the economic development of the Bruderhof indicates, the sectarians have had no compunction about taking charity from the world. In Germany charitable support was informal but significant. In Britain, and possibly in Paraguay, it was institutionalized by the formation of a company of 'Friends of the Bruderhof'. The sectarians regard themselves as God's agents on earth, and gratefully accept any help which God sends them via his witting or unwitting agents. Arnold's vision of a network of self-supporting mission stations was not realized in his lifetime, and at no time have the communities of the Society of Brothers remotely approached self-sufficiency. The voluntarily impoverished sectarians in North America until very recently accepted gifts of used clothing and furniture from sympathizers, but, while throughout the early years at the Rhönbruderhof and in Paraguay (the periods when the sectarians suffered the greatest poverty) the group engaged in various charitable activities, today they extend little more than abstract compassion to the world. Eberhard Arnold's insistence that the Bruderhof witness should include charity and active contact with destitute and suffering persons in the world is at present ignored.

Social composition

The members of the Bruderhof seek to achieve such a degree of unity in submission to the Spirit that all the 'inhuman' barriers which exist between men in the world will be dissolved and replaced by true fellowship unmarred by distinctions of property, class, education, nationality or race. They emphasize that all men can, potentially, live 'the life' if they will only answer the promptings of the Spirit, and acknowledge their inner longing for ego-less community.

The sectarians state that they expect the 'imminent' transformation of the world into the Kingdom of God, but such statements do not bear literal interpretation. The future transformation of the world is a definite event which, in a sense, 'impends' over the whole history of mankind, and, ideally, all men should lead their lives with constant reference to this event. The Bruderhof do not expect all of mankind to be immediately converted to their way of life, but, aided always by the Spirit of God, they hope to provide a growing and deepening witness to the coming order.

The 'open-door' policy of extending hospitality to all who visit the hofs (subject of course to their good behaviour and desire to make progress spiritually), gives expression to the sectarians' concept that, from time to time, God will send them individuals to aid them in their witness. The Spirit of God finds its clearest expression in the united hofs, which are its true earthly home, but it also 'moves in' the corrupt world, and in individuals in the world. As a result, some individuals will be led by the Spirit to reject their worldly selves, and a happy few of these enlightened persons find their way to the group.

No mass conversions have been made by the sect (although the members of several small communitarian groups have joined simultaneously, or shortly after one another), but there have been periods of relatively intensive evangelistic activity, especially in the English hofs after the Second World War, and during the early years in North America. Although standards of admission to the sect were considerably relaxed in some areas in the nineteen fifties, generally the process of transformation of status from casual guest to full member has been prolonged, and closely scrutinized and regulated, and at times perhaps one-half of the persons 'requesting the novitiate' have been refused entry to it.

Numerically, the nucleus of seven adults and five children at Sannerz in 1920, increased to a total of about fifty by 1922. The débâcle of that year left seven adults at Sannerz, and Arnold appears to have made more rigid distinctions among the population of the group after this experience. By 1930, there were 80 persons (comprising twelve families) at the Rhön-bruderhof, by 1934, 180, and in 1938, after the sectarians had reassembled in England, there were 120 adults and 90 children.

Approximately 350 persons migrated to Paraguay in 1941, and a decade later, the hofs there had expanded, almost entirely as a result of natural increase, to a total of 600 persons. In addition, in 1951, there were almost 200 persons at the English Wheathill Bruderhof. In 1956–7, the world total of the Bruderhof was about 1,200, of whom 700 were in South America, 250 in the United States, 200 in England and the few remaining members at the small 'Sinntalhof' in Germany. The numbers of the group probably continued to rise until 1959, and may have reached a world total of 1,500, but in 1962, after the purge, the total population had fallen to about 800. Today, the three American hofs have a total permanent population of somewhat less than 900 persons.

The sectarians have always insisted on their capacity to overcome all barriers of class and education, and, until recently, have stressed the heterogeneity of the persons 'sent' to them. While statements describing the members of the group as ranging from tramps to émigré aristocrats are, or were, quite accurate, it remains true that in Germany, England and the United States, the majority of converts to the sect have come from middle-class, or lower middle-class backgrounds. Many members speak, or have written, of the poverty they endured prior to their conversion, but such poverty was usually voluntary, and the shock of the experience of privation was an important factor in stimulating the individual's revulsion against modern middle-class society. Significantly, while a number of members are said to have come from 'farming families', very few appear to have earned their livings by practical agriculture prior to joining the sect, and the great majority of the sectarians are essentially urban in background.

The same range of former religious affiliation as of social status can be found in the group, but again, while converts have been drawn from, or were once connected with, virtually every major denomination and sect in Europe and North America, most came from orthodox religious families. Persons of former Quaker persuasion or sympathies appear to be strongly represented in the North American hofs, but many of the converts have passed through a variety of loose religious affiliations, and some have also been members of short-lived communitarian ventures.

The majority of the converts made in North America (with the exception of the few drawn from the Hutterites) have received, or at one time embarked on, some form of college education, but the contemporary sectarians remain convinced that the Bruderhof life appeals to all men.

In the early years in Germany more women than men were attracted to the sect, but today there does not appear to be any marked predominance of females, at least among the young and middle-aged adults. Most members marry at quite an early age, and the few older unmarried adults occupy rather an awkward position in a sect which places a great emphasis on the joys of family life. Individual 'singles' are 'adopted' by specific families (as are all guests), and share many familial meals, and spend a large part of their short periods of free time with their family. It must be emphasized that large families are normal in the Society of Brothers, and consequently, throughout the history of the sect, approximately half of its population has consisted of persons under the age of eighteen. The sectarians state that in recent years about half of their children have eventually become members of the Brotherhood, usually after being temporarily exposed to some of the rigours of life in the world, and after undergoing the same screening process as novices from 'outside'.

Relations with the world

The broad pattern of the group's relationships with the world has been indicated above, and the discussion in this section will be as short as the rather complex nature of the material permits. The sectarians' general attitudes to persons and institutions in the world will be examined briefly before considering the special case of their relations with the Hutterites, their evangelical activities and attitudes to the state.

Because he regarded the world as choked by Mammon – as a place where lust, violence, deceit, greed and the 'sickness of the emphasized ego' pervaded and corrupted all human relationships – Eberhard Arnold regarded even the best-intentioned of worldly groups as tainted with sin. He reserved his most vehement denunciations for the denominations, whose condonation or enthusiastic espousal of the First World War had been important in influencing the development of his absolute pacifism. Arnold stressed that his Church-community was not a church in the worldly sense, but that part of its task was to wage the 'sharpest warfare' with the denominations which coated 'unchristian nations with an apparently christian whitewash' (cited in *The Plough*, spring 1938, p. 2).

The true Church was not to be confused with the hypocritical denominations, but neither was Christianity to be found in the sects, which were too narrow and selfish in their concentration on individual salvation, and their refusal to interest themselves in – to 'take responsibility for' – the sufferings of all mankind. While Arnold condemned the selfishness of sectarians generally, it must be remembered that he regarded such groups as the Quakers as partial witnesses, and looked on them with considerable, if rather condescending, approval. Further he looked with some degree of favour on all 'enlightened' political and religious reformist groups, and acknowledged the generosity of their impulses while deploring the incompleteness of their response to worldly evils. However, Arnold felt (as do the contemporary sectarians) that all communitarian groups which lacked deep religious impulse (and in this context depth implied proximity to the ideals of the Bruderhof) must necessarily fail, because the members did not appreciate the severity of the constant struggle which must underlie all efforts to establish true fellowship.

The Bruderhof and the Hutterites – identification and disenchantment

The motives which impelled Arnold and his closest associates to seek incorporation into the Hutterian Church appear to have been compounded of respect for the longevity and pertinacity of the Hutterian witness and of evangelical and financial considerations. Arnold certainly hoped that the Hutterians would be so moved by the story of his followers' struggles that they would grant extensive aid to the Bruderhof, and he appears also to have expected to re-kindle the past zeal of the Hutterites. Emmy Arnold stated that at the time of Arnold's journey to America, the Bruderhof 'cherished the hope that new life would break through in the Hutterian movement as it had often done already' (Emmy Arnold, 1964, p. 127).

In the course of his repeated journeys through the Hutterite colonies, Arnold condemned the tripartite division of the Hutterian Church, and the economic inequalities which existed between the Hutterite communities. Arnold's strictures appear to have temporarily stimulated the zeal of some of the Hutterites, but he also experienced what to him appeared to be the 'negative' qualities of the Hutterian leaders – their suspiciousness, extreme caution and conservatism, cultural narrowness and sobriety of manners – all of which clashed with the Bruderhof's positive estimation of simplicity, openness, spontaneity and financial impetuosity. Despite some disillusioning experiences in North America, the assurances of aid which Arnold wrung from the Hutterites greatly heartened him, and he returned from North America with a large quantity of manuscripts which he had agreed to translate from the Hutterite Tyrolese dialect.

The enthusiasm of the sectarians began to wane when the full amount of aid expected from the Hutterites was not forthcoming, and when the implications of Hutterite behavioural restrictions became apparent. The women of the Bruderhof readily accepted the Hutterite dress, and indeed, according to Emmy Arnold (1964, p. 128), 'felt something like a fulfilment in the simple peasant costumes'. The men were less enthusiastic about the dark fustian suits worn by the Hutterites, and the necessity to grow beards and relinquish smoking, and the middle-class sectarians generally were upset by the prohibition of pictures, photographs and all instrumental music. In Emmy Arnold's words (1964, p. 129):

> Giving up pictures, and even more, musical instruments, seemed to us a greater sacrifice [than the dress reforms]. Yet we were willing to give up even these, if it would lead to greater simplicity. But often a picture had so much to say! And the wandering together and sitting together with flutes and guitars, and all the beautiful folk songs and songs of religious awakening – all this seemed to belong to our life.

By 1934, the 180 persons at the Rhönbruderhof were in danger of splitting into two camps; on the one hand a small group who identified completely with the Hutterians, and who wanted to read and study nothing but Hutterian writings, and on the other, led by the Arnolds, the majority whose enthusiasm for the Hutterians was less than their desire to be a 'living witness'. After much conflict, and probably some expulsions, the more 'rigid' members were restored to clarity, and the Arnolds celebrated yet another triumph against a particularly insidious manifestation of evil – the threat of 'legalism' which sought to stifle the spontaneity of the Bruderhof life.

Throughout the period from 1938 to 1941, when the whole of the group was in England, sporadic contact was maintained with the Hutterians. However, with their migration to Paraguay the sectarians were effectively isolated from Hutterite surveillance, and many of the converts made by the revived group in England were probably more attracted by communitarianism *per se*, than by the possibility of leading lives approximating to those of sanctified sixteenth-century peasants. After the war, the sectarians in both countries virtually abandoned any pretence of conforming to Hutterite behavioural regulations.

Rumours of the prevalence in the Bruderhof of such iniquitous practices and events as smoking, folk-dancing, plays and concerts, reached the Hutterite leaders in the late nineteen forties. In response to Hutterite remonstrances, the Bruderhof sent two persons to reassure the Hutterians of their orthodoxy, and to request aid. The Hutterites were impressed by the emissaries and responded generously to the appeals, and, in response to an invitation by the Bruderhof delegates, sent two senior members of the Church to visit the Paraguayan hofs.

The Hutterite visitors were shocked to find the earlier rumours confirmed, and on their return to Canada, a heated correspondence was exchanged in which the Hutterites accused the Bruderhof of worldliness and prevarication, and the latter accused the Hutterites of having sacrificed the Spirit of the Word of God to its letter. Both sides were intransigent, and for more than a year the two groups had no contact with each other.

In 1953, the Bruderhof requested to be allowed to send members to the Hutterite colonies to work as missionaries in the surrounding regions. Some of the Hutterite leaders openly denounced this scheme as part of a plot to take over the Hutterian Church, and the request was refused, but a group in one colony, Forest River in North Dakota, disassociated itself from the decision, and invited a small number of Bruderhof missionaries.

A party led by Eberhard Arnold's eldest son duly arrived, but found themselves almost as isolated in North Dakota as in Paraguay. Although the Hutterites admired the Bruderhof members' culture and knowledge, they were less enchanted with their reluctance to undertake long hours of labour in the spring and harvest seasons. In 1955, the Forest River colony split again, and the Bruderhof members and their supporters moved first to Woodcrest, and subsequently to the Oak Lake Bruderhof, which was established in Pennsylvania in 1957. The hapless Hutterites who remained at Forest River after the defection of the Bruderhof members were placed under the 'Meidung', a ban of total exclusion from the Church, and were only readmitted to the Hutterian Church in 1963 (see Peters, 1965, pp. 173–8).

The total disruption of the Forest River colony by the Bruderhof put an end to all intercourse between the two sects. In 1957, a Servant of the Wheathill Bruderhof stated with perhaps inapposite bitterness that the Hutterites were 'cultureless peasants', but acknowledged that they were good farmers. Judgments expressed by the Bruderhof about the Hutterites today are inclined to be more temperate, and somewhat regretful and compassionate in tone.

Bruderhof evangelism

In the history of the Society of Brothers evangelism has taken second place to concentration on internal order, and the strengthening of the faith of persons already committed to the sect. Generally, Bruderhof evangelism has been literary and passive – the sectarians have corresponded readily with persons who initiated such correspondence, and have been eager to receive visits from all persons (except those whose interest was most obviously specious) who expressed an interest in their way of life. However, the intensity of Bruderhof evangelism has varied at different times in the sect's history, and, for purposes of exposition, five unequal time periods may be distinguished: Eberhard Arnold's lifetime, the years between his death and the migration to Paraguay, and, separately, the three decades from the date of this migration in 1941 to the present.

Throughout Arnold's lifetime, he and his followers were primarily concerned with struggling to establish and maintain the 'miracle' of their communal lives. By 1927, the year of the establishment of the Rhönbruderhof, Arnold appears to have become dissatisfied with the slow expansion of the group, and in 1928, when the sectarians learned of the existence of the Hutterians, Arnold prophesied a great numerical, social and geographical extension of 'the cause'. No such rapid expansion occurred, but after Arnold's death the group continued to grow slowly.

Once the sectarians had reassembled in England, they embarked on a relatively vigorous evangelical programme. They did not confine themselves solely to literary evangelism, but made several missionary and fund-raising journeys to towns in the north and midlands of England, where they spoke at the homes of sympathizers. A periodical was launched in 1938, which contained accounts of the group's history and appeals for aid, and news of a number of communitarian, co-operative and separatist meliorist ventures, all of which were interpreted as presaging a rapid expansion of the Church-community. In addition, in August 1940, two members were sent to witness to the Hutterites in North America, and to visit a small group of Hungarians in Ontario, who had expressed a wish to unite with the Bruderhof. Neither venture was successful, and the 'witnesses to the west' eventually rejoined the group in Paraguay.

For perhaps six years after the move to Paraguay, the difficulties experienced in establishing the three hofs in that country virtually precluded evangelism, and in Britain, the leaders of the Wheathill hof appear to have been primarily concerned with the maintenance of order among the more recent converts. Once the initial problems had been overcome in Paraguay, the sectarians had little evangelical success among their Mennonite neighbours, or among the Catholic Indians of the region, some of whom they employed on their estancia.

However, as already indicated, in the late nineteen forties the leaders of the Paraguayan hofs made contact with a number of small communitarian groups in North America, and in 1952 dispatched a party of missionaries to the United States. The interest evoked by these representatives greatly encouraged the sectarians, and in 1953 it was resolved to establish a small hof in the United States. In North America the sectarians appear to have employed the same small-scale evangelical techniques as in Europe. By 1956, the almost total absorption of two small pacifist communities, individual converts and drafts of members from Paraguay had brought the population of Woodcrest to 160. In 1957 the Oak Lake hof was established, and in 1958, Evergreen was founded in the United States, and Bulstrode in England, the population of each of these hofs being supplemented by members from Paraguay.

The evangelical concerns of the sectarians in England were clearly revealed in the pages of the group's periodical. After the expediently and economically enforced isolation of the nineteen forties, they turned enthusiastically to the world. From 1953, they sent parties of speakers to large towns in the midlands, and organized a number of work camps for members of pacifist religious organizations. In the middle years of the nineteen fifties, *The Plough* contained reports of such communitarian ventures as the Israeli Kibbutzim and some Tolstoyan groups, and, in a wave of enthusiasm in 1956, the sectarians commenced the study of Esperanto to aid them in their projected 'world task' of out-reach.

At the Interbruderhof Conference held in Paraguay in 1956, the sectarians decided to run down the Paraguayan hofs in order to concentrate the major part of their efforts and resources in North America, and also decided to found a new hof in a part of England closer to major centres of population than Wheathill. Early in 1958 the first of the Paraguayan hofs was closed, but the establishment of Evergreen and Bulstrode in this year brought the total number of hofs to nine in five countries, and the total population of the group to perhaps 1,300 persons.

Despite the conventional unanimity reached at the Primavera Interbruderhof Conference, the decisions taken there generated much controversy, and intra-hof rivalries and jealousies were exacerbated by the implicit condemnation of the Paraguayan leaders, who had failed to 'extend their witness'. Further, a number of the members regarded the move to an industrial economy as a betrayal of Eberhard Arnold's teachings, and many of the sectarians were loath to leave the South American hofs which had been established at the cost of much hardship.

By 1960, all pretence of unanimity in the English and Paraguayan communities had been abandoned, and in this year, the English group severed its connections with a number of religious and political reformist groups, and cancelled plans for a conference of all persons interested in communitarianism. Publication of the periodical ceased without notice after the spring 1960 issue, in which the decay of bourgeois civilization was said to be manifested in the apathy and aimlessness of the British population. Somewhat contradictorily, another article criticized all those persons who involved themselves with such organizations as War on Want and the Campaign for Nuclear Disarmament, both of which had earlier been endorsed by the Bruderhof. The writer inveighed against such reformers, and stated (*The Plough*, spring 1960, p. 8) that, in view of the corruption of the world:

> it must become clear, at least to those who call themselves Christians,
> that no amount of removing the fruits, or pruning, will alter the
> nature of the tree, nor the root from which it springs.

The American hofs had never published a periodical, and in 1959 the 'Woodcrest Service Committee' which had nominally existed to organize charitable projects in the world, was disbanded. During the period of purge the sectarians were entirely occupied with their internal problems, and guests were not received at the hofs. For several years after the purge, the sectarians concentrated on winning back a number of the persons who had left the communities, and on the complicated process of disbanding the hofs outside the United States. (Bulstrode, the last hof outside the United States, was closed in 1966.)

The recent evangelical activities of the group have been confined to correspondence and the sale of literature to interested individuals, and infrequent communications with a number of communitarian groups. Few external converts have been made in recent years, and under the leadership of Heinrich Arnold, who has now dominated the American hofs for fifteen years, the sectarians are concentrating their energies on the chimerical search for absolute unity. They state that they are in a period of 'creative withdrawal', but it seems likely that both the older sectarians who have survived the purge, and the younger members who have been brought up to view the world as a place to be shunned, have little real desire to venture again into the 'strongholds of Mammon'.

The testimony against impurity – marriage, the family and education

Eberhard Arnold and his followers castigated the hypocrisy of the German bourgeoisie in sexual matters, but, unlike many of the other post-First World War separatist groups, they did not react against conventionality by glorifying permissiveness. On the contrary, Arnold insisted that lives of Christian witness should be characterized by their purity and faithfulness, and in his writings occasionally expatiated on the related evils of alcohol and venereal disease. Persons entering the sect were obliged to regularize their sexual relationships by marriage (which involved a special ceremony, plus civil registration) or to relinquish them, and Arnold stated categorically that the marriage of a Bruderhof member to an outsider was unthinkable. For Arnold, family life was at once the nucleus of, and the training ground for, the development of the selfless love which his followers were to feel for all men, and his enthusiasm for the joys of family life was such as to lead him to reject birth control which annihilated the 'little souls' who wait in vain to be called out of eternity (Arnold, 1965a, p. 130).

Children in the sect are shielded from knowledge of sexual matters until at least early adolescence, and sexual experimentation, masturbation and adolescent flirtation are not merely frowned upon, but if detected are treated as abhorrent. The adolescents of both sexes engage as a group in many projects and recreational activities, but there are few opportunities for clandestine relationships to develop, and if such relationships were detected by other members of 'the youth' they would be reported to the hof executive. Bruderhof authors in North America (author is perhaps too dignified a term for the writers of introductions to collections of the writings of Eberhard Arnold) condemn sexual permissiveness and argue that its fruits can only be suffering and the deadening of sensitivity and of the capacity to love (see for example, Arnold, 1965a, p. 8).

If an unmarried man feels attracted to an unmarried woman, he will confide in the Servant of the hof, and the Servant, via his wife the House-mother, will sound the feelings of the woman. If the attraction is mutual, and if the proposed match is favoured by the executive, the couple will be paired together in work, or otherwise given special opportunities to explore their feelings for each other. (Only sentiments are explored, the idea of a 'trial' of sexual compatibility would be abhorrent to the sectarians.) Engagements and marriages are celebrated by the whole hof with special love-meals, and after their short honeymoon the couple take up residence in their own apartment.

As indicated in the discussion of social control, children are believed to be essentially pure, innocent and, in a sense, naturally spiritually minded. The child's ego is believed to be little developed and, consequently, he possesses that clarity of 'vision' which all adults must struggle to attain. The education and broader socialization of children in the sect is intended to preserve and to foster this innate selflessness, and to enable the child to defend himself against evil forces.

Throughout most of their history the sectarians have maintained their own nurseries, kindergartens and junior schools, and, while the basic curriculum in the latter is necessarily similar to that in schools in the world, much emphasis is placed on group projects, mutual aid and co-operativeness. The facilities provided at Woodcrest are excellent, and almost certainly are similar in the other hofs.

The sectarians seek not only to foster co-operativeness and to exterminate selfishness in their children, but also to develop their sense of responsibility for the sufferings of mankind and for the behaviour of other children, and apparently many of the more enlightened children are zealous in admonishing their peers. According to Emmy Arnold, at the instigation of the youthful Heinrich Arnold, some of the children at Sannerz organized themselves into a 'Sun Troop', and held their own religious meetings, and sought to awaken the spiritual perceptions of the other children. Arnold wrote approvingly of the actions of these juvenile inquisitors (*The Plough*, autumn 1939, p. 68):

There is no truly living education without complete universality. The children, as a group, sense this fact so deeply that again and again they feel urged and compelled to extend the children's community by winning more children for the fight against what is evil.

The children attending high school are regarded as being engaged in a particularly fierce battle against evil. They are exposed to the temptations of the world at the time when their developing sexuality poses great problems of self-control. Their task is to preserve themselves from contamination (R. Arnold, n.d., p. 95):

They can if they are determined, remain free from the corrosion of a false social pressure to become 'counterfeit adults', and from the forced pre-occupation with sex which has spread like a sickness through our American high-schools.

The children are not entirely unaided or unsupervised in this struggle. They travel to and from school in groups, and are discouraged from participating in extra-curricular activities, or from making friends with 'outsider' school-fellows. The likelihood of such friendships developing is in any case lessened by the Bruderhof children's lack of pocket money, their ignorance of films and television, their sexual naïvety and somewhat well-worn and old fashioned clothing. (The girls usually wear their hair in plaits, use no cosmetics and their dresses are full, and at least knee-length. The best short way of describing the dress of the adult sectarians, is to say that they look like urban middle-class people who have dressed casually and 'rustically' for an evening of square dancing.)

Until the middle of the nineteen fifties, the sectarians were primarily engaged in agriculture, and this fact, in combination with their poverty and a persistent disdain for all things bourgeois, appears to have generated some measure of contempt for the 'artificiality' of higher education. However, at the 1956 Conference, it was recognized that technically educated personnel would increasingly be required in the American hofs, and additionally, it was thought desirable that young persons should experience something of the world in order to enable them to make an informed decision whether or not to enter the novitiate of the sect.

Since 1956, a large proportion of the young people have undergone some form of higher education or technical or professional training, most frequently of a form immediately utilizable within the hofs. However, the 'collegers' are not thrust out into the world in complete isolation or independence. Generally they attend college in groups, lodge with carefully vetted families, and usually return to their hofs at each weekend and throughout the greater part of their vacations.

Attitudes to the state and persecution

The Bruderhof members' attitudes towards the state are ambivalent, but primarily negative. The power of the state is recognized as the only force which acts to curb the forces of evil in the world, but the state itself, being essentially worldly, can only establish some degree of order and co-operation among its subjects by the use of deceit and violence. Arnold described the state as a 'wild beast of hell, an offspring of evil' but admitted its utility in keeping (by means of the use of violence) a balance between men's hostile instincts (*The Plough*, spring 1938, p. 3).

A later writer (Mettler, 1960, pp. 10–11) put the sectarians' conception of the role of the state more temperately:

> Any state has a necessarily temporary function and has to serve until –
> from within, from the very roots upwards – a creative structure of
> communal civilisation embraces all the people in that state.

Until this 'imminent' blossoming of world-wide fellowship from the seed of the Bruderhof communities, the sectarians seek to avoid association with the sins of the state, while living in the privileged position of ambassadors of the coming order – protected by the 'murderous might' of terrestrial government, but owing ultimate allegiance only to the laws of God's Kingdom.

In practical terms, as already indicated, the sectarians do not vote, and regard the holding of any post which 'upholds the order of law' as incompatible with true Christianity. They affirm rather than swear oaths, and especially seek to avoid complicity in the militarism of governments, but pay whatever taxes are demanded of them, and accept state schooling for their children.

Eberhard Arnold taught that, in view of the corruption of the world, spiritual struggle and persecution were inevitable concomitants of lives of Christian witness, and, according to his wife, the discovery of the numerous martyrs of the early Hutterites greatly strengthened the sectarians' faith, and made them aware that, even after five years of rustic privation at Sannerz, they had not plumbed the depths of suffering, or 'persevered to the end'.

Arnold frequently dwelt on the terrible power of the forces of evil which raged against the Church-community (1965a, p. 55):

We stand in the midst of this world as a fighting and persecuted group, persecuted for the sake of the cause of complete community of faith and unity of God's people.

These lines were originally written some months after Hitler's rise to power, and in the darkest period of the sect's history, but remain applicable to the self-conception of the sectarians today. The group's courageous pacifism caused them to be harried from Germany, and in conjunction with the German nationality of the majority of the sectarians, led them to undergo a considerable degree of obloquy in pre-Second World War England. However, in view of the rather dramatic statements made by the sectarians, it is worth pointing out that the group's martyrology consists of three members who were imprisoned for some months in Germany, and of one woman associate who was interned for a short time in England. No members of the sect appear to have suffered physical violence, and throughout most of the history of the group it has enjoyed the tolerance of its neighbours, and in addition, the financial and moral support of a number of less 'revolutionizing' groups and persons.

In the contemporary United States the group's pacifism is officially recognized, and the sectarians appear to be regarded by persons in the neighbourhood of the hofs with a tolerance which is compounded of equal measures of respect for their principles, and pity for the 'eccentricity' of their isolated lives. However, the sectarians continue to insist that the forces of evil are ever-vigilant for a chance to invade and destroy God's ark on earth, and still frequently refer to their sufferings at the hands of the Nazis. They justify their continued separation from the world as necessary if they are to provide a true witness, and deplore in particular the depravity of American Society, and in general the wickedness of a world in which (Arnold, 1965a, p. xv):

Every attempt to establish a beachhead under the banner of God's Kingdom rouses violent opposition. A committed stand for purity is attacked by impurity.

Chapter 7

Conclusions

The visions and mission of utopian sects

The utopian sect is inspired by a detailed vision of earthly society transformed as a result of the abandonment of existing social institutions and their replacement by those divinely revealed social arrangements which the sectarians believe can alone extirpate the corruption of the world.

The mission of the utopian sect is to strive to bring this vision to fruition; to transform the world from a domain of evil into the final, everlasting Kingdom of God. To this end the sectarians retreat from the world to cultivate their spirituality and to establish a nucleus of the Kingdom; once this nucleus is established, they seek converts in the confident expectation that men will soon appreciate the superiority of their new form of society.

In this majestic task the sectarians are, at least initially, sustained by an activist and conditional or *quid pro quo* conception of their relationship with God. Utopian sectarians believe themselves to be endowed with some measure of the power of the Holy Spirit, and they undertake the task of transforming the world in the expectation that their spiritual and physical endeavours will be rewarded and furthered by fresh outpourings of divine power, but they believe, or come to believe, that should they prove unworthy of God's confidence, His grace will be withdrawn from them. As builders working to God's blueprints, and as stewards of the Kingdom on earth, they feel themselves to be subject, in a peculiarly intensive way, to divine scrutiny and injunctions. Every praiseworthy effort of the group and of the individual will be rewarded, every transgression punished, and the sectarians literally believe that the whole future of the world depends on their actions.

Although initially the sectarians' confidence in their capacity to effect the destruction and replacement of earthly institutions may be very great, the utopian vision is essentially gradualistic. The world is occupied by the forces of evil, and must be reclaimed and purified piece by piece. The utopian conception of the earth peacefully transformed by the actions of men operating under divine guidance differs fundamentally from the deterministic, apocalyptic visions of millennial sectarians. In fact, in some cases and social contexts, utopianism appears to represent a form of reaction to, and resolution of, repeatedly aroused and disappointed millennial expectations.

Each of the three sects was inspired by a version of the utopian vision, and the mission of each was essentially activist and optimistic, but also gradualistic and conditional. Of course the details of the visions and associated responses to the world of the three sects differed, as did the durability of their utopian conceptions. None the less, in the formative years of their development each was endowed with a utopian mandate which (while the clarity, urgency and literalness of these mandates varied) provided the rationale for the existence of each group, the basis for its subsequent development and the primary justification for the sectarians' endeavours.

During some fifty years (roughly the period from 1780 to 1830) the Shakers' utopian enthusiasm reached sustained heights which were unequalled by the other two sects. Evangelical success in the north-eastern parts of the United States and in the frontier areas of Kentucky and Ohio convinced the Shakers of the validity of their inspiration, and of the 'overcoming power' of their testimony, and they exerted themselves greatly in attempts to bring about a rapid reconstitution of the world.

Even in this period of confident expansion (when the membership of the group rose from a handful to some five thousand persons) the leaders of the sect occasionally warned their followers that the continued bestowal of God's gifts to the group was dependent upon sustained and increasing purity and evangelical endeavour. The conditional nature of the relationship existing between God and His servants was repeatedly and emphatically stated in the purificatory internal revival of 1837 to 1847, after which fewer converts were made, optimism declined, and the utopianism of the sect faltered and waned.

Noyes's utopian conceptions developed in the period from 1834 (the year in which he announced his complete salvation from sin) until 1847, when he and his followers 'resolved' that the Kingdom of God was established *in nucleo* in their group. By so resolving, the members of the Putney Association indicated unequivocally that they expected their efforts and sacrifices to be rewarded by ever-increasing infusions of the divine power which would enable them to conquer the selfishness of the world, and the devilish manifestations of death and disease.

Even in the full flush of their utopianism the Oneida communists' expectations of the transformation of the world were more gradualistic than those of the early American Shakers. They strove to enlighten the world and to extend their communities, and hailed a range of events and social movements as presaging widespread acceptance of their teachings and style of life, but the literary nature of Oneida evangelism limited its appeal, and caution regarding the world's possible reaction to their sexual arrangements led them to view intending converts with considerable suspicion. The Community's utopianism persisted fitfully for more than a decade after the founding of the Oneida Community proper, but (at least in the case of the leader and his immediate companions) expectations of bringing about an almost total reconstitution of worldly institutions were subsequently replaced by an amelioristic, partly reformist response to the world.

The pristine vision and response to the world of the Bruderhof bore the hallmark of utopianism (active participation in the construction and promulgation of the terrestrial Kingdom of God) but the expectations of the group were always less immediate and more attenuated than those of the Shakers and Oneida Community. Eberhard Arnold and his followers regarded the Sannerz Community and the Rhönbruderhof as 'mission stations' through which the power of the Holy Spirit would flow to combat the individualism of worldly society and replace it by the organic community ordained by God, but, during the sect's existence in Germany, evangelism took second place to the cultivation of internal unity, and the sectarians rarely sallied forth into the world of Mammon.

Subsequently, some members of the groups in England, Paraguay and the United States were concerned to 'spread their light', but the tensions arising from Arnold's somewhat vague dual commitment of the group to separation from the world and to evangelism culminated in the period of purge from 1958 to 1961, and the eventual triumph of the introversionist majority under the leadership of Heinrich Arnold.

The social prerequisites for the development of utopian sectarianism

The utopian vision of the deliberate and almost total replacement of the existing social structure is almost inconceivable in settled societies in which men's status is ascribed at birth, and in which values, customs and behaviour patterns are endowed with the sanctity of immemorial and unquestionable tradition. Utopian conceptions can arise only where there exists a considerable degree of widespread awareness of the mutability of social institutions and arrangements, and some developed perception (not necessarily highly sophisticated or theoretically articulated) of the importance of socialization and the wider social structure as determinants of the personality and behaviour of the individual.

The utopian sect's gradualistic vision of the future can be understood as a radical, religiously inspired version of the broader idea of progress. This vision rests on the activistic conception that, under the beneficent direction of God, men can attain this-worldly bliss through the rational 'moralization' of the institutional structure of society – this moralization being the condition of the continuing improvement and eventual perfection of the individual.

The attempt to translate the utopian vision into reality (an attempt which is intrinsic to the vision as here discussed) can be made only in societies in which there exists some considerable measure of religious and political liberty and consequently of personal autonomy. In such social contexts it is possible for individuals and groups to attempt to 'contract out' of existing institutions and, to some extent at least, of prevailing morality and generally accepted social obligations.

Further, while the utopian sect does not aim to separate itself completely from the wider society (as might an extreme, internally recruiting introversionist group) as this would vitiate the possibility of evangelism, it does seek to segregate itself communally. The short-term aim of the utopian sect is to establish itself in a position which, *vis-à-vis* the wider society, may be termed one of 'viable detachment'. The attainment of such a position implies that the sectarians are freed from the threat of annihilation or debilitating persecution, and that they can undertake some measure of evangelism, while maintaining a very high degree of communal and individual isolation from what they feel is the contaminating influence of the world.

Ann Lee's contribution to the inspirational millennialism of the Wardley group was her insistence that salvation could only be attained by embracing celibacy. Enunciation of this tenet in the industrial slums of late eighteenth-century Manchester brought her few followers and much ridicule and persecution, but in the United States her simple admonitory message was refined by Joseph Meacham and other talented American converts into a complex utopian theology.

The fundamental works of the Shaker theologians reflected the practicality, activism, theological optimism and the more general awareness of virtually unlimited but unrealized opportunities which characterized many of the frontier settlers of the newly independent United States. The Shakers offered communistic endeavour as an alternative to the risks and rigours of individual enterprise, and more important (at least to the first waves of converts) a sublime communal task and path to perfection in place of intermittent revival-induced convictions of salvation, subsequent backsliding, and the psychological torments attendant upon the individual's realization of his persistent vulnerability to temptation.

Noyes's religious ideas developed in a broadly similar (if somewhat more sophisticated) social and intellectual context to those of the American Shakers. His original radical perfectionism and later fully developed utopianism appealed to persons who had been repeatedly subject to revivalism, and had participated in some of the whole spectrum of religiously inspired reformist movements which were the practical fruits of the 'ultraism' which reached a peak in New England and New York in the late eighteen thirties.

Noyes's utopianism was fully developed by 1847, but the hostile reaction evoked in the settled and respectable community of Putney by revelation of the sexual arrangements of the Kingdom of God necessitated the removal of the group to the backwoods. There, in the margins of civilization, in the 'wilderness of Oneida', the sectarians temporarily achieved a high degree of isolation from the outraged proponents of conventional morality. Knox (1950, p. 558), the Catholic theologian, succinctly outlined the conditions of transient frontier isolation in which immigrant (and also indigenous) introversionist and utopian sects found themselves in nineteenth-century America:

> Once you had landed, safe from the storm and prelates' rage, a vast continent stretched before you; and if your neighbours did not like you – commonly they did not – you had only to stake out your claim on some hitherto uncultivated region, build your New Jerusalem and wait quietly for the Second Advent. In fifty years time you had become an immemorial landmark, and reporters were crowding round to write up your old-world seclusion.

In the case of the Bruderhof, even before the First World War Eberhard Arnold had begun to despair of what he felt were the superficial endeavours of conversionist groups to redeem sinful individuals. The wartime sufferings of the German people were succeeded by the humiliations of defeat, economic collapse and persistent political insecurity, and like many of his compatriots Arnold was led to denounce the entire value system, institutional structure and bourgeois culture of Wilhelmian Germany.

Instead of violent political solutions, or proposals for institutional reform, Arnold offered his small band of urban, middle-class, pacifist supporters a vision of a community, and eventually of the world inhabited by 'peasant like' selfless individuals bound together in and by the egoless love of God. Communitarianism was an integral part of Arnold's vision, but in his lifetime the group did not achieve economic independence, and in contrast to the situation of the Shakers and Oneida Community, the non-existence in Germany of unsettled tracts of free or cheap land precluded the possibility of maintaining large numbers of converts in vicinal segregation.

Even the small degree of moral and institutional autonomy which the group had achieved by the nineteen thirties was deemed intolerable by Nazi totalitarianism, and the hostility experienced by the sectarians in England, and their subsequent isolation among a primitive, Catholic-influenced population in Paraguay strengthened the introversionist leanings of the majority of the sectarians, who tended to neglect Arnold's injunction that the sect should engage actively in reconquering the world for God.

The social circumstances of the emergence of the Bruderhof of course differed greatly from those of the Shakers and Oneida Community. Despite this, all three groups were alike in that they emerged in periods when value patterns and institutions were in flux, or were being subjected to intensive critical scrutiny, and the leaders were alike in their conviction that the corruption of men was primarily the product of corrupt institutions.

The internal dynamic and changing response to the world of utopian sects

In the introductory chapter it was indicated that in recent years the main thrust of the sociological study of sectarianism has been away from the simplistic formulations of Troeltsch and Niebuhr towards a more sophisticated appreciation of the ideological and structural diversity of sectarian groups. Implicit in such an appreciation is the investigation of the potential for development of particular types of sects; an investigation which in part rests on consideration of the dynamic inherent in the sect's response to the world, and on broader consideration of the characteristic patterns of mutation or transformation of that response.

The belief system of a utopian sect sanctions a dual commitment: to isolation and to evangelism. The sectarians try to avoid contamination by the world, but they also seek to excel the social arrangements and morality of the world, and to demonstrate their excellence to persons living in the world.

Of these two ideologically derived components of the response of the sect to the world isolation is strategically prior to evangelism. It is the condition of the development of the spiritual qualities which the sectarians believe will guarantee an eventual world-wide acceptance of their ideal form of society. In practice, after the initial stage of the establishment of communitarianism, and while the sect's utopian response persists, both commitments are likely to claim the attention of the sectarians, and undue emphasis on one commitment tends to partially offset the effects of prior concentration on the other.

Extreme isolation from the world inhibits proselytization, while evangelism poses threats to the social and ideological purity which is believed to be a condition of the success of the sect's mission. In consequence, the development of a utopian sect is characterized by alternate periods of evangelistic activity involving relative openness to the world, and periods of intensified separation from the world.

The utopian response to the world is fraught with ambivalence, and the dual ideological commitment inherent in this response creates an area of strategic ambiguity in the sect. As a result of this ambiguity (in combination with the inspirationalism which will be discussed below) the leaders of a utopian sect are endowed with a considerable amount of flexibility in their choice of policy, and each choice can, at least temporarily, be legitimated in terms of the mission of the sect, and the religious beliefs which underlie this mission.

In consequence, the failure of the sect to achieve its ultimate goal of world transformation can, at any one period, be attributed in part to prior over-concentration on one aspect of the sect's dual commitment, and the very ambiguity of the utopian response (and of course the exploitation of this ambiguity by the leaders) may well be a factor contributing to the durability of that response. Thus it may be argued that the group has failed to make converts because it has concentrated too exclusively and too long on the development of internal purity and spirituality. Conversely, withdrawal from the world may be advocated as a means of developing the spiritual qualities necessary to attract converts, and, associatedly, may be recommended as a means of purging the group of 'impurities' and tensions arising from earlier excessive contact with the world.

This pattern of alternating periods of relative openness to the world and of preparatory and purificatory withdrawal is evident in the history of each of the three sects, but was exhibited in most marked and persistent form by the Shakers. The Shakers largely withdrew themselves from the world during the Ministry of James Whittaker, and 're-opened their testimony' in 1797, a decade after his death. They temporarily curtailed their evangelism and engaged in minor purificatory revivals in 1816 and 1827, and again 'withdrew their testimony' throughout the great internal revival of 1835 to 1847. During each period of retreat the leaders of the sect emphasized the need for the cultivation of greater degrees of spirituality, and prophesied that such efforts would be rewarded by massive accessions of converts and a rapid increase in the number of Shaker societies.

The Oneida Community proper was founded in 1848, and after a year's labour Noyes judged that this first 'visible branch' of the Primitive Church was established on a viable basis, and so removed himself and his closest associates to Brooklyn to undertake what he claimed was the higher task of literary evangelism. During the years at Brooklyn, Noyes's utopian enthusiasm was at a peak, and he evidently expected that widespread publication of his religious and social doctrines in conjunction with the standing example of the Oneida Community would be sufficient to effect a speedy conversion of the superior elements of the American population to 'Bible communism'.

Late in 1854, the financial difficulties of the Community, coupled with the ineffectiveness of his literary evangelism, led Noyes to anathematize American society and to return to Oneida. There he initiated a programme of purification and 'consolidation' of the sect. After 1860, his conception of the nature of the regeneration of mankind became increasingly gradualistic, or in his term 'geological'. His interests turned first to the radical expedient of breeding a new, morally superior race of men, and subsequently to a wide variety of proposals for social reform and to the general study of communitarianism and social experiments.

Arnold's dedication of his Church-community to 'conquering the earth' was less frequently and less vehemently reiterated than the evangelical injunctions of the leaders of the Shakers and of the Oneida Community. However, shortly before his death, Arnold emphasized the need for 'outreach' (and evangelical considerations had been among the factors which prompted his allegiance with the markedly introversionist Hutterians) and evangelism was enthusiastically undertaken for several years after the migration to England and later by some members of the Paraguayan and re-established English hofs.

The threat which evangelism posed to the fragile 'unity of the Spirit' became abundantly clear to the more introversionist-tending members of the sect by the late nineteen fifties, and for the decade since the purge of 1958 to 1961, the group has maintained a posture which the sectarians describe as one of 'creative withdrawal' from the external society.

The paragraphs above indicate the dynamic inherent in the utopian response to the world. Summary consideration must now be given to the effects of repeated disappointment of the utopian vision of bringing about an almost total replacement of the institutions of the world.

The degree of success of a utopian sect (in contrast to the success of sects which are primarily concerned with the attainment of other-worldly salvation) is empirically assessable in terms of converts made and the consequent extension of the supposedly ideal form of society. Evangelical success is interpreted by the sectarians as betokening God's approval of their endeavours. Evangelical failure may for some considerable time be attributed to an unanticipated degree of corruption of the world and to the spiritual inadequacy of the sectarians themselves, but if evangelism remains unsuccessful or disappointing after repeated efforts to 'strengthen' the members and purify the group, the effects are likely to be drastic.

In such a case of repeated or prolonged evangelical disappointment many of the sectarians (especially the younger, more independent and less committed adults) are likely to leave the group which to them manifestly appears to have lost the 'overcoming power' of the Holy Spirit. The persons who remain (and whose motives for so doing will be considered below) gradually adjust themselves to the disappointment of their utopian hopes in ways which represent an interpretation or modification of one of the two contradictory commitments which were inherent in the original utopian vision. The modified responses to the world which were exhibited in varying degrees by members of the Shakers and the Oneida Community can be termed, albeit clumsily, 'apathetic introversionism' and 'exemplary reformism'.

Those sectarians whose response develops into apathetic introversionism gradually relinquish all but the vaguest and most remote hopes of transforming the world, and become increasingly preoccupied with the practical side of communal life and with devotional matters; especially those pertaining to other-worldly salvation. Their attitude to the external society which has spurned their teachings and way of life remains for long one of suspicion and hostility; but in time resentment of the world is likely to be replaced by resignation to the continued existence of worldly evil, and, concomitantly, some aspects of the more arduous or irksome ascetic practices and other patterns of behaviour which originally served to distinguish the sectarians from the world are relinquished.

Apathetic introversionism develops as a direct response to the sense of futility and despair generated by repeated disappointment of utopian hopes. The espousal of exemplary reformism appears as an attempt to counter this despair by revitalizing the sect through demonstrating the continuing importance, but changed nature, of its mission.

The proponents of exemplary reformism do not (as for example do the more purely reformist Quakers) regard the performance of good works as the primary task of their group, although typically they look with approval on such good works and on reform-oriented movements generally. They attempt to make the best of the world's rejection of their utopian 'light', and argue that this rejection only demonstrates the degree of their superiority to the world, and hence that their task is to stand as a moral and social exemplar of the heights to which the more enlightened of men can aspire. The self-conception of such sectarians changes from that of being persons destined to bring about the total reconstitution of human society, to that of being the vanguard of human progress, whose task is to inspire men to improve their institutions and their lives.

Both types of response to evangelical disappointment appeared most plainly and in sharpest opposition among the Shakers in the second half of the nineteenth century (who of course, being celibate, were entirely dependent on external recruitment for their expansion and survival). As the facts of numerical decline became impossible to ignore in the years after the Civil War, the great majority of persons who remained in the group appear to have sought solace in contemplation of its past achievements, in the orderliness of their communal lives and in personal devotions. The ageing, predominantly female sectarians paid scant heed to Eads's orthodox exhortations to greater austerity and communal discipline; and were probably largely indifferent to, or incapable of appreciating, the sophistry with which Evans tried to persuade an unresponsive world that the Shakers were uniquely qualified to be its guides and mentors.

The vigour, ambitiousness and ineffectiveness of the exemplary reformism of Evans and the other 'progressive' Shakers was rivalled by that of Noyes and his immediate associates once their utopian fervour had declined. Despite devoting the five years after his return from Brooklyn to purifying the Oneida Community, Noyes was still unable to realize his hope of 'rolling back the tide of sin'. He was incorrigibly innovative and impetuous, and in the eighteen sixties not only embarked on the stirpicultural experiment, but also conquered his earlier repugnance to American society, and proclaimed that the United States lacked only his inspiration and the social techniques of 'Bible communism' in order to fulfil its manifest destiny of civilizing the world.

In the early eighteen seventies, indifference to his proposals, and mounting internal dissension and external opposition led Noyes to view the Oneida Community not, as earlier, as the nucleus of the terrestrial Kingdom, but as one, imperfect, type of 'Socialism'. However, the imperfection of his creation did not prevent Noyes from regarding himself as the person most qualified to direct the socialist and communitarian movements of America.

Noyes's changed conception of his mission was evidenced in numerous articles in the sect's periodical; the reaction of the rank and file Perfectionists is somewhat harder to assess. With their increasing prosperity after the Civil War the zeal of many of the older sectarians for publicity and evangelism dwindled to extinction; and for some years the majority appear to have been content to bask in a sense of moral and intellectual superiority, and to lead comfortable, highly sociable, but none the less introverted lives.

Concern for personal salvation probably increased slightly in the Community in this period, but must have been considerably inhibited (as compared with the Shakers, whose theology retained many elements of orthodox eschatology) by the fact that the sect remained at least formally committed to the abolition of death and disease from the world.

Noyes's reformist ambitions and intellectual vagaries distressed many of the older sectarians, who remained more loyal to their leader's original utopianism than he did himself, and the spectacle of his declining health shook the faith of many, and led to a gradual decline in his authority. By 1875, Noyes was a prophet who had intellectually outdistanced many of his older followers; had ceased to command the loyalties of the young, and who was conspired against by some of his lieutenants. The extent of apathy, insecurity and manifest dissatisfaction and conflicts in the sect encouraged its opponents, and was evidenced by the sectarians' capitulation to the demand that they abandon complex marriage, and their subsequent voluntary relinquishment of economic communism.

In comparison with the utopian visions which inspired the Shakers and the Oneida Community, that of Eberhard Arnold was less radical, more mystical and less immediate, and the response to the world of the sect in recent years has become unequivocally and increasingly introversionist. This mutation of the response of the Bruderhof can be undertood as a reaction to the conflicts and dissension which resulted from the somewhat indiscriminate evangelism of the nineteen fifties (and, as will be argued later, indicates some of the difficulties associated with the maintenance of utopianism in industrial societies). The abandonment of evangelism poses no such threat to the Bruderhof as did evangelical failure to the Shakers, as the extremely high birth rate in the sect permits it to maintain its numbers through internal recruitment, even if more than half of the young persons should leave the sect for the world.

The future development of the Bruderhof can only be a matter for speculation, but it seems likely that, at least during the lifetime of the present leader, the introversionism of the group will be maintained, and may even continued to be intensified. The group will probably expand slowly as a result of internal recruitment, as well as the conversion of those few individuals who are 'sent' to the sect, and who there find at least an illusion of independence and freedom from the competitiveness, individualism, bureaucratization and anonymity of life in the contemporary United States.

The theologies of utopian sects

Sects may emerge in three main ways: as a result of schism, through organized revival or by crystallizing around the teachings of a leader or prophet. Schism may occur as a result of disputes concerning a wide range of topics – organizational questions, devotional practices and the like – but generally the arguments of both parties to the dispute become couched in doctrinal terms. The schismatic sect is likely to emerge with a fully developed theology which may differ in seemingly only very minor details from that of the parent group.

Sects which develop through organized revivals are typically originally endowed with a simple conception of the 'true way of life' and of the consequent road to salvation, and may only gradually develop a comprehensive theology. The same is true of sects with charismatic origins. Typically the leader initially proclaims a simple message or programme which, over time, and often only after the leader's death, is elaborated and becomes the basis of a comprehensive body of religious teachings.

Each of the three sects examined in this study had charismatic origins and in each the original simple, if dramatic, mission, conceptions and injunctions of the founder were subsequently developed (in the case of the Oneida Community and Bruderhof, largely by the founders themselves) into a coherent body of teachings or a full fledged systematic theology which explained and justified the mission of the group; identified its precursors and, conversely, traced the past development of the forces of evil which the sectarians sought to drive from the earth. The developed theologies of utopian sects can be characterized summarily as gradualistic in the expectations they engender, this-worldly in orientation and informed by a conception of continuing inspiration.

The theologians of each sect explicitly or implicitly rejected orthodox millennial conceptions of an apocalyptic overthrow of worldly society. Instead they regarded the primary eschatological event – the Advent and the associated inauguration of the terrestrial Kingdom of God – as past, or as realized or re-embodied in their own organization.

An essentially, but not unqualifiedly optimistic vision of the future is intrinsic to utopian theologies. The eschatological event having occurred, the future promises to be one of cumulative progress towards the worldwide establishment of God's Kingdom; but this progress remains conditional on the sectarians' struggles to improve themselves spiritually and so to render themselves fit recipients of the power of the Holy Spirit. Such conceptions permit of a wide range of chronological interpretations. The sectarians may expect an almost immediate or extremely slow transformation of the world. Although, presumably largely because of past experience of millennial disappointment, none of the theologians of the three sects ventured to predict the precise date when God's work would be completed on earth, the early Shakers certainly expected that Ann Lee's inauguration of the fourth historical dispensation would lead to the rapid establishment of the celibate 'earthly heavens'. Similarly, in the eighteen fifties, Noyes and his followers triumphantly proclaimed the imminent abolition of sin, disease and death. However, experience of the resilience of worldly institutions led both groups to increasingly gradualistic interpretations which approximated to the less radical expectations of Eberhard Arnold, and eventually to the quasi-metaphorical rather than literal statements of contemporary members of the Bruderhof.

The theologians of each sect urged their followers to 'look to the earth' as the setting in which the struggle between good and evil would be resolved, and emphasized that the salvation of the earth and of the individual was only possible in the context of collective endeavour. A this-worldly orientation is of course an essential component of the utopian response to the world, but such an orientation is not exclusive to the utopian sect, nor does it entirely preclude orthodox, other-worldly eschatological considerations of salvation and damnation. Such secondary other-worldly considerations were most prominent in the basic theological works of the Shakers, which were compiled more than twenty years after the death of Ann Lee. The Shaker theologians and the later inspired instruments emphasized the magnitude of the task undertaken by the sect, but promised that all those who struggled faithfully on earth, but died before God's work was completed, would receive heavenly rewards of the highest order. These teachings, which contained strongly marked compensatory elements, and promised that in heaven the lowly and despised Shakers would receive the tribute and submission of the mighty of the earth, indubitably facilitated the development of passive devotionalism as a response to evangelical disappointments in the second half of the nineteenth century.

As long as the members of the Oneida Community expected that their efforts would bring about a speedy breakdown of the 'partition between heaven and earth', and so effect the abolition of sin, disease and death, the theological writings of the group laid little emphasis on other-worldly salvation, although Noyes readily accepted that the most depraved of men, the 'seed of Satan', would suffer an eternity of torment. With the decline of utopian expectations and as increasing numbers of the sectarians fell victim to the unremitting power of death, the joys of other-worldly salvation were increasingly referred to in the sect's periodical.

The contemporary members of the Bruderhof, who appear to regard themselves as a gathered remnant protected by their communal fellowship from the general evils of the world and from the specific seductions of reformism, volunteer little information regarding the after-life, but probably take post-mortem rewards for granted. Persons joining the sect from the outside world have typically been associated with such sects as the Quakers, whose eschatology is attenuated, and within the Bruderhof they quickly learn that to discuss individual salvation is to betray vestiges of self-seeking egotism. Similarly, the sectarians make no reference to damnation, and presumably regard the wretchedness of lives led in separation from the love of God as sufficient punishment for even the most heinous of earthly transgressions.

The founders of the three sects believed themselves to be directly inspired by the Spirit of God, and to be the 'vessels' through which the word of God was to be made known to all mankind. They claimed to be the recipients, not just of their original dramatic revelations, but of continuous, or at least intermittent, divine inspiration. As the sects' utopianism developed, and as the complexity of the task involved in these responses became apparent, so there developed a conception (intimately related to the *quid pro quo* nature of the sectarians' understanding of their relationship with God) that the details of the mode of accomplishment of God's plan would be gradually revealed to the sectarians.

Theologically this conception was expressed in various doctrines of continuing and progressive inspiration. Thus the members of the Shaker Ministry were regarded as the heirs of Ann Lee and as the 'fount' of the revelations which guided the development of the group. Noyes proclaimed himself to be the pre-eminent 'child of inspiration', and Arnold, as the instrument of God and 'Word Leader' of the Bruderhof, had the self-appointed task of articulating the will of the Spirit, which was most clearly manifested in the united fellowship of the Brotherhood.

The belief in continuing inspiration – the idea that God's word and will for his people on earth will be progressively opened up to them – is not unique to the utopian sect, but in combination with the ambiguities of the utopian response which have been discussed earlier, it endows the leaders of a utopian sect with the capacity to exercise a high degree of flexibility in exegesis and in policy, and with a whole range of possible rationalizations for the group's non-attainment of its ultimate goal.

Within limits, such flexibility allows the sect to adapt itself to changing social circumstances without necessarily completely repudiating past practices or social attitudes, and without the need for condemnation of the instigators of these practices. Past leaders may be acclaimed and revered for having proclaimed and obeyed the word of God as it stood in their time, even while departures from their practices and teachings are justified in terms of subsequent 'higher' revelations. Thus, encouraged by the passivity or apathy of the Shaker Ministry in the second half of the nineteenth century, Evans was able to present an increasingly gradualistic and reformist interpretation of the mission of the sect as involving seven testimonies against evil. He discussed Ann Lee with some measure of condescension as the woman who had 'lived up to the light accorded her' by inaugurating the first testimony – that against sexuality. Similarly, Noyes adduced higher revelations to justify his changing ambitions and conception of his mission.

Belief in continuing inspiration creates the possibility of theologically legitimating changes in policy and social attitudes, and so of minimizing the disruptive effects of these changes. Further, such a belief may be an important factor in stimulating or at least maintaining the commitment of the sectarians by enhancing their self esteem. While belief in the validity of the group's inspiration persists (an extremely important proviso), each generation of sectarians will tend to regard themselves as, in a sense, doubly enlightened, superior to the world, and also superior to earlier members of the group whose lives were governed by less advanced revelations of the will of God.

In sects which lack a clearly defined and effective authority structure (as for example do many pentecostal groups) belief in continuing inspiration is extremely likely to be a divisive factor, as each member may lay claim to revelation. The divisive potential of inspirationalism was clearly recognized by the authoritarian leaders of the three sects analysed here. The early Shaker theologians and the Ministry at the time of 'Mother Ann's Work' restricted the scope and the recipients of legitimate inspiration, and ingeniously adduced revelations to justify this limitation. Noyes emphasized that he was the arbiter of all subordinate inspiration; and in the Bruderhof the 'leadings of the Spirit' which meet with the necessary unanimous approval are generally those vouchsafed to, or articulated by, the Servant and executive of the group.

The members of utopian sects exhibit a marked tendency to attribute unexpected happenings (even of the most minor kind) to the direct operation of God or of the forces of evil. In each sect fortunate occurrences or fruitful ideas were hailed as gifts from the Spirit, or at least from benign spirits. Conversely, practical misfortunes, derelictions and evil impulses (and in the Oneida Community ill-health) were attributed to the operation of the devil, or of his incarnate or spiritual myrmidons.

These conceptions can be understood as low-level corollaries of the idea of continuing inspiration, and as serving to remind the sectarians that their lives, however secure, restricted or monotonous they might at times seem, were spent in the immediate and hazardous service of God. It seems likely, although it is impossible to substantiate the contention, that this tendency to invest even trivia with cosmic significance is developed to the highest degree among the contemporary Bruderhof, who suffer no persecution or hardship, and whose introversionism and rejection of reform militates against their identifying with any persecuted minority (as did the Shakers with the American Indians and the Oneida Community with the Jews), but who seek to justify their introversionism in terms of the 'unclean and devilish' spirits which rage in the external society.

Conclusions

Charisma and the utopian 'social contract'

All three of the sects examined in this work had their origins in small unstructured fellowships which develop around leaders who were charismatic in that, with varying degrees of emphasis, they claimed supernatural inspiration and extraordinary missions and powers and derived their authority from their followers' acceptance of these claims. Ann Lee believed herself to be the female counterpart of Christ and announced that celibacy was the one road to salvation. Noyes proclaimed that, the Second Coming being past, perfect holiness was potentially attainable by all men, and that he was commissioned to inaugurate the Kingdom of God on earth. Arnold considered himself to be the most recent in a line of witnesses to the true Christianity which had flourished for a time in the Primitive Church, and further to be an instrument of God whose task was to sow the seed of the new order on earth. The conviction that their leader was endowed with a divine warrant and with extraordinary power inspired the sectarians (many of whom appear to have been otherwise practical and empirically minded men) to undertake the prodigious task of regenerating the world by transforming its institutions.

In each of the three sects, specific personality traits and the more general social and intellectual predilections of the founder were expressed in the *Weltanschauung* of the group, and more concretely, were built into its social structure. Consideration of this fact gives rise to a form of paradox or irony – charismatic authority (using the term in the 'undiluted' Weberian sense) is instrumental in inspiring men to attempt to establish a final form of society which will be 'infused' with the love stemming from the Holy Spirit. This love, being perfect and, in the sectarians' conception, impersonal, will put an end to all personal authority, including charismatic authority. The founders of utopian sects, markedly forceful, egotistical and idiosyncratic personalities, thus aim, more or less consciously, to bring about the conditions of their own extinction – a state of affairs in which individualism and idiosyncrasy will be extinguished by the diffuse, undifferentiated love of God.

An additional point which should be made in connection with the charismatic origins of the utopian sect is that the very nature of its mission and response to the world renders it necessary for the sociologist to exercise some caution when discussing the 'routinization' of the charisma of the founder of a utopian sect. The charismatic authority of the leader of a utopian sect rests on his followers' acceptance of the genuineness of his inspiration, and this inspiration is demonstrated by the success of his mission – the construction and promulgation of an alternative form of society.

Such a conception of his mission necessarily involves the leader of the sect in organizational matters (it is he who enunciates God's blueprint and who, with his followers, actively engages in translating this blueprint into reality) but such involvement does not inevitably lessen or vitiate this charismatic authority, even if, as is typically the case, the leader concerns himself with matters of an essentially utilitarian kind.

For example, in 1848 Noyes concentrated his attention on establishing the Oneida Community on a viable basis; a task which involved his direction of the initiation of craft industries, the construction of buildings and even the establishment of a schedule of daily activities. His involvement with, and successful completion of, these utilitarian tasks did not diminish or change the quality of Noyes's authority over his followers. On the contrary, it greatly enhanced his charisma, which was only eroded years later when his prophecies had been repeatedly falsified and his health had begin to fail.

The above remarks pertaining to charisma and the associated exploration of the practical implications of the utopian response to the world should not be allowed to obscure the fact that the utopianism of each sect gradually developed from a matrix of simpler religious teachings. Shaker utopianism was developed from Ann Lee's dramatic admonitory message, and, concomitantly, the expedient communism and communalism practised by the sectarians at Niskeyuna was invested with extreme ideological significance, and became the basis of Shaker 'gospel order'. Noyes's utopianism only developed after more than a decade in which he suffered repeated evangelical disappointment and much personal rejection and vilification; and Arnold's eventual concern to translate the principles of the Sermon on the Mount into reality was the product of disillusionment with the compromises of denominational and evangelical groups, in conjunction with his wartime experiences and subsequent contacts with the religiously-oriented wing of the German youth movement.

The utopian response appears as a complex product of sustained dissatisfaction, disappointment and eventual despair of the religious and social condition of the world. The members of a utopian sect have abandoned hope of reforming the world by limited practical measures or of effecting its spiritual regeneration from within, but they have not abandoned their concern for persons living in the world.

To the sectarians the world appears to be, in the Hobbesian sense, a state of nature. The lives of men in the world are 'solitary' in that they are estranged from God; 'poor, nasty' and 'brutish' as a result of this estrangement and the consequent dominance of the forces of evil, and 'short' in that there is little hope of attaining salvation in the midst of worldly corruption.

To escape, and ultimately to put an end to this state of affairs, the sectarians enter into a 'social contract' which they regard as cemented by the Spirit of God. They abandon the world in order to establish what they believe is the embryo of the form of society which will eventually replace the corruption of the world.

The difficulties attendant upon the construction and promulgation of an alternative society are many, and, somewhat ironically, while the original social contract is usually made between the sectarians 'in faith'; this original is usually replaced or supplemented by a contractual instrument which is in accordance with the legal forms of worldly society. Thus the Shakers' original oral covenant was in 1795 supplanted by a written covenant which, in response to a variety of exigencies – claims from seceders and relatives of converts, challenges from opponents of the sect and the fiscal, military and educational demands of the state – was repeatedly clarified, modified and strengthened.

It would be unnecessarily repetitious to present even a summary examination of the variety of problems faced by the sectarians in their attempt to construct a more or less self-sufficient, rationally ordered *Gemeinschaft*. However, reference to the successive modifications of the contractual basis of the Shaker sect raises the more general point that the successful solution of each of the problems faced by the utopian sect (for example, that of winning special tax status, or recognition of pacifist principles) strengthens and re-entrenches the organizational structure of the group, but to some extent compromises the sect with the world, and demonstrates the sect's dependence for its continued existence on the toleration of the external society. As a result, while the organizational structure of the group becomes more firmly established, the original utopian vision and convictions which provided the initial motivation for the development of that structure are steadily eroded.

The variety, and ideological sources, of the strategies which enable the leaders of the sect temporarily to divert attention from, or explain, the group's non-attainment of its ultimate goal have already been indicated. The fact remains that as the sect becomes increasingly compromised with the world, and as these compromises and the eventually apparent lack of success of the group are rationalized by an ever more gradualistic interpretation of its mission; so the enthusiasm of the sectarians and the capacity (and ultimately even the desire) of the leaders to mobilize their followers for the 'conquest of the earth' declines.

Once the faith which inspires the utopian vision and response has been fundamentally shaken, even the most complex mechanisms of social control can do little to restore it. The communitarian structure of the group is likely to persist for some considerable time after the utopian spirit has departed, and may, as with the majority of the Shakers in the late nineteenth century or the contemporary Bruderhof, serve as a defence for, respectively, apathetic or purer forms of introversionism. Conversely, the persisting organizational structure may be adduced (as by Noyes before the complete collapse of his 'Bible communism', or as in the last writings of the Shakers) as demonstrating the practical, if limited, benefits and feasibility of sustained communism and communalism.

Social control in the utopian sect

Sects are voluntaristic religious organizations which typically seek to foster exclusive adherence to their ideology, and to mould their members' behaviour into a high degree of conformity with normative principles which are derived directly from this ideology. To attain these related ends – to elicit cognitive and behavioural compliance from their members – sects employ a wide variety of techniques of social control and (primarily but not exclusively) normative sanctions of varying degrees of severity.

The aim of the utopian sect is more radical and more all-encompassing than that of most other types of sect. The utopian sect literally aims to bring every aspect of its members' lives into conformity with its ideological principles. The utopian sect is thus committed to establishing a truly totalitarian degree of control over its members.

More specifically, the techniques of social control of a utopian sect are employed in order to attain two broad and closely related, but chronologically and conceptually distinguishable ends. First, to purge the individual of the corruption of the world from which he has been drawn. Second, to protect the individual and hence the group from renewed contamination by the world, and, concomitantly, to render the individual a fit inhabitant of the Kingdom of God on earth, and to inspire him to defend and extend that Kingdom.

The phraseology employed by the members of a utopian sect to denote the ends to which their techniques of social control are directed is similar to that used by many other sects, but is capable of a somewhat more literal interpretation. The individual must become 'dead' to the world in order that he should be capable of the 're-birth' which establishes him as fit to become a full member of the utopian sect and hence to be rendered (to use the Bruderhof terminology) into a 'cell' or 'building block' of the Kingdom of God.

Superficially, becoming dead to the world implies becoming indifferent to worldly concerns. More radically, it implies the destruction of individualism and egotism; such destruction being the condition of the 'exhumation' and eventual 're-birth' of the individual as a selfless, regenerated personality.

In each of the three sects here examined a distinction was drawn between the point when the individual began to die to the world, and the commencement of the process leading to full regeneration. Entry to the novitiate of the Shakers and Bruderhof and the first 'voluntary' revival-induced conversion experienced by many members of the Oneida Community prior to their joining the sect were alike understood as giving expression to the individual's desire to renounce the world and to 'crucify' his selfish personality. Entry into the Church order of the Shakers, baptism into the Bruderhof and the second conversion 'involuntarily' wrought by the Holy Spirit on worthy members of the Oneida Community betokened the individual's full commitment to the particular sect, and his embarkation on the spiritual journey which, at least potentially, would lead him to full regeneration.

The strategies and general methods of social control (implying here techniques of re-education or re-socialization as well as means of maintaining commitment to the ideals of the group) employed in utopian sects are best distinguished and described in summary fashion before turning briefly to examine the combinations of the techniques employed in the individual sects. Three types of modes of control may be conceptually distinguished. First, 'situational' or 'physical' controls; second, 'normative' controls; and third, more overt and individually specific 'technical' methods which may serve to discipline recalcitrants and more generally to instil the desired patterns of thought and behaviour into the sectarians.

Despite the pronounced ideological and consequent social divergences between the three sects, the ideal personality of each group (the 'childlike man' of the Shakers and Bruderhof, the 'regenerated man' of the Oneida Community) was broadly delineated in similar adjectival terms. The aim of the control mechanisms of the three sects (all of which regarded the Primitive Church as, if not ideal, at least a worthy model) was to produce men who were fit to be the instruments of God. Such men were to be courageous and zealous, but also disciplined, subordinated, humble and essentially and especially self or ego-less, and could only be produced as a result of intensive individual and communal spiritual endeavours, in conjunction with unremitting vigilance against the powers of evil that sought to prevent the sect executing its divinely appointed task by subverting the individual sectarians.

Turning now to consideration of the first – physical or situational – type of control exerted by the utopian sect, the maintenance of a high degree of communal and individual separation from the world is of course a *sine qua non* of the utopian response, and requires little further comment beyond a reiteration of the fact that the utopian sect does not seek (even if it could attain) total separation from the external society. The utopian sect's commitment to evangelism necessitates the maintenance of, as an absolute minimum, literary contacts with the world and facilities for scrutinizing potential converts. In fact, in all three cases reviewed here, the range of contacts was considerably more extensive. Missionaries were periodically sent into the world, economic transactions and relations with the state were regularized, and visitors and aspirant converts were received and accommodated by the sectarians.

Despite the variety and frequency of contacts with the world, each point of contact was to some extent 'insulated' by formal or informal patterns of behaviour which protected the values and commitment of the sectarians from unnecessary challenges, accentuated the distinctions prevailing between the sectarians and worldly persons, and quite explicitly functioned to guard the sectarians from corruption by the world or to counteract such corruption as was deemed inevitable.

Thus the trustees who occupied a pivotal position between the Shaker families and the external society were thought to be especially exposed to worldly evil in all its forms, and in consequence, their conduct and comportment in the world was subject to especially minute regulation and scrutiny. Members of the Oneida Community who had travelled outside the Community for any considerable length of time (and even those persons who had been particularly exposed to the evil influences emanating from visitors to the sect) were decontaminated on their return by a refreshing 'bath' of criticism, and the Bruderhof children who receive their high school education outside the hofs are effectively debarred from more than superficial and largely impersonal contact with 'outsider' children. In each sect individual contacts with the world were frowned upon, or at least carefully controlled, and among the Shakers and the Bruderhof, knowledge of day-to-day events in the external society was largely gleaned from edifying readings – edifying in that they illuminated the evils of the world and reminded the sectarians of their privileged positions.

In all three groups the desire for privacy was the subject of reiterated condemnation, as was the formation of cliques, special attachments and even indulgence in individualistic recreational activities or the cultivation of intellectual interests which, being relatively esoteric, were hence largely incommunicable. All such prohibitions were intended to foster the destruction of the ego and to bring about its replacement by, literally, a collective consciousness, or almost total other-directedness. The very structure of utopian communitarianism – the small total population of the communities, their internal stratification (especially the partial isolation of converts from full members), the group performance of economic, recreational and devotional activities – was in large part intended to facilitate this process by permitting almost constant surveillance of each member by his spiritual superiors, and perhaps more important, by his peers.

Within the tightly-bounded physical confines of each group the sectarians were subject to unremitting moral exhortation, and specific normative injunctions laid emphasis on the fact that the spiritual welfare of the sect was the concern and responsibility of every member. Failure to make known other's derelictions, or even suspected attitudinal irregularities, was to condone their sins, and hence to participate in their guilt.

Normative and situational constraints together provided the basic social context in which the regeneration of the individual could take place. In each sect regeneration was additionally fostered by the reiteration of the moral principles of the group in literal and symbolic form in worship and recreational activities, and more specifically was promoted by overt instruction, and by the employment of the third mode of control – those

technical methods of social control which were at once educative, therapeutic, punitive and cathartic.

These techniques were educative because they served to inculcate in a
particularly forceful manner the moral and behavioural *desiderata* of the sect;
therapeutic in that they were intended to remove all vestiges of the 'diseased'
worldly personality; punitive as their employment involved potent normative
sanctions; and cathartic in that they permitted the expression of accumulated
tensions, or legitimized the immediate expression of sentiments which might
otherwise have posed threats to the continuance of communal life. Among
the Shakers confession of sins was a prerequisite for entry to the novitiate or
junior order of the sect but delinquent individuals were frequently required
to make full, abject and repeated confessions of their lamentable conduct
and spiritual state, and the elders of the group had a clear appreciation of
the humiliating and mortifying effects of such 'voluntary' confessions.

The system of mutual criticism practised in the Oneida Community was,
in combination with Noyes's daily instructive home-talks, regarded as the
fundament of the group's communal existence, and its function in channel-
ling gossip and providing release for the strains inherent in close-knit
communal life were recognized and lauded. The First Law in Sannerz of
the Bruderhof is manifestly a simple prohibition of the informal control
techniques of gossip, ridicule and ostracism which operate in all 'uninten-
tional' communities, but it provides the basis for the system of brotherly
remonstrance which acts as a sharp corrective for persons who manifest
even minute secondary symptoms of egotism. Further, the Law's requirement that all doubts and grievances should be immediately and publicly
'opened' provides an extraordinarily effective method of preventing the
development of cabals and factions, by rendering the collective expression
of grievances illegitimate, and so automatically convicting the aggrieved
parties of harbouring evil spirits and threatening the unity of the group.

The structural, normative and technical methods of control summarily
described above provide a striking demonstration of the ways in which
normative commitment to religious organizations may be maintained and
stimulated, and go far towards explaining the often overlooked, minimized,
or misunderstood durability of such voluntary commitment. However, this
point having been made, the range of sanctions backing the techniques of
control of the utopian sect must be briefly considered. The positive sanctions
– the enjoyment of the approval of one's co-religionists, the sense of participating in God's ultimate task, hopes of sublime rewards in this world and
the next – were indubitably of prime importance in stimulating the spiritual
and physical endeavours of the sectarians, but when energy and convictions
temporarily flagged, a range of negative sanctions – remonstrance, reduction
of privileges of worship or of rank, degrees of institutionalized ostracism
and ultimately expulsion – could be invoked against the errant individual.

While such negative sanctions were again primarily normative in that they depended for their full impact on the individual's continued basic acceptance of the belief system of the sect, the extra-normative, economic aspect of the most serious sanction – expulsion – should not be overlooked. In each sect the individual's degree of ideological commitment was in part expressed by a parallel degree of economic commitment. The novice or probationer was required to dedicate his labour and property without expectation of recompense for work, or interest on his property if he should secede. More important, persons making a full commitment were required to dedicate their labour without recompense, and, additionally, to consecrate their property irrevocably to the group.

In each sect the full rigour of these contractual agreements was frequently mitigated by payments of quittance money, and sometimes the return of consecrated property, to persons who departed amicably. However, in many cases when full members were expelled or seceded after heated and protracted disagreements, the individual was, literally and legally, thrust into the world with nothing more than the clothes on his back. Economic considerations must have added an important dimension to the threat of expulsion, and it seems likely that fear of the world, of loneliness and of the possibility of destitution, combined to prompt many of the sectarians (especially the older ones) to maintain an outward semblance of belief even when their faith had drastically declined or was entirely lost.

The modes and general techniques of control discussed above were employed in each of the three sects, but there was a marked difference in the style and emphasis of the control mechanisms utilized by, on the one hand, the Shakers, and on the other, the Oneida Community and the Bruderhof. The Shaker techniques of control were relatively unsophisticated, and were rightly compared by many observers to those of an army. Shaker 'gospel order' was characterized by its overt authoritarianism, which was manifested in the rigid hierarchical authority structure extending upwards from the elders and trustees of the individual families to the Central Ministry at Mount Lebanon, and by the formal regimentation of every aspect of the lives of the sectarians.

Among the Shakers, normative injunctions were predominantly pro-hibitive in form, and the desire to provide a living witness of the harmony of Shaker life in contrast to the chaotic individualism of the world led to an insistence on almost complete uniformity of conduct. Of course among the prohibitions contained in the various Shaker 'statute books' there were also a number of scattered positive injunctions – to be charitable, diligent and the like – but it can fairly be stated that every aspect of Shaker life was characterized by repression. Sexual repression was the key which opened the door to eventual salvation, but the initial act of 'embracing the cross' of celibacy was only the first step in the individual's progress towards the extirpation or expungement of every aspect of his degenerate self.

The tension generated by the repression which was attendant upon, and a condition of, the Shakers' desire to demonstrate their power to 'defy the Old Adam' by living in celibate bi-sexual families appears to have found partial expression in the worship of the sect, and more particularly in the variety of physical gifts which were manifested to the sectarians in the course of their devotions. Such gifts were especially numerous and ecstatic during the periods of internal revival when utopian hopes were fostered and their fulfilment made explicitly conditional on renewed asceticism and greater humility and obedience to the dictates of the leaders.

During the revival periods a strictly delimited measure of informality and of what can best be termed 'licensed disorder' was tolerated by the leaders of the sect. Such tension-releasing 'manifestations' rarely posed a serious threat to the authority of the elders and ministers, and should not be thought of as constituting a form of Saturnalia in which ranks, roles and privileges were temporarily reversed. Rather the Shaker indulgence in 'promiscuous' gifts was analogous to the drunken horse-play which is informally condoned on certain occasions among the lower ranking officers of normally highly disciplined élite regiments.

The Oneida Community and Bruderhof relied less on prohibitions than on exhortation and 'silent example', coupled with occasional criticism and remonstrance, to foster the desired rebirth of the individual. A number of definite prohibitions existed in both sects, but the conduct of the members was not guided by any codified set of rules and regulations, and, despite the existence of settled observances and a pattern of daily routine, the members of both groups frequently exclaimed their 'horror of forms'.

Such protestations can be understood as indicative of the sectarians' attempts to resolve a sociological and psychological paradox; they attempted to introduce at least a semblance of spontaneity into what was essentially a planned and tightly controlled social environment. They sought to 'crystal-lize out' the 'joyous', harmony-creating aspects of the affectual relationships which prevail in a true *Gemeinschaft*, while systematically attempting to establish virtually all relationships on a diffuse, non-exclusive basis, and deyning expression to, or 'criticizing away' the ambivalent, aggressive, selfish or malicious aspects of affectual relationships.

This tendency was, and is, most marked in the Bruderhof, whose eulogies on the virtues of the peasantry and favourable conception of the moral character of children, betray a deep-rooted romanticism and a desire to see only with the eye of faith which discerns the good but not the evil. The members of the Bruderhof have been predominantly drawn from the urban middle classes, and the 'ceremonial informality' which characterizes their lives, and their associated desire to render even trivial events the subject of special festivities, represent a reaction to the culture of modern industrial societies in which genuine occasions of (to use Durkheim's phrase) 'spontaneous effervescence' have largely been replaced by de-mystified, commercialized and often only token, observances and celebrations.

The utopian sect seeks to maintain constant vigilance against external evil and insidious internal corruption, but in each group there were periods when social control was relatively relaxed and periods when it was stringent. The periods of increased stringency coincided with the periods of withdrawal from the world, which were also periods of purification and purge. During these purificatory periods deliberate attempts were made to revitalize the group by strengthening the convictions of the sectarians, and so endowing them with fresh zeal and power to combat the indifference, scepticism or hostility of the world. Each revival temporarily rekindled the hopes of the sectarians, but each revival was also accompanied by purges and defections, and it appears that the members who weathered the storm of the revival period were more inclined to acquiescence, ritualism and at least incipient introversionism than to conversionist fervour.

As the utopian hopes of the Shakers and Oneida Community declined, so the sectarians gradually ceased to be convinced of the need for asceticism, or even for maintaining a high degree of separation from the world, and all but the most extreme sanctions became ineffective as ideological commitment dwindled. The Bruderhof represents an exceptional case; the complex informal mechanisms of control continue to elicit compliance, but the employment of these techniques to cement the unity of the group is no longer a 'preparatory work', but has become an end in itself. Outside the Church-community there is no true joy, and no chance of regeneration, and the sectarians appear unwilling to take the risks attendant upon spreading joy and light in the world.

Economy, sexual relations and the family in utopian sects

The seemingly disparate topics denoted by the above heading have been discussed at length in the analytic chapters and have in part been alluded to earlier in these conclusions, and so merit only brief further consideration. The utopian sect exerts a degree of control over its members which in its intensity, extent and unremitting nature is only approached by some introversionist sects, which also seek, more or less consciously, to sacralize every aspect of life.

This similarity between utopian sects and the more extreme introversionist groups having been noted, it is important to emphasize the distinction between the self-conceptions and aims of the two types of sect. Extreme introversionist groups (for example the Hutterites and the Old Order Amish Mennonites) separate themselves from the world in order to defend a way of life which to them is natural. Their conceptions are a-historical; they seek to preserve what they believe to be the social forms, and associated patterns of human relationships which are essentially 'right' in that they are pleasing to God and so are in some measure infused by the Holy Spirit.

Typically such introversionist sectarians attempt to maintain a form of peasant culture in the midst or, more usually, on the margins or remoter areas of modern industrial societies. They regard themselves as a gathered remnant and do not conceive their task to be that of transforming the world, but more simply that of maintaining an island of righteousness as a 'dwelling place' for the Holy Spirit until such time as earthly things come to an end.

In contrast, utopian sectarians do not seek to preserve a way of life, but to build anew – to construct an order of society which is, and can be seen to be, in complete conformity with certain basic religious principles. Building anew does not necessarily imply a complete rejection of the institutional structure of the external society; but it does imply the critical inspection of every aspect of that structure, and the rejection and replacement of those cultural items and behaviour patterns which are deemed to be incompatible with the group's religiously derived imperatives.

The establishment of a considerable degree of economic independence is of course a prerequisite of introversionism and of the attainment of the state of 'viable detachment' from the world which, potentially, permits the utopian sect to maintain its purity while undertaking some measure of evangelism. As indicated, the more extreme introversionist sects usually seek to preserve a 'sacralized' peasant culture. They typically regard agriculture and agriculturally-related crafts as the only economic activities which meet with full divine approval. They reject the world as the domain of evil, but frequently are not averse to making use of those worldly products which assist them in their task of maintaining and perfecting a sacrosanct enclave.

The position of the utopian sect in regard to economic matters is more complex. Each group here examined modelled itself on the Primitive Church, and each assumed that economic communism was implicit in true Christianity. Agriculture was recognized to be a necessary condition of self-sufficiency; but self-sufficiency is not the sole goal of the utopian sect. Consequently, other economic activities may be undertaken, and some measure of independence forgone, if these activities appear to afford a greater possibility of promulgating the divinely inspired form of society throughout the world.

After the gathering of the sect, the Shakers rapidly developed a range of craft industries, and sought to demonstrate the Shaker virtues in their dealings with persons in the external society, and in the quality of their products. Noyes initially regarded agriculture (more accurately horticulture) as the only economic basis appropriate to the regenerate life. However, in the eighteen fifties, his enforced experience of the 'unedifying' nature of subsistence farming, coupled with his desire to spread the gospel of holiness by means of a daily newspaper under the editorship of Jesus Christ led him to abandon his earlier simplistic economic programme.

After the Civil War, the Oneida communists were supported by their own and their hired hands' labour in the group's various industrial establishments, and Noyes proclaimed that the manufacture of traps was part of God's plan in that it assisted in 'ridding the earth of vermin'. Arnold believed that the Church-community should be agriculturally based, but the Bruderhof did not achieve financial independence until the early nineteen sixties, when the semi-industrial production of toys was developed to the exclusion of agriculture. Paradoxically, production for the world has been the factor permitting the group's present high degree of ideological and social detachment from the world.

Utopian sects are innovative in the sense that they seek to construct a complete alternative world; but of the three sects examined here only the Shakers were markedly innovative in the more specific technical sense, and were credited with, or laid subsequent claim to, a wide variety of inventions and of improvements to manufacturing processes. Only a tentative explanation of Shaker innovativeness can be adduced, but it seems plausible that sexual repression, in combination with the hierarchical structure of the group and the anti-intellectualism of the Shaker elders, combined to direct the energies of many of the lower-ranking members towards practical concerns.

Junior members of the sect could only move very slowly upwards through its hierarchy; theological speculation was largely debarred by the authoritarianism of the elders and evangelism was the province of the most trusted senior members. In consequence, many of the younger members appear to have sublimated their sexual energies, and possibly their procreative desires, in the only way open to them – by developing high standards of craftsmanship and expending considerable energy and effort to improve the practical arrangements of the 'earthly heavens'.

The goal of establishing a new order on earth leads to the critical appraisal of existing arrangements; even the most fundamental and most 'delicate'. The three sects each sought to abolish sin by replacing those social arrangements which engendered it, or were conducive to its development. For the Shakers, the tap-root of sin was sexuality, for the Oneida Community and the Bruderhof it was selfishness, which was primarily manifested in intimate and exclusive, as distinct from diffusely benevolent, relationships. Each sect was directly or indirectly led to appraise the sexual relationships of the world, and each attempted to apply new, rational, or semi-rational, 'revealed' principles to sexual relations in general and to the institution of the family in particular.

The Shaker solution to the problem of sin was the most direct. Sin was to be abolished by the adoption of celibacy and the consequent abolition of the family, and, when all the world had become Shakers, the 'world of generation' would come to an end, and the earthly heavens would, presumably, persist throughout eternity. The Oneida Community's 'social' (as distinct from economic) solution to the all-besetting evil of selfishness was to institutionalize a pattern of sexual arrangements which, by putting a moral premium on sexual diversity (but not on sexual indulgence), was intended to militate against the development of exclusive attachments, and the disruptive tensions they engendered. The children of the sectarians (very few in number before the inauguration of stirpiculture) were reared communally, and were taught to regard all adult sectarians as their parents.

The Bruderhof solution of the problems posed for communal life by sexuality and the institution of the family is less radical than those of the Shakers and the Oneida Community. The family is neither abolished, nor is it made co-extensive with the community, but even while the joys of family life are extolled, the relationships within the family are weakened. Individual families occupy separate apartments, but the sheer size of the average family, the use of communal facilities within the apartment houses and the consequent lack of privacy, together with the prohibition of demonstrations of affection for particular persons, combine to prevent the development of any intimacy save sexual intimacy between spouses; and to speak of, or even to allude to sexual intimacy is abhorrent to the sectarians.

The accumulation of dependants by a utopian sect

Persons are attracted to, and become members of, religious sects for a wide variety of reasons, and usually as a result of a complex concatenation of social and psychological circumstances. In consequence, it must be admitted that general discussions of the motives of persons adhering to particular sects are almost inevitably largely inferential and largely speculative. None the less, it is necessary to summarize some of the scattered points made above in regard to the motives of persons adhering to a utopian sect at different stages of its development.

The initial espousal of religious utopianism appears as the response of persons who have, in a sense, 'passed through despair' and who from a position in which they variously abhorred the world; expected its overthrow; awaited the total abolition of sin; or merely sought an irrevocable conviction of their salvation, have developed a gradualistic conception of the redemption of the world and, associatedly, of the redemption of the individual.

The utopian conception that man's task is to build a new world under God's guidance bridges the gap between theologically posited future salvation and the individual's desire to experience his 'saved state' in the present. The faithful member of a utopian sect believes that his every action is performed directly under the eye of God, and that in helping to build the earthly Kingdom, he is ensuring himself an exalted position in that Kingdom.

The first generation of adherents to a utopian sect (or the persons who join or remain in a sect whose response is in process of transforming into a utopian one) appear to be primarily motivated by strongly held religious convictions. (These convictions may of course legitimate or give covert expression to other 'interests' or motives. Thus the Shakers in a sense legitimated feminism and were literally ruled by 'Mother' Lucy Wright for some twenty years at a time when feminism was non-legitimated in the wider society.) The followers of Joseph Meacham and Lucy Wright who spread the Shaker testimony throughout New England and parts of the frontier were indubitably convinced that, despite vigorous persecution, they would effect a speedy transformation of the world. Similarly, the persons who joined Noyes in the desolate Oneida Reserve were probably convinced that, once the gospel of holiness was translated into concrete institutional forms, its appeal would be irresistible. The early members of both sects considered that it was their God-given duty to create the conditions of their own salvation, and this belief inspired what would otherwise have been tedious, and largely pointless, labours.

In each group, immediately after the utopian message was announced and rudimentary communitarian forms instituted, would-be adherents were accepted simply on the basis of their professions of faith. However, as the leaders developed a clearer conception of the magnitude of their task (and concomitantly developed and explored the practical implications of the distinctively utopian *quid pro quo* conception of their relationship with God), so discipline was tightened, and lukewarm or intransigent members left, or were expelled from the group.

The task of putting the sect on a viable basis, or to use Noyes's apologetic phrase, 'of winning the power to be', may preoccupy the sectarians for many years, but, once communitarian forms are established (and to a lesser extent even in the period of this establishment) the utopian response is likely to be sapped by evangelical disappointment, and by differential secession and recruitment. The tendency of the established utopian sect is to accumulate dependants – persons who regard the sect as a place of refuge from the world – and who have little desire to do more than lead comfortably secluded and gratifyingly sanctified lives.

The reactions to the shock of evangelical disappointment exhibited by persons remaining in the sect have already been discussed, but it should be emphasized that, with the disconfirmation of the utopian vision, and in part as a result of the purges and purificatory 'works' which are initiated in order to counteract evangelical failure, numbers of persons leave the sect. The individuals who secede or are expelled are likely to be predominantly the younger members (who have, objectively, less to fear from the world), and to be the more enterprising, talented and courageous individuals who are able to muster the resolution necessary to embark on what is, almost literally, a new life in the external society.

While many of the younger members leave the sect, the few converts made are likely to be seeking security and peace rather than the immense challenge of replacing the social structure of the world. Once the utopian vision had been repeatedly or drastically disconfirmed, the secession of the enterprising, the apathy and disillusionment of the persons who remain and who are, in a sense, trapped in the sect, and the accession of converts seeking sanctuary, combine to promote the development of some form of intro-versionist position, and, usually, the decline of the group's moral, social and intellectual vigour.

A final point should be made in this section with regard to the influence of the children of the sectarians on the group's development. Niebuhr depicted the second, internally recruited generation as a kind of fifth column which sapped the vigour of a sect's rejection of the world, and so brought about its transformation into a denomination. The grossness of Niebuhr's generalizations was indicated in the introduction, but it is interesting to note that, while the dissatisfaction of the younger members of the Oneida Com-munity was in part instrumental in bringing about its demise, the second and subsequent generations of the Bruderhof have apparently effected a mutation of the sect's response in a manner which finds expression in an intensified rejection of the world.

The divergent influences of the second and subsequent generations in the two sects can in part be attributed to the differing emphases of socialization, and the specific attitudes to education which prevailed in the Oneida Com-munity and the Bruderhof. The upbringing of the Oneida children was governed by Noyes's insistence that 'improvement' should be the watch-word of the Community. They were taught not so much to fear the world, as to look on it with some measure of compassion, and were encouraged intellectually in order that they might rise above the world, and be living demonstrations of the efficacy of 'Bible religion'. As a result of their exposure to worldly knowedge, the small but crucial group of younger adults (includ-ing, most importantly, Noyes's son) learned that Noyes's whole style of thought was outmoded (or at least unfashionable) and came to regard him, not as the vessel of God, but as a deluded, decrepit autocrat.

In contrast, until recent years only a few of the children of the Bruderhof received more than the legal minimum of formal education and were taught (and still are) explicitly and implicitly, to shun the world as a place in which evil spirits were only partially held in check by the power of government; which in itself was potentially a corrupt and raging 'wild beast of hell'.

By no means all of the children of the Bruderhof heed these warnings, but the high birth rate of the group ensures that, even if many are lost to the world, the sect's population will be maintained by relatively timorous, unenterprising or merely acquiescent individuals who have suffered an uncomfortable brush with the world, or who have never ventured into it.

The 'life chances' of the utopian sect in the modern world

Taken together the three sects analysed here span a period of some two hundred years – from the middle decades of the eighteenth century to the present – and while all three for a time exhibited a utopian response to the world, the characteristics of the individual responses varied from what may be termed (without pejorative connotations) the 'primitive' utopianism of the Shakers, through the intermediary response of the Oneida Community, to the 'modernist' attenuated response of the Bruderhof.

The Shakers' utopian conceptions may be termed primitive in that they were developed out of a crude matrix of denunciatory millennial teachings, and retained a large element of orthodox other-worldly eschatological doctrines. The vision elaborated by the early American Shakers was direct and explicit (and persisted as the primary source of inspiration of the sectarians for upwards of four decades); the techniques of social control practised in the group were authoritarian and relatively simple, and the Shakers' attitude to their (primarily agricultural) economic activities was pragmatic and unromantic, if reverential.

The utopianism of the Oneida Community was likewise refined out of millennial expectations, but millennialism of a somewhat less hysterical and violently condemnatory kind than that of Ann Lee, and other-worldly elements were largely, but not entirely, eschewed from the sect's theology. Social control in the Oneida Community rested on an interesting mixture of personal charismatic authority and sophisticated 'rehabilitative' techniques and the group, which emerged in the period when the United States was undergoing the trauma of early industrialization, was at first committed to agriculture as the only basis for the regenerate life, but within a decade was re-established on a manufacturing basis.

The 'modernist' utopianism of the Bruderhof (by far the most marginal and debatable of the responses exhibited by the three sects) developed not from orthodox millennial expectations, but out of profound disillusionment with the institutional structure of twentieth-century industrial society, and with the life style of the German bourgeoisie. Other-worldly considerations exist only in an extremely attenuated form in the teachings of the sect; the techniques of control are highly sophisticated, and the sectarians have shown a persistent tendency to romanticize pre-industrial society, and especially to idealize the quality of the relationships existing in such forms of society.

The above gross characterization of the three sects prompts consideration of a final question – that of the 'life', and indeed the 'birth' chances of utopian sects in the modern world. Such consideration must, of its nature, be speculative (and only a few tentative general statements will be adduced), but, this fact admitted, it appears that utopian sects as here conceived – religious groups which partially retreat from the world with the avowed intention of eventually re-structuring worldly society according to a better model – are not very likely to emerge in modern societies, and, should they emerge and survive for a time, their utopian response will probably very rapidly be modified into some form of introversionism.

Indubitably, there exists a high degree of enthusiasm for communalism or 'community building' of one kind or another in most modern industrial societies. This enthusiasm is especially marked in those societies or areas of societies in which life is to a particularly high degree impersonal, anonymous and outwardly demystified, and in which human relationships are largely impermanent and are conducted within a framework of specific roles.

The strains of life in such societies have certainly generated something of a hunger for 'true community' or, less ambitiously but perhaps more pathetically, for 'warm, meaningful relationships', and have led large numbers of (predominantly, but not solely) young people to romantic identification with various types of 'noble savage' or 'Robinson Crusoe' figures, and to attempt to drop-out of society into one of a tremendous range of 'intentional' communities.

The existence of widespread dissatisfaction with the institutional structure and quality of life of modern societies is indisputable, but such dissatisfaction is not in itself a guarantee of the emergence of utopian sects, as distinct from introversionist sects or secular retreatist groups. This is not the place to enter into the convoluted sociological debate on the implications and extent of secularization, but it can fairly be stated that orthodox or quasi-orthodox religious imagery and conceptions are no longer as familiar to the majority of men as they were to the persons who attended the revivals which Shaker evangelists frequented, or who participated in the ultraist reform movements of the eighteen thirties.

Today 'religious conceptualizers' (or at least those whose conceptions are of a God who takes such an interest in His creation that He is liable to descend to particular individuals and reveal to them His plan for the redemption of the world) are relatively rare, and most self-confessed religious persons betray little expectation of even a fairly remote transformation of the world by direct divine action, or by the labours of men working under divine surveillance.

In the first section of this concluding chapter it was suggested that the development of some rudimentary measure of sociological awareness, implying at least a crude conception of the mutability of social arrangements, was a necessary condition for the emergence of utopian sects. However, the relatively high degree of sociological awareness (again not necessarily clearly articulated or consciously apprehended) found in Western industrial societies would appear to militate against the development and maintenance of the convictions conducive to the emergence and persistence of utopian sects.

The members of the three sects analysed in this work laboured to construct a new order of society in accordance with what they believed to be a divine blueprint. They were (for a time at least) convinced both of the originality of their conceptions and efforts, and of their capacity to maintain a sufficient degree of detachment from the world to enable them to perfect their social arrangements. Today, convictions of originality and of independence are much harder to maintain.

In the present era of mass communications, and of a consequent constant search by journalists and reporters for 'newsworthy' material, it would be extraordinarily hard for any nascent utopian who engaged in evangelism to remain without knowledge of the structural and ideological variety of past and present 'intentional' communities, and would be even harder for him to convince others of the originality of his conceptions, and of their power to replace the existing institutional structure of the world. Theoretically at least, such knowledge of previous 'social experiments' may be fruitful and intellectually bracing, but in practice it is likely to have a damping effect on enthusiasm, and it is much less easy for an individual to devote his life to establishing a model of society which he knows has already been tried, than to devote his life to establishing what he believes is a unique prototype of the 'new order'.

Similarly, the possibility of establishing a high degree of independence from the external society has diminished in the last century, as unsettled areas have become fewer and as the state has appropriated new functions and further-reaching, if not always obvious, powers to itself. In consequence, an emergent sect which sought to establish itself in a high degree of independence from the world, but which retained sufficient ties with the world to facilitate evangelism (the *sine qua non* of 'genuine' utopianism) would be likely to be compromised with the world from the very outset of its endeavours, and the extent of its compromises would be evident to the sectarians themselves, and to possible converts.

While the emergence and especially the persistence of new utopian sects appears to be unlikely in modern industrial societies, there remains the possibility that such sects may arise in some of the underdeveloped countries of the world. Utopian sects would be most likely to appear in countries, or regions of countries, where tribal and kinship ties have been eroded, and where profound dissatisfaction with established religious organizations is combined with the persistence of religious conceptions, and the possibility of establishing a measure of vicinal segregation, and a measure of detachment from the claims of a tolerant, weak or indifferent state.

Parts of South America and Africa may yet give birth (or may have given birth unnoticed) to utopian sects, whose members, naïve and credulous as they may appear to persons in the world, will for some time be dedicated to the sublimely altruistic task of constructing a new form of society according to God's blueprint, and so of ridding man of sin and misery by freeing him from corrupt institutions.

The continuing decline of the Shakers

The facts of the Shakers' prolonged decline after 1905 need only be summarized very briefly. A few persons were admitted to membership of the group in this century, but the majority were middle aged or elderly, and probably performed the functions of 'companions' or housekeepers to the venerable sectarians.

By 1910, the population of the group had fallen to a total of approximately a thousand persons, and in that year the last society in Ohio – Union Village – was disbanded. The western saga of the Shakers ended suitably on a slightly raffish note in 1922, when the South Union, Kentucky, society was auctioned. Of the ten surviving members, seven moved to Mount Lebanon, and the three others, including a couple who married shortly afterwards, each received 10,000 dollars as their share of the money realized by the sale of the society property.

The decline of the sect was slower in the east, and is still continuing. The Shirley, Massachusetts, society was disbanded in 1908; Enfield, Connecticut, in 1917; Enfield, New Hampshire, in 1918; Harvard, Massachusetts, in 1919. In 1931, the fifteen members left at the Alfred, Maine, society transferred to Sabbathday Lake after being given a farewell party by the town of Alfred. In 1938, the Watervliet, New York, society (which occupied the site of the original settlement at Niskeyuna) was disbanded, and the three remaining female members moved to Mount Lebanon.

In 1947, the sect had less than fifty members, and the society at Mount Lebanon, New York, once the home of the Shaker Ministry, was sold. Finally, the society at Hancock, Massachusetts, was closed in 1960.

Two societies remain: Canterbury, New Hampshire, and Sabbathday Lake, Maine, which in 1970 were reported to have a combined population of fifteen sisters, the last male Shaker having died in the early nineteen sixties.

The buildings and lands of the defunct societies were put to a wide variety of uses, and the societies at Harvard, Massachusetts, and Pleasant Hill, Kentucky, have been largely restored and are open to the public. Shaker furniture and smaller artifacts are much sought after by collectors, and articles of Shaker manufacture were exhibited in the United States' pavilion at Expo '70 in Japan.

The Shakers themselves appear to have taken their decline philosophically. In 1949 the Canterbury Shakers were reported to regard the sect as having been an influence for good in the world, and stated that their past charitable actions had been made redundant by public social service agencies. With resignation to the death of the sect ascetic practices were almost entirely abandoned, and an anonymous reporter (*Life*, 17 March 1968, p. 68) stated of Sabbathday Lake: 'Today television antennas sprout from their roofs and every sister has seen the movie "The Sound of Music" at least once.'

Chronology of the Shakers

1736	Ann Lee born.
1747	Wardley group secedes from Quakers.
1758	Ann Lee joins Wardley group.
1762	Ann Lee marries.
1772	Ann Lee conceives herself divinely inspired to reveal sexual relations as the source of all sin.
1774	Ann Lee and followers sail for America.
1776	Shakers gather at Niskeyuna.
1779	New Lebanon revival.
1780	Joseph Meacham joins Shakers. Ann Lee imprisoned.
1781–3	The missionary journeys of the 'three witnesses'.
1784	Ann Lee dies. James Whittaker succeeds her as leader. Sect has approximately 1,000 associates.
1785	Shaker testimony 'withdrawn from the world'. Worship formalized after this date.
1787	James Whittaker dies. Joseph Meacham succeeds him.
1788	The 'gathering' of the sect – the institutionalization of communitarianism.
1792	'Gospel Order' fully established.
1795	By the end of this year, eleven societies were established.
1796	Joseph Meacham dies. Lucy Wright succeeds him.
1797	Shaker testimony 'reopened to the world'.
1799–1806	Great Kentucky revival.
1803	Upwards of 1,300 members.
1805	Shaker missionaries arrive in Kentucky.
1807	'Sympathetic revival' in north, after evangelical success in south-west.
1808	Youngs publishes the 'Shaker bible'.
1812	Upwards of 3,000 members.
1816	Lucy Wright initiates the purification of the sect.
1821	Lucy Wright dies.
1823	Upwards of 4,000 members. Peak membership in south-western societies.
1826	By this year, six societies founded in Kentucky and Ohio. No successful societies founded after this date.
1827	Another period of revival and purification of the sect.
1830	Frederick Evans joins the sect.

1835	Upwards of 5,000 members (peak of somewhat less than 6,000 a decade later).
1837–47	The prolonged internal revival – 'Mother Ann's Work'.
1837	Philemon Stewart receives his first revelations.
1840	Ministry commences to censor spiritual 'communications'.
1842	New rituals established by revelation.
1842–3	The peak of 'Mother Ann's Work'.
1843	Frederick Evans appointed chief elder of New Lebanon novitiate.
1844–6	Converts made among disappointed followers of William Miller.
1847	The spirits leave the Shakers and visit 'the world'. Approximate date of commencement of failure of Shaker evangelism.
1860	5,200 members.
1863	Shakers granted immunity from conscription.
1869	Evans's autobiography published. Evans appears as *de facto* leader of the sect.
1870	Day of prayer allotted for preservation of the sect.
1871	Periodical established. Evans visits Britain.
1874	2,400 members. Females outnumbered males two to one.
1887	Evans's second visit to Britain.
1891	1,700 members.
1892	Harvey Eads dies.
1893	Frederick Evans dies.
1899	Publication of periodical ceases at end of this year.
1900	Upwards of 1,300 members. Three major societies already closed.
1902	Services of group closed to public.
1905	White and Taylor publish last significant Shaker work.
1910	Approximately 1,000 members.

Chronology of the Oneida Community

1811	John Humphrey Noyes born.
1821	Noyes's father retires to Putney, Vermont.
1831	Noyes 'humbles himself to God' after attending revival meeting. Enters Andover seminary.
1832	Noyes transfers to Yale Theological College.
1833	Noyes helps establish New Haven 'Free Church'. Noyes concludes that second coming of Christ occurred in AD 70.
1834	Noyes claims his personal freedom from sin. His licence to preach is revoked. Noyes travels to New York and suffers prolonged 'spiritual experiences'. Subsequently establishes a periodical with James Boyle.
1835	The 'Brimfield experience'.
1836–7	Noyes establishes the 'Putney Bible School'.
1837	Garrison publishes Noyes's denunciation of the government of the United States. Gates publishes Noyes's *Battle-Axe* letter.
1838	Noyes marries Harriet Holton.
1841	Noyes's father dies, and his estate is divided among his children. Noyes's son, Theodore, is born.
1843	'Putney Association' established.
1844–5	Noyes develops contraceptive technique of 'male continence'.
1846	'Complex marriage' clandestinely instituted.
1847	Noyes publishes *The Berean*. The members of the Putney Association 'resolve' that their group is the nucleus of the Kingdom of God on earth. Noyes cures Harriet Hall, and is later arrested on charges of adultery and fornication. Later flees to New York City.
1848	Noyes calls on followers to join him at Oneida Reserve. Group has 87 members by end of year. Mutual criticism instituted.
1849	Noyes and his closest associates move to Brooklyn.
1850	170 members.
1851	Mary Cragin drowned.
1854	Zenith of Noyes's journalistic ambitions and achievements.
1855	Noyes returns to Oneida, and commences its purification. Admissions to Community greatly restricted from this year.
1860	250 members.
1867	All property of group formally transferred to four 'owners'. Noyes openly publicizes complex marriage.
1868	'Stirpicultural experiment' commenced.

1870   Noyes's physical condition begins to deteriorate. His *History of American Socialisms* is published.

1873   Mears emerges as chief opponent of the Community.

1874   The 'Towner family' admitted. 270 members in all.

1875   Control of stirpiculture passes, temporarily, to a formal committee.

1877   Noyes confers Presidency of the Community on his son Theodore.

1879   Mears calls conference of all opponents of the Community. Noyes flees to Canada. Complex marriage abandoned. 300 in this peak year.

1880   Agreement to reorganize domestic and economic arrangements of the Community concluded.

1881   Economic communism ends on 1 January.

1882   'Townerite party' in Corporation decisively defeated.

1886   Noyes dies.

Chronology of the Bruderhof

1883	Eberhard Arnold born.
1908	Arnold decides not to enter State Church.
1909	Arnold marries Emmy von Hollander.
1913	Arnold diagnosed as tubercular, moves to Tyrol.
1914–15	Arnold called to reserve unit, but soon discharged.
1915	Arnold appointed literary director of German Christian Student Union publishing house.
1919	Arnold speaks at Marburg conference of Christian Student Union.
1920	Schlüchtern Conference. Arnold establishes Sannerz Community.
1922	Mass defection from Sannerz.
1926	45 persons at Sannerz.
1927	Rhönbruderhof established.
1928	Arnold corresponds with the Canadian Hutterites.
1930–1	Arnold visits Hutterite communities in North America and is received into Hutterite Church.
1933	Bruderhof members register protest against Nazi regime.
1934	Almbruderhof established in Liechtenstein.
1935	Arnold visits England, dies in Germany in November.
1936	Farm purchased at Ashton Keynes in Wiltshire.
1938	Members reassemble at the Cotswold Bruderhof. Some 200 members.
1941	350 members migrate to Paraguay.
1942	Wheathill Bruderhof established in England.
1950	Hutterite delegates visit Bruderhof in Paraguay.
1951	World total of about 800 members.
1952	Small community established in Uruguay. Missionaries sent from Paraguay to United States.
1953	Bruderhof asks to send members to the Hutterite colonies. Request refused except by Forest River Colony, in North Dakota.
1954	Woodcrest community established in New York State.
1956	Interbruderhof Conference held in Paraguay.
1957	Oak Lake community established in 1957 in Pennsylvania. Community Playthings passes into Bruderhof control. Total membership approximately 1,200 persons.
1958	Bulstrode community established in England. Evergreen community established in Connecticut.
1958	World total perhaps 1,500 members. First Paraguayan community closed.

1958–62   Period of purge and retrenchment.
1960   Wheathill closed. Publication of periodical ceases.
1962   Total membership about 800 persons.
1964?   Heinrich Arnold acknowledged as leader of sect.
1965   Sales of toys voluntarily restricted.
1966   Bulstrode closed.
1970   Membership about 850 persons, in three communities in the United States.

Bibliography

Works published by the Shakers

Allen, C. (1897), *A Full Century of Communism* . . . , Pittsfield, Massachusetts.
Anon. (1816), *Testimonies of The Life* . . . , Hancock, Massachusetts.
Anon. (1823), *Concise Answer* . . . , Union Village, Ohio.
Anon. (1830), *A Revision and Confirmation of the Social Compact* . . . , Harrodsburg, Kentucky.
Anon. (1833) *General Rules of the United Society* . . . , Union Village, Ohio.
Anon. (1847), *Condition of Society* . . . , Union Village, Ohio.
Anon. (1851), *A Brief Exposition* . . . , New York.
Aurelia (A. G. Mace) (1899), *The Aletheia* . . . , Farmington, Maine.
Bates, P. (1849), *The Divine Book* . . . , Canterbury, New Hampshire.
Doolittle, M. A. (1880), *Autobiography* . . . , Mount Lebanon, New York.
Dunlavy, J. (1818), *The Manifesto* . . . , Pleasant Hill, Kentucky.
Eads, H. L. (1879), *Shaker Sermons* . . . New Lebanon, New York.
Eads, H. L. (1884), *Discourse on Religion* . . . , South Union, Kentucky.
Evans, F. W. (1853a), *Tests of Divine Inspiration* . . . , New Lebanon, New York.
Evans, F. W. (1853b), *A Short Treatise* . . . , Boston.
Evans, F. W. (1859), *Shakers Compendium* . . . , New York.
Evans, F. W. (1869), *Autobiography of a Shaker* . . . , Mount Lebanon, New York.
Evans, F. W. (1871), *Religious Communism* . . . , London.
Evans, F. W. (1877), *Shakerism* . . . , New Lebanon, New York.
Evans, F. W. (1890), *Two Orders – Shakerism and Republicanism*, Pittsfield, Massachusetts.
Fraser, D. (1887), *The Music of the Spheres* . . . , Albany, New York.
Green, C. and Wells, S. Y. (1823), *A Summary View* . . . , Albany, New York.
Green, C. and Wells, S. Y. (1851), *A Brief Exposition* . . . , New York.
Leonard, W. (1853), *A Discourse* . . . , Harvard, Massachusetts.
Lomas, G. A. (1873), *Plain Talks Upon Practical Religion* . . . , Albany, New York.
Mace, F. (1838), *Familiar Dialogues* . . . , Portland.
McNemar, R. (1807), *The Kentucky Revival* . . . , Frankfort, Kentucky (reprinted New York, 1846).
McNemar, R. (1818), *An Address to the State of Ohio* . . . , Lebanon, Ohio.
McNemar, R. (1833), *The Constitution of the United Societies* . . . , Watervliet, Ohio.
Meacham, J. (1870), *A Concise Statement* . . . , Bennington, Vermont.
Pattison, M. (1873), *Social Gathering* . . . , Albany, New York.
Pelham, R. W. (1874), *A Shaker's Answer* . . . , Boston.

Philos Harmoniae (1833), *A Selection of Hymns and Poems* . . . , Watervliet, Ohio.

Stewart, P. (1843), *A Holy, Sacred and Divine Roll and Book* . . . , Canterbury, New Hampshire.

Wells, S. Y. (ed.) (1827), *Testimonies Concerning the Character* . . . , Albany, New York.

White, A. and Taylor, L. S. (1905), *Shakerism: It's Meaning and Message* . . . , Columbus, Ohio.

Youngs, B. S. (1808), *The Testimony* . . . , Lebanon, Ohio.

PERIODICALS

The Shaker, January 1871–December 1872.
Shaker and Shakeress, January 1873–December 1875.
The Shaker, January 1876–December 1877.
The Shaker Manifesto, January 1878–December 1883.
The Manifesto, January 1884–December 1899.

Works concerning the Shakers

Andrews, E. D. (1932), *The Community Industries of the Shakers*, Albany, New York.

Andrews, E. D. (1940), *The Gift to be Simple* . . . , New York.

Andrews, E. D. (1963), *The People Called Shakers* . . . (revised edition), New York.

Andrews, E. D. and F. (1937), *Shaker Furniture*, New Haven.

Andrews, E. D. and F. (1966), *Religion in Wood*, Bloomington, Indiana.

Anon. (1843), *A Return of Departed Spirits* . . . , Philadelphia.

Anon. (1846), *Some Lines in Verse about Shakers* . . . , New York.

Anon. (1849), *Report of the Shakers' Examination* . . . , Concord, New Hampshire.

Baker, A. (1896), *Shakers and Shakerism*, London.

Brown, J. (1812), *Account of the People Called Shakers* . . . , Troy, New York.

Desroche, H. (1955), *Les Shakers Americains* . . . , Paris.

Dyer, J. (1819), *A Compendious Narrative* . . . , Concord, New Hampshire.

Dyer, M. (1818), *A Brief Statement* . . . , Concord, New Hampshire.

Dyer, M. (1822), *A Portraiture of Shakerism*, Concord, New Hampshire.

Dyer, M. (1824), *A Reply to the Shakers* . . . , Concord, New Hampshire.

Dyer, M. (1847), *The Rise and Progress of the Serpent* . . . , Concord, New Hampshire.

Elkins, H. (1853), *Fifteen Years in the Senior Order of Shakers* . . . , Hanover, New Hampshire.

Haskett, W. (1828), *Shakerism Unmasked* . . . , Pittsfield, Massachusetts.

Lamson, D. (1848), *Two Years Experience Among the Shakers* . . . , West Boyleston, Massachusetts.

Melcher, M. F. (1941), *The Shaker Adventure*, Princeton.

Neal, J. (1947), *By Their Fruits* . . . , Chapel Hill, North Carolina.

Piercy, C. B. (1916), *The Valley of God's Pleasure* . . . , New York.

Sears, C. E. (1916), *Gleanings from Old Shaker Journals*, New York.

Smith, J. (1810), *Shakerism Detected* . . . , Paris, Kentucky.

Symonds, J. (1961), *Thomas Brown and the Angels*, London.

Visitor (Silliman, B.?) (1832), *The Peculiarities of the Shakers*, New York.

Wickliffe, R. (1832), *The Shakers* . . . , Frankfort, Kentucky.

Bibliography

Works published by the Oneida Community

Anon. (1849), *First Annual Report* . . . Oneida Reserve, New York.
Anon. (1850), *Second Annual Report* . . . , Oneida Reserve, New York.
Anon. (1851), *Third Annual Report* . . . , Oneida Reserve, New York.
Anon. (1867), *Handbook of the Oneida Community* . . . , Wallingford, Connecticut.
Anon. (1875), *Handbook of the Oneida Community*, Oneida, New York.
Barron, A. and Miller, G. N. (1875), *Home-Talks*, Oneida, New York.
Cragin, G. (ed.) (1850), *Faith Facts* . . . , Oneida Reserve, New York.
Noyes, J. H. (1838) *The Way of Holiness* . . . , Putney, Vermont.
Noyes, J. H. (1840), *A Treatise on the Second Coming of Christ*, Putney, Vermont.
Noyes, J. H. (1843), *The Doctrine of Salvation* . . . , Putney, Vermont.
Noyes, J. H. (1847), *The Berean* . . . , Putney, Vermont.
Noyes, J. H. (1848), *Confessions of John H. Noyes* . . . , Oneida Reserve.
Noyes, J. H. (?) (1853) (Anon.), *Bible Communism* . . . , Brooklyn.
Noyes, J. H. (1869), *Salvation from Sin* . . . , Wallingford, Connecticut.
Noyes, J. H. (1870), *History of American Socialisms*, Philadelphia.
Noyes, J. H. (1871), *Dixon and His Copyists*, Wallingford, Conecticut.
Noyes, J. H. (1872), *Male Continence*, Oneida, New York.
Noyes, J. H. (1875?), *Essay on Scientific Propagation*, Oneida, New York.
Noyes, J. H. (1878), *Paul's Prize*, Oneida, New York.
Noyes, T. R. (1878), *Report on the Health of Children* . . . , Oneida, New York.

PERIODICALS

In addition to his collaboration with James Boyle on the first six issues of *The Perfectionist* (which was published monthly in two volumes, August 1835–March 1836) Noyes published independently:

The Witness, vols 1, 2, 20 August 1837–18 January 1843.
The Perfectionist, vols 3–5, 15 February 1843–14 February 1846.
The Spiritual Moralist, vol. 1, nos 1, 2, 13, 25 June 1842. (No further numbers were published.)
The Spiritual Magazine, vols 1, 2, 15 March 1846–17 January 1850. vol. 2, no. 13 to vol. 2, no. 24, 5 August 1848–17 June 1850 continued as:
The Free Church Circular, vol. 3, no. 1 to vol. 4, no. 16, 28 January 1850–28 June 1851.
The Circular, vol. 1, no. 1 to vol. 12, no. 52, 6 November 1851–25 February 1864.
The Circular (new series), vol. 1, no. 1 to vol. 13, no. 10, 21 March 1864–9 March 1876. (From vol. 8, no. 1, 2 January 1871, this periodical was formally entitled the *Oneida Circular*.)
The American Socialist, vol. 1, no. 1 to vol. 4, no. 52, 30 March 1876–25 December 1879.

Works concerning the Oneida Community

Bishop, M. (1969), 'The great Oneida love-in', *American Heritage*, vol. 20, no. 2, 1969, pp. 14–18, 86–92.
Carden, M. L. (1969), *Oneida: Utopian Community to Modern Corporation* Baltimore.

(Carden's work contains a detailed account of the vicissitudes of the Oneida Joint Stock Corporation, and for this reason an appendix dealing with events after 1881 appears to be redundant.)

Eastman, H. (1847), *Noyesism Unveiled* . . . , Brattleboro, Vermont.

Edmonds, W. D. (1948), *The First Hundred Years, 1848–1948*, Oneida, New York.

Estlake, A. (1900), *The Oneida Community* . . . London.

Mc'Gee, A. N. (1891), 'An experiment in human stirpiculture', *The American Anthropologist* vol. 4, no. 4, 1891, pp. 319–25.

Miller, G. N. (1894?), *After the Strike of a Sex* . . . , London.

Noyes, G. W. (ed.) (1923), *Religious Experience of John Humphrey Noyes* . . . , New York.

Noyes, G. W. (ed.) (1931), *John Humphrey Noyes* . . . , Oneida, New York.

Noyes, P. (1937), *My Father's House*, London.

Noyes, P. (1958), *A Goodly Heritage*, New York.

Parker, R. A. (1935), *A Yankee Saint* . . . , New York.

Robertson, C. N. (ed.) (1970), *Oneida Community: An Autobiography 1851–1876*, Syracuse.

Wordon, H. M. (1950), *Old Mansion House Memories* . . . , Oneida, New York.

Works published by the Bruderhof

Anon. (n.d.), *The New Bruderhof Community* . . . , Ashton Keynes, Wiltshire.

Anon. (1939?), *The Call of the Hour* . . . , Ashton Keynes, Wiltshire.

Anon. (1940?), *The Cotswold Bruderhof* . . . , Ashton Keynes, Wiltshire.

Anon. (1964), *Eberhard Arnold* . . . , Rifton, New York.

Anon. (n.d.), *The Secret Flower*, Rifton, New York.

Arnold, E. (1938), *The Individual and World Need*, Ashton Keynes, Wiltshire.

Arnold, E. (1939a), *God and Anti-God*, Ashton Keynes, Wiltshire.

Arnold, E. (1939b), *The Early Christians* . . . , Ashton Keynes, Wiltshire.

Arnold, E. (1940a), *The Peace of God*, Ashton Keynes, Wiltshire.

Arnold, E. (1940b), *The Hutterian Brothers* . . . , Ashton Keynes, Wiltshire.

Arnold, E. (1965a), *Love and Marriage*, Rifton, New York.

Arnold, E. (1965b), *When the Time was Fulfilled* . . . , Rifton, New York.

Arnold, E. (1967a), *Why We Live in Community*, Rifton, New York.

Arnold, E. (1967b), *Salt and Light* . . . , Rifton, New York.

Arnold, Emmy (ed.) (1963), *Inner Words* . . . , Rifton, New York.

Arnold, Emmy (1964), *Torches Together* . . . , Rifton, New York.

Arnold, R. (ed.) (n.d.), *Children in Community*, Rifton, New York.

Hindley, S. and M. (1943), *Work and Life at the Bruderhof in Paraguay*, Bromdon, Shropshire.

Lejeune, R. (1963), *Christoph Friedrich Blumhardt* . . . , Rifton, New York.

Mettler, A. (1960), *A New Perspective*, Bromdon, Shropshire.

PERIODICAL

The Plough, spring 1938–summer 1940; (new series) spring 1953–winter 1957; (new series) spring 1958–spring 1960.

Bibliography

Works concerning the Bruderhof

Anon. (1964), 'Something long forgotten: Christian community', *Christian Century*, vol. 81, 1964, p. 1159.

Armytage, W. H. G. (1959), 'The Wheathill Bruderhof, 1942–1958', *American Journal of Economics and Sociology*, vol. 18, no. 3, 1959, pp. 285–94.

Fretz, J. W. (1953), *Pilgrims in Paraguay*, Scottdale, Pennsylvania.

Hall, F. B. (1957), 'Revival of Christian Community', *Christian Century*, vol. 74, 1957, pp. 1283–5.

Ineson, G. (1956), *Community Journey*, London.

Kolko, F. (1954), 'Housewarming at the Woodcrest Bruderhof', *Co-operative Living*, vol. 16, no. 1, 1954, pp. 4–5.

Merchant, W. (1952), 'The Bruderhof Communities – I,' *Co-operative Living*, vol. 3, no. 2, 1952, pp. 13–15.

Merchant, W. (1952), 'The Bruderhof Communities – II', *Co-operative Living*, vol. 3, no. 3, 1952 pp. 4–6.

Merchant, W. (1952), 'The Bruderhof Communities – III', *Co-operative Living*, vol. 4, no. 1, 1952, pp. 8–11.

Sorokin, P. A. (ed.) (1954), *Forms and Techniques of Altruistic and Spiritual Growth*, Boston.

Schoeps, J. (1956), *Die Letzen Dreissig Jehre*, Stuttgart.

Tillson, D. S. (1958), 'A Pacifist Community in Peacetime . . .' (thesis), Syracuse University.

Whitworth, J. (1971), 'The Bruderhof in England: a chapter in the history of a utopian sect', *Yearbook of the Sociology of Religion in Britain*, no. 4 1971, pp. 84–101.

Zablocki, B. D. (1967), Christians Because it Works . . .' (thesis), Johns Hopkins University. (Zablocki's works provide a detailed description of the lives of contemporary members of the Bruderhof, and contain an extremely interesting discussion of the psychological dynamics of the group.)

Zablocki, B. D. (1971), *The Joyful Community*, Baltimore, Maryland.

Studies in the sociology of religion

Becker, H. (1932), *Systematic Sociology* . . . , New York.

Berger, P. L. (1954), 'The sociological study of sectarianism', *American Sociological Review*, vol. 21, no. 4, 1954, pp. 467–85.

Berger, P. L. (1969), *The Sacred Canopy*, New York.

Clark, E. T. (1937), *The Small Sects in America*, Nashville.

Cohn, N. (1957), *The Pursuit of the Millennium*, London.

Faris, E. (1955, originally published 1928), 'The sect and the sectarian', reprinted in *American Journal of Sociology*, vol. 60, no. 6, 1955, pp. 75–87.

Festinger, L. (*et al.*) (1956), *When Prophecy Fails*, Minneapolis.

Johnson, B. (1957), 'A critical appraisal of the church–sect typology', *American Sociological Review*, vol. 22, no. 1, 1957, pp. 88–92.

Kliewer, F. (1957), 'Die Mennoniten in Brasilien', *Stadenjahrbuch* (São Paulo) 5, 1957, pp. 233–46.

Lofland, J. (1966), *The Doomsday Cult*, Englewood Cliffs, New Jersey.

Bibliography

Martin, D. A. (1962), 'The denomination', *British Journal of Sociology*, vol. 13, no. 1, 1962, pp. 1–14.

Martin, D. A. (1965), *Pacifism . . .* , London.

Niebuhr, H. R. (1929), *The Social Sources of Denominationalism*, New York.

Stark, W. (1967), *Sectarian Religion*, London.

Troeltsch, E. (1912), *The Social Teaching of the Christian Churches*, London (translated by Olive Wyon, 1931).

Pope, L. (1942), *Millhands and Preachers*, New Haven.

Vollmer, H. M. (1957), 'Member commitment and organisational competence in religious orders', *Berkley Publications in Society and Institutions*, vol. 3, no. 1, 1957, pp. 13–36.

Wach, J. (1947), *Sociology of Religion*, London.

Wilson, B. R. (1958), 'Apparition et persistence des sectes . . .' , *Archives de Sociologie des Religions*, no. 5, 1958, pp. 140–50.

Wilson, B. R. (1959), 'An analysis of sect development', *American Sociological Review*, vol. 24, no. 1, 1959, pp. 3–15.

Wilson, B. R. (1961), *Sects and Society*, London.

Wilson, B. R. (1963), 'Typologie des sectes . . .' , *Archives de Sociologie des Religions*, no. 16, 1963, pp. 49–63.

Wilson, B. R. (ed.) (1967), *Patterns of Sectarianism*, London.

Yinger, J. M. (1946), *Religion in the Struggle for Power*, Durham, North Carolina.

Other works cited or consulted

Armytage, W. H. G. (1961), *Heavens Below . . .* , London.

Armytage, W. H. G. (1968), *Yesterday's Tomorrows . . .* , Toronto.

Arndt, K. J. (1965), *George Rapp's Harmony Society . . .* , Philadelphia.

Barnett, H. G. (1953), *Innovation . . .* , New York.

Becker, H. (1946), *German Youth: Bond or Free*, London.

Bennett, J. W. (1967), *Hutterian Brethren . . .* , Stamford, California.

Bestor A. E. (1950), *Backwoods Utopias . . .* , Princeton.

Bury, J. B. (1920), *The Idea of Progress*, London.

Cleveland. C. C. (1916) *The Great Revival in the West, 1797–1805*, Chicago.

Cross, W. R. (1950), *The Burned-over District*, Ithaca, New York.

Curtis, E. R. (1961), *A Season in Utopia . . .* , New York.

Davenport, F. M. (1905), *Primitive Traits in Religious Revivals . . .* , New York.

Dixon, W. H. (1868), *New America*, London.

Egbert, D. D. and Persons, S. (1952), *Socialism and American Life* (two vols), Princeton, New Jersey.

Fry, A. R. (1939), *Victories Without Violence*, London.

Gide, C. (translated by Row, E. F.) (1930), *Communist and Co-operative Colonies*, London.

Hillquit, M. (1910), *History of Socialism in the United States*, New York.

Hinds, W. A. (1902), *American Communities* (revised edition), Chicago.

Hine, R. V. (1966), *California's Utopian Colonies*, London.

Holloway, M. (1951), *Heavens on Earth . . .* , London.

Hostetler, J. A. and Huntingdon, G. E. (1967), *The Hutterites in North America*, New York.

Infield, H. F. (1955), *The American International Communities*, Glen Gardner, New Jersey.

Kaplan, B. and Plaut, T. F. A. (1956), *Personality in a Communal Society* . . . , Lawrence, Kansas.

Knox, R. A. (1950), *Enthusiasm* . . . , London.

Lifton, R. J. (1961), *Thought Reform* . . . , London.

Mackintosh, H. R. (1964), *Types of Modern Theology*, London.

Nordhoff, C. (1875), *The Communistic Societies of the United States* . . . , New York.

Owen, R. D. (1831), *Moral Physiology*, New York.

Peters, V. (1965), *All Things Common*, Minneapolis.

Ruether, R. R. (1970), *The Radical Kingdom*, New York.

Schambaugh, B. M. H. (1932), *Amana That Was and Amana That Is*, Iowa City.

Smelser, N. (1949), *Theory of Collective Behaviour*, London.

Smith, T. L. (1957), *Revivalism and Social Reform* . . . , New York.

Stockham, A. B. (1896), *Karezza, Ethics of Marriage*, Chicago.

Sweet, W. W. (1930), *The Story of Religion in America* . . . , New York.

Sweet, W. W. (1944), *Revivalism in America* . . . , New York.

Tuveson, E. L. (1948), *Millennium and Utopia* . . . , Berkeley, California.

Tylor, C. (1898), *The Camisards* . . . , London.

Warfield, B. B. (1931), *Perfectionism*, New York.

Webber, E. (1959), *Escape to Utopia* . . . , New York.

Index